The Implied Spider

AMERICAN LECTURES ON THE HISTORY OF RELIGIONS

Sponsored by the American Academy of Religion, New Series, Number 16

This volume is the sixteenth to be published in the series of American Lectures on the History of Religions for which the American Council of Learned Societies, through its Committee on the History of Religions, assumed responsibility in 1936, and for which the American Academy of Religion assumed responsibility in 1995.

Under the program the Committee from time to time enlists the services of scholars to lecture in colleges, universities, and seminaries on topics in need of expert elucidation. Subsequently, when possible and appropriate, the Committee arranges for the publication of the lectures. Other volumes in the series are Martin P. Nilsson, *Greek Popular Religion* (1940); Henri Frankfort, *Ancient Egyptian Religion* (1948); Wing-tsit Chan, *Religious Trends in Modern China* (1953); Joachim Wach, *The Comparative Study of Religions, Christianity* (1959); Robert Lawson Slater, *World Religions and World Community* (1963); Joseph M. Kitagawa, *Religion in Japanese History* (1966); Joseph L. Blau, *Modern Varieties of Judaism* (1966); Morton Smith, *Palestinian Parties and Politics That Shaped the Old Testament* (1971); Philip H. Ashby, *Modern Trends in Hinduism* (1974); Victor Turner and Edith Turner, *Image and Pilgrimage in Christian Culture* (1978); Annemarie Schimmel, *As Through a Veil: Mystical Poetry in Islam* (1982); Peter Brown, *The Body and Society: Men, Women, and Sexual Renunciation in Early Christianity* (1988); W. H. McLeod, *The Sikhs: History, Religion, and Society* (1989); and Caroline Walker Bynum, *The Resurrection of the Body in Western Christianity, 200–1336* (1995).

The Implied Spider

POLITICS & THEOLOGY IN MYTH

Wendy Doniger

Columbia University Press

NEW YORK

Columbia University Press
Publishers Since 1893
New York   Chichester, West Sussex
Copyright © 1998 Wendy Doniger
Library of Congress Cataloging-in-Publication Data
Doniger, Wendy.
The implied spider : politics and theology in myth / Wendy Doniger.
p.   cm.—(Lectures on the history of religions ; new ser., no. 16)
Includes bibliographical references and index.
ISBN 0-231-11170-3
1. Myth—Study and teaching—Methodology. 2. Mythology—Study and
teaching—Methodology. I. Title. II. Series.
BL304.D54   1998
291.1'3'01—dc21   97-26476
CIP

Casebound editions of Columbia University Press books are printed
on permanent and durable acid-free paper.
Printed in the United States of America
Designed by Linda Secondari
c 10 9 8 7 6 5 4 3 2 1

For Bruce Lincoln and David Tracy

Contents

Acknowledgments

Some of the ideas in this book began to germinate in print in various places: "Myths and Methods in the Dark," the 1995 Ryerson Lecture, published in *The University Record* (of the University of Chicago), October 12, 1995, and then in the *Journal of Religion* 76, no. 4 (October 1996): 531–47; "The Theological Uses of Double Vision," *Criterion* 34, no. 3 (Autumn 1995); "The Microscope and Telescope of a Liberal Education," *Shenandoah: The Washington and Lee University Review* 46, no. 1 (Spring 1996): 78–88; and "Minimyths and Maximyths and Political Points of View," in *Myth and Method*, edited by Laurie Patton with Wendy Doniger (Charlottesville: University Presses of Virginia, 1996), 109–27. I also gave an early version of parts of these lectures at the Wellfleet Library in August 1996, where I benefited particularly from the input of Victor and Jacqueline Gourevitch; and I worked on them in Key West in December 1996, with great help from Annie Dillard and Bob Richardson. Throughout the process of revision and expansion, Katherine Ulrich proved a spectacular research assistant, who made the index and, without a murmur, always delivered the goods even in response to idiotic requests like "Can you find this somewhere in Plato (or Peirce)?"

But my primary debt of thanks is to the American Academy of Religion and the American Council of Learned Societies, who invited me to give the 1996–97 American Lectures on the History of Religions. At each lecture, I met with lively discussion and helpful contributions, only a fraction of which are actually accounted for in the endnotes of the book. I would like, therefore, to take this opportunity to thank, at Cornell University, Dominick LaCapra, Mieke Bal, Tim Brennan, Roald Hoffmann, Alison Lurie, Edward Hower, Michael Steinberg, Michael O'Flaherty, and Rachel Nussbaum; at Duke University, Miriam Cooke; at the University of North Carolina at Chapel Hill, Joanne Waghorne and Jack Sasson; at Emory University, Mara Miller, Vernon Robbins, Laurie Patton, Paul Courtright, and Joyce Burkhalter-Flueckger; at the University of Michigan at Ann Arbor, Sarah Caldwell, Ralph Williams, Val Daniels, and Lee Schlesinger; at the University of Missouri at Columbia, Jill Raitt, Joel Brereton, and Paul Johnson; and at the University of Chicago, Lorraine Daston, Clark Gilpin, Tikva Frymer-Kensky, Hugh Urban, Wayne Booth, Tim Child, Glenn Most, William Schweiker, Judith Kegan Gardiner, Frank Reynolds, Jean Bethke Elshtain, Jonathan Z. Smith, and, as always, David Tracy and Bruce Lincoln, to whom I wish to dedicate this book about the interaction between theology (Tracy), politics (Lincoln), and myth (me).

The Implied Spider

Introduction

Myth and Metaphor

This book is about why and how myths from different cultures should be compared. I will take up the "how"—the actual method, the step-by-step procedure that a comparatist may follow (in contrast with the theory of what a myth is)—in chapters 4 and 5. But in the first three chapters, and in the final one, I will take up the "why" of comparative mythology.

I will be talking about all sorts of stories; but the points that I wish to make are particularly relevant to myths, one discrete subdivision of the broader category of "story." It is customary in scholarly approaches to myth to begin with a definition. I have always resisted this, for I am less interested in dictating what myth *is* (more precisely, what it is not, for definitions are usually exclusivist) than in exploring what myth *does* (and in trying to demonstrate as inclusive a range of functions as possible). Defining myth requires building up the sorts of boundaries and barriers that I have always avoided and that this present work is specifically designed to combat. I do not wish, for instance, to limit myths to stories involving supernatural beings (though many myths do), and though there are important differences among myths and epics, legends, history, and films, in many ways I think these texts function similarly and should be studied together. I certainly would not limit myths to written texts, let alone ancient written texts; they may be written or oral, ancient or contemporary.

On the other hand, I would also narrow the field of my concern in certain ways: all myths are stories, but not all stories are myths. In my definition, myths raise religious questions (which of course means that I should define religious questions, and I will in chapter 3). But my remarks are intended to apply only to the rather narrow field of comparative mythology within the broader field of the history of religions (which would include doctrines, rituals, ethics, and so forth), not the entire discipline of religious studies (which would include philosophy of religions, psychology of religions, and so forth). Other considerations would certainly have to be taken into account in an argument for comparison within these larger arenas. And it is worth keeping in mind at all times that myth is not an active force in itself but a tool in the hands of human beings—and different human beings will not only use it in different ways, but define it in different ways. The word may seem to be the same, but—like the narratives it represents—it will have different meanings in different contexts.

Let us begin with what a myth is *not*: a myth is not a lie or a false statement to be contrasted with truth or reality or fact or history, though this usage is, perhaps, the most common meaning of myth in casual parlance today. But in the history of religions, the term *myth* has far more often been used to mean "truth." What makes this ambiguity possible is that a myth is above all a story that is *believed*, believed to be true, and that people continue to believe despite sometimes massive evidence that it is, in fact, a lie.[1] For example, Sudanese storytellers often begin with this formula:

> I'm going to tell a story.
> [Audience] Right!
> It's a lie.
> Right!
> But not everything in it is false!
> Right![2]

In its positive and enduring sense, what a myth *is* is a story that is sacred to and shared by a group of people who find their most important meanings in it; it is a story believed to have been composed in the past about an event in the past, or, more rarely, in the future, an event that continues to have meaning in the present because it is remembered; it is a story that is part of a larger group of stories.[3] This definition of myth owes much to David Tracy's definition of the classic,[4] which (like a myth, in my view) is highly private in its expression but public in its effect and reception.[5]

Plato used the word in both senses, to mean "lie" and "truth." On the one hand, Plato was the great demythologizer (if not the first), as Mircea Eliade noted long ago;[6] Plato "deconstructed" the myths of Homer and Hesiod, contrasting the fabricated myth with the true history.[7] But since people have to have myths, Plato was willing to construct new ones for them,[8] and so he invented the drama of the philosophical soul and made it a reasonable, logical myth[9] to challenge the old myths of centaurs and so forth. He transformed ancient mythic themes to make the myth of Eros[10] and the myth of the creation of the universe,[11] and he actually applied the word *myth* (which he called *muthos*, since he spoke ancient Greek) to the story of the world that he created in the *Phaedo*[12] and to the myth of Er that he created at the end of the *Republic*.[13] The myths that Plato didn't like (that were created by other people, nurses, and poets) were lies, and the myths that he liked (that he created himself) were truths. And this ambivalence in the definition of myth endures to the present day.

I will make further claims for myth in each chapter of this work, claims that could be taken as part of a cumulative working definition (the only sort of definition that I am comfortable with): in chapter 1, that myth combines distant and near views; in chapter 2, that it is greater than the sum of its parts; in chapter 3, that it expresses cross-cultural human experiences; and in chapter 4, that it expresses both an idea and its opposite, reveals— or sometimes conceals—certain basic cultural attitudes to important (usually insoluble) questions, and is transparent to a variety of constructions of meaning. Throughout this work, I will argue that a myth is not bounded by a single text and will use the word *myth* to refer not to any single version (which I would call a text or a telling) but to the narrative that underlies the whole series of tellings, encompassing them all.

In a previous discussion of comparative mythology, I argued that myths from other peoples' cultures often provide us with useful metaphors that are more refreshing than our own.[14] The metaphor that I used to make that point about metaphors, the tale of the hunter and the sage, has turned out to be more refreshing for readers than anything else in that book— such as, for instance, my ideas about comparative mythology. In this present work, I wish simultaneously to use certain metaphors to explain what comparative mythology is and should be, and to argue more theoretically that comparison *is* a kind of metaphor, and that we all think metaphorically and comparatively.

(The wonderful thing about metaphors is that they are simultaneously real and unreal. When I presented an early version of chapter 1 as a lecture in Atlanta, two evolutionary biologists came to it, thinking that it was about *real* microscopes and telescopes. They stayed through the whole lecture and talked to me afterward about the double vision in their fields, the unfortunate schism between people who focus on tiny details and people who dream about the big picture, and the difficulty of getting them to talk to one another.)

I might have used another metaphor for comparison instead of metaphor: translation.[15] In fact, *metaphor* and *translation* are English derivatives from related Greek and Latin words for the same thing: "bringing across" (Greek *phor*, Latin *fero, latus*—"to bring"; Greek *meta*, Latin *trans*—"across"). We are always translating when we speak to someone else, and of course dramatically more so when we speak to someone in a foreign language; as every translator knows, we can't really translate, but we do.[16]

The belief that we can't translate some things at all, or compare them, seems to me as idiotic as the scene in *The Land of Oz* in which the Scarecrow, who has become King, meets Jack Pumpkinhead, who believes that since they live in different sectors of the Land of Oz they must speak different languages. Pumpkinhead begins it by insisting, "I don't understand your language. You see, I came from the Country of the Gillikins, so that I am a foreigner. . . . So it will be impossible for us to understand one another." So the Scarecrow sends for the allegedly bilingual Jellia Jamb and offers Jack a chair. But Jack insists, "If you wish me to sit down you must make a sign for me to do so." The Scarecrow pushes him violently into the chair and asks politely, "Did you understand that sign?" "Perfectly," declares Jack. The interpreter then arrives and translates Jack's harmless greeting into, "He says that your Majesty's brains seem to have come loose," and the Scarecrow muses, "What a fine thing it is to understand two different languages." But when the Scarecrow instructs the interpreter, "Ask him, my dear, if he has any objection to being put in jail for insulting the ruler of the Emerald City," Jack indignantly protests, "I didn't insult you!" "Tut—tut!" cautions the Scarecrow; "wait until Jellia translates my speech. What have we got an interpreter for, if you break out in this rash way?" Finally, the interpreter confesses that the languages of both the Gillikins and the Munchkins "are one and the same!" Greatly relieved, the Scarecrow says, "Then, I might easily have been my own interpreter!" "It was all my fault, your Majesty," Jack apologizes, looking rather foolish, "as I thought we must surely speak different languages, since we came from different countries."[17] We must all be our own interpreters sometimes, perhaps more often than we realize. Translation requires a leap of faith very much like the leap that, I will soon argue, is required by comparison. We are always moving between worlds, trying to make sense of and orient our lives, and the trick of comparison is the trick of translating between these worlds.

I will begin, in chapter 1, by assuming that we can compare myths and that they can be politically inspiring rather than repressive; that the cross-cultural comparison of myths is pragmatically possible, intellectually plausible, and politically productive.[18] As a matter of fact, this book arose out of my need to justify, retroactively, the method I had already blithely used in writing a book comparing myths from, inter alia, ancient Judaism, ancient India, Shakespeare, and the contemporary American cinema.[19]

Then in chapters 2–6, which are composed in a different, more argumentative genre, I will problematize both of these assumptions, or rather, reveal the ways in which other people have problematized them by asserting that myths can't be compared and that they are antipolitical. And I will attempt to answer those objections and defend my position. I would hope that a reader of this book, particularly the first chapter, if asked whether she believed in comparative mythology, might answer like the man asked if he believed in baptism, who replied, "Believe in it? I seen it done." But for those of little faith, I have written the rest of the book.

Chapter 1

Microscopes and Telescopes

Myths as Textual Lenses

In this first chapter I will consider the metaphor of the microscope and the telescope in the functions and the analysis of myths, and will demonstrate my method by comparing texts from two traditions, the Hebrew Bible and Hindu mythology. Let me begin by arguing that the microscopic and telescopic levels are intrinsically combined within the myths themselves.

One way to begin to define myth is to contextualize it on a continuum of all the narratives constructed of words (poems, realistic fiction, histories, and so forth)—all the various forms of narrations of an experience. If we regard this textual continuum as a visual spectrum, we may use the metaphor of the microscope and/or telescope to epitomize the extreme ends of this narrative vision. The end of the continuum that deals with the entirely personal (a realistic novel, or even a diary), the solipsistic ("This never happened to anyone but me"), is the microscope; this is where I would situate a dream or the entirely subjective retelling of an experience. Some novels on this end of the continuum may be contrasted with myths in several respects. These novels depend on the individual; character is all important; these novels say, this could only happen to this one person or at least only did happen to this one person. In most myths, by contrast, character, except in the broadest terms (young or old, wise or foolish), doesn't count at all; myths say, this could happen to anyone. Yet some novels are more like myths than others; many novels assume that the drama of a few representative men and women speaks to our condition. And while "romantic realism," a phrase denoting a detailed description of a particular event or person that simultaneously conveys another meaning, is often used to categorize some novels, it also applies to certain myths in which a detailed description of an actor vividly suggests the myths' applicability not only to many individuals but also, sometimes, to certain abstract concepts.

T. S. Eliot hoped that James Joyce would beget a lineage of mythological novelists: "In using the myth, in manipulating a continuous parallel between contemporaneity and antiquity, Mr. Joyce is pursuing a method which others must pursue after him. . . . Instead of narrative method, we may now use the mythical method."[1] To me, the mythical method *is* the narrative method, but a very special sort of narrative method, which Joyce employed not only in the obvious way of fashioning his novel after Homer's *Odyssey* (as John Updike built the double focus, contemporary and realistic on the one hand, and ancient and mythic on the other, into his novel *The Centaur*), but in constantly invoking mythic tropes, constantly fiddling with the lenses. Writing about the novels of John Dos Passos, Joseph Epstein said, "Use a wide-angle lens and you cannot expect to go very deep; use the closeup and you lose breadth of detail. It has been given to very few novelists—Balzac, Dickens, Tolstoy, and, at moments, Stendhal—to do both things well."[2] But in my view, it has been given to a number of mythmakers. It is in part a matter of degree: the mixture of the cosmic and the banal is different in different novels, and also in different myths.

At the other end of the continuum from the personal, the abstract end—the telescope—is the entirely general and the formal: a theoretical treatise, or even a mathematical formula. "Euclid alone has looked on beauty bare," as Edna St. Vincent Millay entitles a poem, and we might locate the barest beauty of a myth in the sort of geometrical abstractions that the anthropologist Claude Lévi-Strauss ends up with, the ultimate algebraic formula into which he distills a myth.[3] On one occasion when scientists wished to send a message to possible life-forms on other planets, who could not be expected to know any of our languages, they sent radio waves with such data as the figure of *pi* (the ratio between the radius and circumference of a circle), which is presumably the same everywhere, without any communication. Here at the telescope end is where we might locate experiences unimaginably great ("This has happened to two million Armenians, six million Jews," or even, "This is happening every day in some one of the billions of other planets in the galaxy"). It is also where we might imagine an ideal experience devoid of any human telling, devoid of subjectivity—though this is a purely theoretical construct.

On this continuum between the personal and the abstract, myth vibrates in the middle; of all the things made of words, myths span the widest range of human concerns, human paradoxes. Epics too, so closely related to myths, have as their central theme the constant interaction of the two planes, the human and the divine, as the gods constantly intervene in human conflicts. Myths range from the most highly detailed (closest to the personal end of the continuum) to the most stripped down (closest to the artificial construct at the abstract end of the continuum); and each myth may be rendered by the scholar in its micro- or macro- form. If prose is general and translatable, poetry particular and untranslatable, myth is prose at its most general, which is one of the reasons why Lévi-Strauss was able to claim that the essence of myth, unlike the essence of poetry, is translatable.[4] And, I would add, myth is cross-culturally translatable, which is to say comparable, commensurable. The simultaneous engagement of the two ends of the continuum, the same and the different, the general and the particular, requires a peculiar kind of double vision, and myth, among all genres, is uniquely able to maintain that vision. Myth is the most interdisciplinary narrative.

The reflecting telescope uses a concave mirror as its eye,[5] and some scholars of myth have used the related images of reflection and transparency to express the ability of myth to capture simultaneously the near and far view, as in the title of A. K. Ramanujan's article about myths: "Where Mirrors are Windows."[6] Also writing about myths (though he was using the word *myth* to describe something very different from what I am talking about in this book), Roland Barthes said, "If I am in a car and I look at the scenery through the window, I can at will focus on the scenery or on the window-pane. At one moment I grasp the presence of the glass and the distance of the landscape; at another, on the contrary, the transparence of the glass and the depth of the landscape; but the result of this alternation is constant: the glass is at once present and empty to me, and the landscape unreal and full. The same thing occurs in the mythical signifier: its form is empty but present, its meaning absent but full."[7]

Scholarly Lenses on Myths

Turning from the myths themselves to scholarly approaches to them, we can choose to focus a microscope on any of an infinite number of levels of magnification within any text and see something very different if we do so, from submolecular structures to large patterns that are also visible to the naked eye. As Cyril Stanley Smith pointed out, speaking of metallurgy but also of much more, you must constantly change the scale in which you view any particular phenomenon, for there are always at least two significant levels above and two levels below what you are looking at at any given moment.[8] Through the microscope end of a myth, we can see the thousands of details that each culture, indeed each version, uses to bring the story to life—what the people in the story are eating and wearing, what language they are speaking, and all the rest. "God is in the details," as Mies van der Rohe said (though he also said that the devil is in the details). But through the telescope end, we can see the unifying themes.

We might distinguish three levels of lenses in methods for the analysis of myths: the big view (the telescope) is the universalist view sought by Freud, Jung, Eliade; the middle view (the naked eye) is the view of contextualized cultural studies; and the small view (the microscope) is the focus on individual insight. In chapters 3 and 4 I will suggest two different, specific ways in which the big view and the small view can be combined in a scholar's work; here let me approach the more general question of scholarly focus.

Where do we set the f-stop? When do we use a wide-angle lens, a zoom lens? Victor Hugo posed this question: "Where the telescope ends, the microscope begins. Which of the two has the grander view? Choose."[9] The subjective nature of this choice, and of vision through any lens, is best demonstrated, I think, by a story that James Thurber told of his youth, when his eyesight was already very poor. It seems that in botany class Thurber could never see anything through the microscope, despite the persistent fiddling of his teacher; but one day, as he stared into it and focused up and down, he saw "a variegated constellation of flecks, specks, and dots," which he promptly drew. The instructor came over hopefully, looked at the drawing, squinted into the microscope, and shouted in fury, "You've fixed the lens so that it reflects! You've drawn your eye!"[10] Annie Dillard too, in her essay "Lenses," describes vividly the difficulties in looking through microscopes and telescopes:

> You get used to looking through lenses; it is an acquired skill. When you first look through binoculars, for instance, you can't see a thing. You look at the inside of the barrel; you blink and watch your eyes; you play with the focus knob till one eye is purblind. The microscope is even worse. You are supposed to keep both eyes open as you look through its single eyepiece.[11]

You "watch your eyes," like half-blind Thurber, in the binoculars; but you must also willingly half blind yourself to see the world of a microscope.

We are always in danger of drawing our own eye, for we depict our own vision of the world when we think we are depicting the world; often when we think we are studying an other we are really studying ourselves through the narrative of the other. Our choice of lens level is arbitrary, but not entirely so, for it is circumscribed by certain boundaries that we ignore to our peril. The choice is heuristic: we choose a specific level in order to make possible a specific task. Where we focus depends on the sorts of continuities we are looking for; in all instances, something is lost and something gained. One particular focus lets us ask just one set of questions, but does not stop other people from focusing in other ways. Taking the two extreme ends as I propose to do, the microscope and the telescope, at the cost of the middle focus (or the focus provided by normal human vision), is another way of expressing my choice to focus on the individual and the human race in general, at the cost of the focus on any ethnic group or historic moment or cultural milieu, a choice I will defend in chapter 3 and apply in the micromyth and the macromyth in chapter 4. My choice of these two extreme points of focus is sustained, though hardly validated, by the tendency of the myths themselves to maintain these polarized foci — though always, of course, with the mediation of culturally specific materials. Let us therefore turn to the myths, to see how they do it.

Myths as Theological Lenses in Job and the Bhagavata Purana

How do texts provide us with microscopes and telescopes? Why do we need them? I will approach these questions first by taking a look at two texts from two different cultures, the Book of Job in the Hebrew Bible and the Sanskrit text of the *Bhagavata Purana*, and then by considering the role of the double focus in human life.

When, in the Book of Job, Job confronts God, the level of focus of the text changes, and that changes the level of focus of the text's readers or hearers. What precedes this transitional point in the text is Job's sufferings, not the sufferings of a Greek hero or a Shakespearean king, but everyday sufferings (admittedly raised to the nth degree), "the heartaches and the thousand natural shocks that flesh is heir to":[12] the loss of our possessions (the destruction of Job's livestock), the deaths of those we love (friends and parents, Job's children), physical illness (cancer and heart disease, boils), injustice. Job tries, in vain, to deal with these problems in the normal human way, with words — words of acceptance, words of denial, arguments with his friends, arguments with his wife, arguments with God. That is, he naturally enough confronts the problem on the plane on which he experiences it, the plane of human experience, human injustice, human grief.

Instead of giving a direct answer to any of Job's arguments—for they cannot be answered—God sends him the voice from the whirlwind. Refusing to deal on the level of argument, of *logos*, on which the problem remains insoluble, the text catapults Job out of the plane of his existence onto another plane altogether, that of *mythos*. It whips the microscope of self-pity out of his hand and gives him, in its place, a theological telescope. The voice of God begins at the beginning, with cosmogony, the making of the world: "Where were you when I planned the Earth? Tell me, if you are so wise. Do you know who took its dimensions, measuring its length with a cord?" This image of the measuring cord holds out a transitory hope of returning us once again to the comfortable and comforting scale of human actions, human trades, something that can be counted, counted on, comprehended, encompassed, measured. But that personal image is immediately swamped by the spectacular, impersonal image of cosmic power: "the morning stars burst out singing and the angels shouted for joy." We are robbed even of the comfort of an everyday metaphor.

The juxtaposition of the comforting image of the measuring cord and the overpowering riddle of creation also occurs in another of the great cosmogonies of the world, the one in the *Rig Veda*, composed in the mountains of northern India about a thousand years before the common era: "The measuring cord was extended across. Was there below? Was there above? Who really knows? Who will here proclaim it?"[13] But the comfort of this metaphor is undercut by two verses that frame it; for the hymn begins, most confusingly, with the statement, "There was neither existence nor nonexistence then," and it ends, most unsatisfyingly, with the suggestion, "Whence this creation has arisen—perhaps it formed itself, or perhaps it did not—the one who looks down on it in the highest heaven, only he knows—or perhaps he does not know."[14]

And when the image of measuring recurs in the *Rig Veda*, again it is submerged in cosmic splendor, and again it is undercut by the unanswered cosmic question: "He by whom the awesome sky and the Earth were made firm, by whom the dome of the sky was propped up, and the sun, who measured out the middle realm of space—who is the god whom we should worship with the oblation?"[15] Later Hindu tradition was troubled by this open-ended refrain and invented a god whose name was the interrogative pronoun *ka* (cognate with the Latin *quis*, French *qui*), Who. One text explained it: The creator asked the sky god, Indra, "Who am I?," to which Indra replied, "Just who you just said" (i.e., "I am Who"), and that is how the creator got the name of Who.[16] Read back into the Vedic hymn, as it was in some of the Vedic commentaries,[17] this resulted in an affirmative statement ("Indeed, Who *is* the god whom we should honor with the oblation") somewhat reminiscent of the famous Abbott and Costello routine ("Who's on first?").

In the Book of Job, too, God poses riddles: "Does the rain have a father?" Stephen Mitchell, the author of the beautiful translation that I am using, comments on this in his introduction: "*Does* the rain have a father? The whole meaning is in the *lack* of an answer. If you say yes, you're wrong. If you say no, you're wrong. God's humor here is rich and subtle beyond words."[18] Beyond words, indeed. The power of the passage lies not in its arguments, its words, but in its images, more precisely in the dizzying way it ricochets back and forth between images of cosmic machismo and of familiar, treasured things. First, the cosmic (though even here connected to the personal, for the great constellations are called by their nicknames): "Can you tie the Twins together or loosen the Hunter's cords? Can you light the Evening Star or lead out the Bear and her cubs? . . . If you shout commands to the thunderclouds, will they rush off to do your bidding? If you clap for the bolts of lightning, will they come and say, 'Here we are'?" Then, in contrast, familiar things evoke family and human reproduction, viewed in the mirror of animal metaphor: "Do you tell the antelope to calve or ease her when she is in labor? Do you count the months of her fullness and know when her time has come? She kneels; she tightens her womb; she pants, she presses, gives birth. Her little ones grow up; they leave and never return." This passage—which repeats the motif of counting and time, measuring again—sets up a tension in the outer frame of the story too, for Job has lost the one thing that is most precious to him of all: his children, his posterity. And is God mocking this value in Job when he tells him of an ostrich who has lost her offspring and does not care?

When, in the end, God has the last word, it is the word beyond words. He mocks Job—"Has my critic swallowed his tongue?" And Job replies, lamely, "I had heard of you with my ears; but now my eyes have seen you. Therefore I will be quiet, comforted that I am dust." This is a comfort that renders words irrelevant; Job says, "I am *speechless*: what can I *answer*? I put my hand on my *mouth*. I have said too much already; now I will speak no more." But this vision, and its brand of comfort, is of course expressed in words, the words of the text, the words of the myth—*mythos*, not *logos*.

Does Job forget the image of the beast who "chews clubs to splinters and laughs at the quivering spear"? We are not told, but it is clear at the end of the story that Job is caught up once again in the snug and smug world of material wealth and family pleasures, the world in which we first encountered him: "So the Lord blessed the end of Job's life more than the beginning. Job now had fourteen thousand sheep, six thousand camels, a thousand yoke of oxen, and a thousand donkeys. He also had seven sons and three daughters"—and a partridge in a pear tree. We arc back in the world of account books and dowries, business as usual. We have moved back from the cosmic measuring cord to the cash register. But we have also moved back to a world in which God has restored to Job what is most precious to him in real life: another set of children, his posterity.

There are many who find this ending a rather lame afterthought, like the second endings that Orson Welles and F. Scott Fitzgerald were asked to write for their Hollywood screenplays, or the Hayes office endings in films where the audience knew that they really did get away with adultery or murder, or the happy endings that Melina Mercouri tacked on to the Greek tragedies in the 1959 film *Never On Sunday* (Medea and the children all went to the seashore).[19] In fact, we have been prepared for this ending by the prologue, in which God and Satan look down through their telescopes and decide to use Job as a pawn in a test of their own powers, much as the Greek gods manipulate men in their own quarrels (as Gloucester says in *King Lear*: "As flies to wanton boys, are we to the gods; they kill us for their sport"[20]). It has not been a game to Job, of course, but at least he does not die at the end, like Lear or a Greek tragic hero; the final restoration attempts to make the story, retroactively, a kind of game to him too, as if he were being invited to see through the divine telescope, to see the god's-eye view of his own sufferings, to torment himself for his own sport. Many readers refuse to accept this invitation. For them, if they identify with Job, it is certainly not a game—it has real consequences in their lives. For the author, perhaps, who kills Job (a fictional creation, after all) for his sport, and more than sport, and who moves the reader for his sport, and more than sport, it is a very serious game indeed.

The trick of undoing it all at the end ("It was all a dream") is not typical of the Hebrew Bible, and so its appearance at the end of the Book of Job adds yet one more puzzle to this puzzling book. (The trick is also used at the end of the story of Abraham and Isaac, when God at the last minute allows Abraham to sacrifice a ram instead of his son. Woody Allen's version of this myth has God answer Abraham's complaints by saying, "I jokingly suggest thou sacrifice Isaac and thou immediately runs out to do it." And when Abraham protests, "I never know when you're kidding," God replies, "No sense of humor."[21] Or, as Stephen Mitchell argued of the Book of Job, "God's humor here is rich and subtle.")

But the "it was just a dream" ending is a staple of myths enacting Hindu theories of illusion, and it makes sense in Hindu mythology, where the idea that evil itself is an illusion is widely accepted.[22] Let us consider two Hindu parallels that use this trick of the illusion-shattering epiphany and thus shed light on the dynamics of the Book of Job. One of these is the *Bhagavad Gita*, a text composed in Sanskrit in the centuries before the common era, in which, on the eve of the great battle in the great epic the *Mahabharata*, the hero Arjuna asks the incarnate god Krishna a lot of difficult, indeed unanswerable, moral questions about the justice of war.[23] Krishna gives a series of rather predictable answers, a bit too glib to satisfy Arjuna's doubts, and then Arjuna asks Krishna to display his true cosmic form. Krishna shows him his doomsday form, the form that J. Robert Oppenheimer recalled when he saw the first explosion of an atomic bomb.[24] And Arjuna cries out, "I see your mouths with jagged tusks, and I see all of these warriors rushing blindly into your gaping mouths, like moths rushing to their death in a blazing fire. Some stick in the gaps between your teeth, and their heads are ground to powder."[25] And right in the middle of the terrifying epiphany, Arjuna apologizes to Krishna for all the times that he has rashly and casually called out to him, saying, "Hey, Krishna! Hey, pal!" And he begs him to turn back into his pal Krishna, which the god consents to do. Again the worshipper is comforted by the banality, the familiarity of human life. Outside the text, however, the reader has been persuaded that since war is unreal, it is not evil; the warrior with ethical misgivings has been persuaded to kill, just as God kills. And this political message is made palatable by the God's resumption of his role as intimate human companion.

The casual intimacy of that brief passage is enhanced by the reader's (or listener's) memory of a kind of fun house mirror image of the *Gita* that occurs in the epic just two books earlier: Arjuna is living in disguise as an impotent transvestite dancing master, who offers his services as charioteer to a certain young prince, Uttara, giving as his reference none other than Arjuna himself, for whom, he says, he used to serve as charioteer. As the battle approaches, Uttara gets cold feet and doesn't want to fight; Arjuna tries to talk him into it, with a kind of parody of the speech that Krishna will give to Arjuna in the *Gita*: "People will laugh at you if you don't fight." Reflexively, in the *Gita* Krishna begins his exhortation by saying to Arjuna, "Don't act like an impotent transvestite; stand up!"[26] (a line whose sexual double entendre was almost certainly unintended but may have operated on a subconscious level). In this proleptic parody, Prince Uttara jumps off the chariot and runs away, and Arjuna, in drag, his skirts flapping, runs after him (people who see him run say, "Gosh, he looks more like Arjuna than an impotent transvestite; that *must* be Arjuna"). Arjuna catches Uttara by the hair and says, "If you won't fight, why don't you at least drive the chariot." And the prince (whom the text describes as "witless and terrified") agrees to this.[27] So the initial apparent inversion of power and status is turned right side up after all; Arjuna is the warrior, and his inferior is his charioteer. Finally Arjuna reveals himself to the prince, who doesn't believe him at first and asks him to recite, and then to explain, Arjuna's ten names (which Arjuna does); then Uttara is convinced, and Arjuna wins the battle. When Arjuna finally reveals his true identity to the king, Uttara's father, the king says, as Arjuna says to Krishna in the *Gita*, "Whatever we may have said to you [when we didn't know who you were]—please forgive us."[28] As Arjuna was to Prince Uttara, so Krishna in the *Gita* is to Arjuna: a creature of great destructive power who velvets his claws for the sake of human affection. (Another brief satire occurs elsewhere in the *Mahabharata*, when Arjuna's blustery brother Bhima meets the great monkey Hanuman [hero of the other epic, the *Ramayana*] and tries in vain to lift his tail; when he asks Hanuman to expand to his full form, Hanuman stops halfway, saying, "This is about as much as you can stand." Bhima agrees that he can't stand to look at Hanuman in this form, any more than he could stare at the sun.)[29]

The passage in the *Gita* is about war and destruction, the passage in Job about creation and destruction. And there are other differences: the illusion in Job has just happened (God "unsays" the sufferings, the deaths), while in the *Gita* the illusory battle is about to happen. But the parallels between them are rightly noted by Stephen Mitchell:

> The only scriptural analogy to God's answer (the other Biblical examples, except for the burning bush, are of a lesser god) is the vision granted to Arjuna in chapter 11 of the [*Bhagavad*] *Gita*. . . . But Job's vision is the more vivid, I think, because its imagination is so deeply rooted in the things of this world.[30]

Mitchell is certainly right about the *Bhagavad Gita*. But there is a second Hindu text that, like Job—perhaps even more than Job—takes refuge "in the things of this world." This is the *Bhagavata Purana*, composed in Sanskrit in South India probably during the tenth century of the common era, which tells a story about the same incarnate god Krishna, but when he was still a little boy with his mortal mother, Yashodha:

> One day when the children were playing, they reported to Yashodha, "Krishna has eaten dirt." Yashodha took Krishna by the hand and scolded him and said, "You naughty boy, why have you eaten dirt? These boys, your friends, and your elder brother say so." "Mother, I have not eaten," said Krishna. "They are all lying. If you believe them instead of me, look at my mouth yourself." "Then, open up," she said to the god, who had in play taken the form of a human child; and he opened his mouth.

Then she saw in his mouth the whole universe, with the far corners of the sky, and the wind, and lightning, and the orb of the Earth with its mountains and oceans, and the moon and stars, and space itself; and she saw her own village and herself. She became frightened and confused, thinking, "Is this a dream or an illusion fabricated by God? Or is it a delusion in my own mind? For God's power of delusion inspires in me such false beliefs as, 'I exist,' 'This is my husband,' 'This is my son.'" When she had come to understand true reality in this way, God spread his magic illusion in the form of maternal love. Instantly Yashodha lost her memory of what had occurred. She took her son on her lap and was as she had been before, but her heart was flooded with even greater love for God, whom she regarded as her son.[31]

What could be more personal, more "deeply rooted in the things of this world," more literally *down to earth* or *earthy* than a small, dirty boy lying about *dirt*? But taking off from this modest moment the myth plummets down and turns the universe inside out, shifting gears entirely, into the warp speed of *mythos*. It is surely relevant that this cosmic vision takes place inside the child's *mouth*, the place of useless words, the place of *logos*, now silenced by the wordless images of the myth—images conveyed, as always, by words. For death, as well as words, comes out of the mouth of God. Yashodha, like Arjuna, like Job, cannot sustain the vertiginous vision of the world beyond the world that she has always regarded as real. T. S. Eliot pointed out (in *Burnt Norton*), "Humankind cannot bear very much reality"; apparently, humankind can't bear very much unreality, either, or very much of what the text presents as an alternative reality.

The myth returns the mother to what the text regards as the level of comfortable illusion. She forgets that her child's mouth is the mouth of God, just as Job, perhaps, forgets the image of the beast whose mouth "chews clubs to splinters" and Arjuna forgets the beast whose teeth ground the heads of warriors to powder in his mouth. Indeed, later in the *Mahabharata*[32] Arjuna reminds Krishna of the time right before the battle when Krishna revealed his divine form, and he adds: "But I have lost all that you said to me in friendship, O tiger among men, for I have a forgetful mind. And yet I am curious about those things again, my lord." Krishna, rather crossly, remarks that he is displeased that Arjuna failed to understand or grasp the eternal secret, and he adds, "I cannot tell it again just like that." Like Arjuna, Yashodha has a forgetful mind, but in this instance Krishna himself gives her that forgetfulness as a gift.

More than that: it is unlikely that anyone, even a Vedantic Hindu, could believe for long that her life was totally unreal.[33] Most people's gut reaction to such stories, as to the end of Job, is that the banal is the real, and the astronomical vision is just so much cosmic bullshit. But the myth as a whole offers a way of balancing the two views so that the reader is not in fact forced to accept either one, or to choose between them.

The threat posed by the combination of the telescopic and microscopic view is well expressed by the eponymous hero of Saul Bellow's novel, *Henderson the Rain King*:

> Being in point of size precisely halfway between the sun and the atoms, living among astronomical conceptions, with every thumb and fingerprint a mystery, we should get used to living with huge numbers. In the history of the world many souls have been, are, and will be, and with a little reflection this is marvelous and not depressing. Many jerks are made gloomy by it, for they think quantity buries them alive. That's just crazy.[34]

Just as the earth mediates between the sun (seen through a telescope) and the atoms (seen through a microscope), so the myth allows us to ground the "huge numbers" in such a way that we do not go crazy or get "gloomy."

There is an old story about a lady who went to a lecture and heard the lecturer say that the universe was going to self-destruct in five billion years, at which she fainted. When they asked her why she was so upset at an event that was five billion years away she heaved a sigh of relief and said, "Oh thank God. I thought he said five *million* years." (Annie Dillard once remarked about such figures, "These astronomers are nickel-diming us to death."[35] And a boy in her novel, *The Living*, feels as if "The spaces between the stars were pores, out of which human meaning evaporated."[36]) The enormous scale of the theological visions in Job and the *Gita* and the *Bhagavata Purana* would, if accepted on their own terms, threaten to dwarf human enterprise. But the myth does not demand that we accept the theological vision; even within the text the actors end up in the everyday world. On the other hand, the myth is not necessarily saying that the ending is more real than the vision that precedes it. On the contrary, its purpose is to challenge us simultaneously to see that our lives are real, and to see that they are unreal. To the question, "Which is the reality?" the myth replies, "Yes."

Myths as Political Lenses

We have seen how myths use different scales of words, different verbal lenses, to link theology with daily reality. The abstract end of the textual continuum may be antipolitical (though certainly not a-political) if it withdraws the gaze from human affairs entirely, to a life of philosophical contemplation or renunciation—religious or other—or eschatological expectation. But the process of generalization, of abstraction from local detail, has a political aspect as well: it is where we begin to look beyond our selfish personal concerns and think globally, environmentally, think of the future, think of what is happening elsewhere on the planet earth, think of the consequences of what we say and do and write for people in political circumstances very different from our own. The wide-angle lens can be political and theological simultaneously, as when we realize the political implications of our own theological assumptions or begin to respect the humanity of political others by appreciating their theologies. And myth is particularly qualified to forge these links. Using microscopes and telescopes to link daily reality with global—indeed, galaxial—politics, myth enables us to do what the bumper sticker urges: think globally, act locally.[37]

The human instinct, the common sense, that resists the theological argument that we are unreal is a political instinct; but there are also ways in which political narratives offer us a telescope not to turn us away from our own lives but to turn us toward the lives of others, including political others. Just as our theological vision is opened up by myths like those discussed above, so too our political vision may be opened up by our own myths; by the juxtaposition of certain texts with the events of our lives; by the comparison of myths from other cultures; and, most of all, by the interaction of political and theological texts acting as lenses for one another. In such texts, theology and politics become lenses for each other; we see each differently, better, through the insights of the other. Here again, if one should ask of politics and theology, "Which is the reality?" the answer is "Yes."

In Thomas Keneally's book *Schindler's List* (and in the film),[38] the hero stands on a high hill, mounted on a high horse, and views, as if through a telescope, the panorama of the liquidation of the Krakow ghetto. Amid all the carnage he sees one little girl, in a red coat, and follows her as she wanders through the scenes of horror, a red thread through the genocidal murder mystery, like the inevitable red dot in a landscape by Corot. (The red dot is the only piece of color in this part of the black and white film, producing a genre shock akin to the sudden burst of technicolor in *The Wizard of Oz*).[39] By seeing her, Schindler sees what he must do. Here, switching from a telescope to a microscope is the move from indifference to compassion; for Job, the move in the other direction is the move from self-pity to something more than indifference—resignation, perhaps, or acceptance. Myth here is a narrative that employs, and demands, radical shifts in perspective.

A fine example of this mythic scope, and an image beyond words (though I must use words to tell about it), occurs in a film about World War I, *Oh What a Lovely War* (1969).[40] This film ends with a kind of quotation of the end of *All Quiet on the Western Front* (1930),[41] the classic film about that war, in which we hear a shot, our hero falls, and we see, against the background of a field of white crosses, a line of soldiers marching away, each turning and staring into the camera for a moment, accusingly, before turning back and fading into the field of graves. At the end of *Oh What a Lovely War*, the hero whom we have come to know and care about in the course of the film—through the cinematic microscope—is fighting in the trenches. He is shot, the movie shifts into slow motion and silence, and we see him sitting on the grass at a picnic on a hill in England with his family, full of the mellow drowsiness of sunshine and wine. He leans back against a tree to take a nap, but the tree becomes a white cross that marks his grave, and he vanishes. As the camera zooms back farther and farther from the cross, enlarging our field of vision, we see that the cross on the grave of the soldier we know is just one cross among the millions of crosses marking the graves on the battlefields of France, one small white tree in a great forest of death. For a second, or perhaps ten seconds, we are able to experience, simultaneously, the intensity of personal grief that we feel for that one soldier and our more general, cosmic sorrow for the astronomical numbers of young men who, as we have long known and long ceased to notice, died in World World I. A similar double vision of another war, the American Civil War, is achieved in the scene in *Gone With the Wind* (1939)[42] when Scarlett O'Hara's horror at the suffering of one soldier is suddenly magnified as the camera zooms back to reveal the horrifying dimensions of the full slaughter, the enormous Atlantan square full of wounded and dying soldiers.

In a *Star Trek* episode,[43] the half Vulcan Mr. Spock, who has the ability to "bond" with other minds, suddenly experiences agonizing pain when he senses the death screams of four hundred Vulcans on a star ship some distance from him. When Dr. McCoy expresses his amazement, Spock says, "I have noticed this insensitivity among wholly human beings. It is easier for you to feel the death of one fellow-creature than to feel the deaths of millions." And when McCoy asks if Spock would wish that empathy upon humans, Spock replies, "It might have rendered your history a bit less bloody." Our myths allow us "wholly humans" a glance through the telescope of Vulcan vision.

"One man's death is a tragedy; the death of a million is a statistic," said Joseph Stalin (who knew whereof he spoke). The myth turns the statistic back into a tragedy, turns the telescope back into a microscope. But sometimes, like Job, we need to change the lens in the other direction. In fury and despair, Job gazes through the microscope at the millions of tiny gnats that are gnawing away at his peace of mind. And the poet magnifies them for us, magnifies the banality of human suffering, the banality of evil, as Hannah Arendt put it. "A mote it is to trouble the mind's eye," as Horatio says to Hamlet,[44] speaking of the way our own eyes magnify the small things that trouble us. This same mote, as Matthew tells us (7.3), is the sign of our selfishness, our inability to see ourselves in proper proportion to other people: "Why beholdest thou the mote that is in thy brother's eye but considerest not the beam that is in thine own eye?"

Whenever the microscope of our ego rivets our gaze to the minutiae of our daily lives, myths may catch our eye and make us see with our telescopes, make us think about the stars and the galaxy and how small the planet earth is. And it is difficult for us to think like this for long. It is difficult for us to go on living with care and concern and at the same time to stay fully aware that "Our lives don't really amount to a hill of beans," as Rick (Humphrey Bogart) says at the end of *Casablanca*[45] when his own love affair, which had seemed all that mattered in the world, is dwarfed by the giant reality of the Nazi threat, seen through the political telescope. But just as Job and Yashodha could not believe for long that their lives were unreal, so we can't live our lives if we think only about the galaxies, or the Nazis, or the children who are dying of starvation or disease or gunshot wounds on the streets of our own cities as well as in wars and famines throughout the world. We can't think about those things for long because we are human and we care about *our* lives, about what video we're going to watch tonight. Yet at the same time we know that there are all those galaxies out there, and all those children. We never entirely forget. This tension in us, in either direction, haunts us and threatens either to dim the intensity of the pleasure that we rightly take in our lives or to weaken our commitment to causes beyond our lives, causes that we undertake for the sake of those who will inhabit this planet hundreds of years after all of us have died.

The difficult choice between the two foci is captured in Reinhold Neibuhr's prayer (now best known as Alcoholics Anonymous's "Serenity Prayer"), which asks for the serenity to bear the things we cannot change, the courage to change the things we can, and the wisdom to tell the difference. But wisdom more often nudges us in the direction of "serenity" or acceptance of other peoples' lives, which we can simply ignore. The sorts of stories I have been discussing—myths like the Book of Job and the story of Krishna and other sorts as well—may inspire a number of different reactions in the reader—regret, guilt, rage. Too often they fail to produce comfort. But sometimes they may shake us out of whatever focus we happen to be stuck in. The tension gives rise to the myth. And this tension may affect us in many different ways, of which one, perhaps the most idealized but very real nevertheless, is to inspire us to strive to keep both of these levels of political vision, the microscopic and the telescopic, alive in us at the same time. But how?

The myth offers a fictive solution to the problem that it raises, but we may carry it back into our lives to make it real. The myth balances simultaneously the conviction that each of us is such a tiny part of the universe that nothing we do is real (in the sense that the Buddha taught, that nothing is permanent); and the conviction that a picnic with our friends and family is a great thing, not a small thing. Myths form a bridge between the terrifying abyss of cosmological ignorance and our comfortable familiarity with our recurrent, if tormenting, human problems. Myths make us reverse the focus, viewing through the telescope of detachment the personal lives that we normally view through the microscope and viewing the cosmic questions through the microscope of intimate involvement.

In the theological myths of Job and Krishna, it was the telescope that provided the shock of another reality. But in political myths, as in *Schindler's List*, it may be the microscope rather than the telescope that gives the shock, when a myth balances simultaneously the comfort of an ancient, general, commonplace truth and the surprise of totally new, totally specific details. In fact, the myth can work in either direction, both in theology and in politics. Lévi-Strauss used the idea of an optical image (a kind of crude microscope) to describe the process of inversions in myths:

> Similar inversions occur in optics. An image can be seen in full detail when observed through any adequately large aperture. But as the aperture is narrowed the image becomes blurred and difficult to see. When, however, the aperture is further reduced to a pinpoint, that is to say, when *communication* is about to vanish, the image is inverted and becomes clear again. This experiment is used in schools to demonstrate the propagation of light in straight lines, or in other words to prove that rays of light are not transmitted at random, but within the limits of a structural field. . . . The field of mythical thought, too, is structured.[46]

One such inversion is precisely the ability of "the field of mythical thought" to translate a microscopic image into a telescopic image, to move us from the infinitely small to the infinitely large. The myths suggest that if your microscope is powerful enough it turns into a telescope, that things really deep down and really far away become one another.

Lévi-Strauss's image of inversion is an inversion of the use of the same image by Marcel Proust:

> Soon I was able to shew a few sketches. No one understood a word. Even those who were favourable to my conception of the truths which I intended later to carve within the temple congratulated me on having discovered them with a microscope when I had, on the contrary, used a telescope to perceive things which, it is true, were very small but situated afar off and each of them a world in itself. Whereas I had sought great laws, they called me one who grubs for petty details.[47]

The "world in itself" inside each "very small" thing, each "petty detail," is the grand vision, the panorama of "great laws," of a great novelist, a mythological novelist.

As we have seen, the microscope too can be an instrument of empathy, but as Andrew Delbanco points out: "If a man surrenders to his designated function, his victims will be no clearer to him than microbes smeared on a slide as seen with the unaided eye. He will not see beyond the blur to the lives consumed—each singular, each a world unto itself."[48] The world within each life is precisely what is embodied in the Hindu image of the world that the mother sees inside the mouth of her child, and that Proust saw in each "very small thing."

Annie Dillard, in her essay on lenses, describes the experience of looking at whistling swans through binoculars, and the experience of coming back out of the world of the binoculars afterward:

> As I rotated on my heels to keep the black frame of the lenses around them, I lost all sense of space. If I lowered the binoculars I was always amazed to learn in which direction I faced—dazed, the way you emerge awed from a movie and try to reconstruct, bit by bit, a real world, in order to discover where in it you might have parked the car.[49]

To find our place in the world after we emerge from the magnified mythological vision, the world of the truly wide screen; to avoid getting the metaphysical equivalent of culture shock or a deep-sea diver's "bends" from coming up (or down) too fast, or from awakening too fast from that other world that we also enter sometimes when we dream but usually forget; and to find our car in a different place from the place where we parked it— that's the trick, and myth is the key.

Sometimes the myth is formed not within a text, but rather in the intersection of our own lives with a text,[50] a telescope that provides a political as well as a theological shock. Delbanco writes of the time when Roosevelt discovered Kierkgaard and understood, for the first time, the Nazi evil; it was "a moment at which this feeling of theatrical distance was obliterated by a shock of recognition."[51] The double vision of a dead philosopher writing about the human condition in general and the immediate problem posed by totally new, totally specific human details produced this particular shock of recognition: Kierkegaard's general insights into human nature allowed Roosevelt to understand not *that* the Nazi evil had occurred (which, by then, he knew) but *how* it could have occurred. /s h u w w e f

Delbanco also wrote about the effect of the publication of John Hersey's *Hiroshima* in a 1946 *New Yorker* magazine:

> Hersey gave the anonymous victims of the nuclear firestorm faces and names. He showed the citizens of Hiroshima in the kitchen, on the porch, putting their children in pajamas in the moments before the bomb fell. He showed them blown about like tossed debris amid window shards and the splinters of what had been roofs and walls. He made it difficult to represent them with a number (70,000 or 100,000, depending on whether one took account of post-blast radiation effects) and a dismissive name (Japs).[52]

Sometimes only fiction can make reality real. A radio advertisement for the play *Miss Saigon* declared, "Saigon: it used to be just a name in the news, but now it's real."[53] The mythic drama claims to make the war real, implying that the "name in the news" was *not* real because it was just a name, not a story. Here I am reminded of the epilogue of George Bernard Shaw's play *Saint Joan*, when Cauchon asks, "Must then a Christ perish in torment in every age to save those that have no imagination?"[54]

But sometimes life itself is the text in which we read the myth of double vision. On the wall of the central room in the house in Amsterdam where Anne Frank and her family hid from the Nazis, two charts are preserved, side by side. One is a column of short, parallel, horizontal lines by which Otto Frank marked the growth of his children over the years, as my father used to mark mine, and I marked my son's. The other is a map of Europe with pins marking the advance of the Allied forces—too late, as we now know, to allow that first chart to grow more than a few poignant inches. They are roughly the same size, those two charts, and they represent the tragic intersection of the tiniest, most banal personal concern and a cataclysmic world event. For me, they are the microscopic and telescopic view of the Holocaust, side by side.

We can use these lenses either to see or to blur a world that we cannot fathom. In great myths, the microscope and the telescope together provide a parallax that allows us to see ourselves in motion against the stream of time, like stars viewed from two different ends of the earth's orbit, one of the few ways to see the stars move. And when we take into account myths not, perhaps, from different ends of the earth's orbit, but at least from different ends of the earth, we have made our mythical micro-telescope a bit longer than the one provided by our own cultures, and we can use it to see farther inside and also farther away—a double helix of the human paradox. To jump ahead to the argument that I will make in subsequent chapters, not just for myths but for comparative mythology, the individual text is the microscope that lets us see the trees; the comparison is the telescope that lets us see the forest. The myth allows us to look through both ends of the human kaleidoscope at once, simultaneously to view the personal, the details that make our lives precious to us, through the microscope of our own eye and, through the telescope provided by the eye of other cultures, to view the vast panorama that dwarfs even the grand enterprises of great powers, that dwarfs the sufferings of Job and of ourselves. Every time we listen to a story with mythic dimensions, about human beings in crisis, and really listen and think about the ways in which it is telling us the story of our own lives—and *not* the story of our own lives—we see for a moment with the double vision of the human microscope and cosmic telescope.

Chapter 2

Dark Cats, Barking Dogs, Chariots, and Knives

The Difference of Dark Cats

In chapter 1 I spoke of the inherent ability of myths to compare the views of the microscope and the telescope, to use different scales of words and different verbal lenses to link theology with daily reality. In this chapter I will argue that this ability suggests that myth is an inherently comparative genre, in a double sense: it both compares and is amenable to comparison. In chapter 1 I also argued that myths may use microscopes and telescopes to link daily reality with global—indeed, galaxial—politics; that some myths open up our political vision just as other myths open up our theological vision; and that there are texts that, in juxtaposition with the events of our lives, open up our political vision. I also suggested that political and theological texts act as lenses for one another. Now I argue that the comparison of myths from other cultures opens up our political vision. Where chapter 1 vertically linked the cosmic and the banal within any single myth, the cross-cultural agenda I consider now looks sideways, constructing links between different tellings of myths in different cultures. My introduction argued for the uses of metaphor; this chapter and the next use three metaphors from the animal world—dark cats, barking dogs, and implied spiders—to advance the argument for comparison.

A rich body of evidence suggests that people compare things all the time, consciously or unconsciously, with useful results. Comparison, is, after all, the basis of our value systems; to the question, "Do you like this, want this?" the answer is often, "Compared with what?" Maurice Chevalier, when asked on his eightieth birthday, "How do you like being eighty, Monsieur Chevalier?" is reputed to have replied, "Considering the alternative, I like it very well." Hilaire Belloc, during the reign of Queen Victoria, remarked of the lurid details of the life of Queen Cleopatra, "How very unlike the domestic arrangements of our dear queen." Comparison is our way of making sense of difference.

Indeed, comparison of things acknowledged to have something in common is the basis of our entire way of making sense of the world, our intellectual taxonomy, our survival system. The caveperson who reasoned, "This saber-toothed tiger looks a lot like that lion I saw yesterday; this animal, too, may try to eat me. Therefore, I should run from this tiger as I ran from that lion" is our ancestor. The one who reasoned, "I've never seen an animal like this before. That lion yesterday had no stripes; this animal has. There is the difference of the mane, too. I wonder if . . ." did not live to bequeath his genes to us.

The problem of the same and the different has become a crucial issue within the field of comparative mythology and for the self-definitions of postmodernism. The simultaneous engagement of the same and the different, the general and the particular, requires precisely the kind of double vision that myth, among all genres, is best able to maintain. David Tracy has argued that we can know others only through analogy, what he calls "similarity-in-difference," recalling that, "The power of the analogical imagination as imagination was honored by Aristotle in his famous dictum: 'to spot the similar in the dissimilar is the mark of poetic genius.' " These "analogies-in-difference" allow one to reflect upon relationships "to other selves, to society, history, the cosmos."[1] Tracy uses a poem by James Tate about likeness and difference as the epigram for his epilogue on the role of the analogical imagination in religious pluralism. The poem speaks of the human need for likeness despite its paradoxical, topsy-turvy nature:

> When I think no thing is like any other thing
> I become speechless, cold, my body turns silver
> and water runs off me. There I am
> ten feet from myself, possessor of nothing,
> uncomprehending of even the simplest particle of dust.
> But when I say, You are *like*
> a swamp animal during an eclipse,
> I am happy, full of wisdom, loved by children
> and old men alike. I am sorry if this confuses you.
> During an eclipse the swamp animal

acts as though day were night,
drinking when he should be sleeping, etc.
This is why men stay up all night
writing to you.[2]

Not to see the likeness in two different things is to miss the similarity of the woman and the swamp animal (who see the similarity of day and night) and the similarity of them and the nocturnal poet (to whom day and night are alike). Difference can be alienating; likeness, even the likeness that confuses night and day, generates love.

At the same time, we must acknowledge that the emphasis on likeness, often epitomized by its critics in the same metaphor that James Tate uses to defend it (the metaphor of not seeing in the dark), has done great harm in the history of the study of other peoples' cultures. Occasionally the metaphor is used to make a positive statement about sameness; thus Francis Bacon, in his essay "The Unity of Religions," argued positively for the mutual resemblance of religions: "All colors agree in the dark."[3] Almost always, however, it is pejorative. In a discussion of sameness and difference in Plato's *Sophist*, the Stranger observes that "the Sophist takes refuge in the darkness of not-being, where he is at home and has the knack of feeling his way, and it is the darkness of the place that makes him so hard to perceive."[4] That is, since all Sophists are in the dark, they are hard to tell apart.

This is best known as a proverb — "In the dark, all cats are gray" — attested, with clear sexist overtones, in early French and English sources. Erasmus, at the beginning of the sixteenth century, cites the "Gallic" saying in his commentary on Plutarch's Adages,[5] and John Heywood, in his *Proverbs* in 1546, remarks, "When all candles be out, all cats be gray."[6] The Germans (or, rather, if I am to avoid the very cultural essentialism and stereotyping that I am here decrying, *some* Germans) apparently made the switch from cats to cows (so Indo-Aryan, so bovine, so domesticating, so redolent of *Kinder, Kü[c]he, Kirche*), and also applied the metaphor to texts rather than to women (or religions). In 1807, Georg Hegel provoked a great and absolutely final break with his very old friend Friedrich Schelling by saying that a naïve philosophy of Oneness in which "everything was the same in the Absolute" (recognizable to everyone as Schelling's doctrine) meant that the Absolute was "like a night, as people say, in which all cows are black."[7] John Hollander incorporates the Hegelian image (presumably, a cow) into his poem "Kinneret":

This night in which all pages are the same
Black: The Hegelians must shut up shop.[8]

But he reverts to the older image of cats in his Fitzgerald-Omar Khayyam-like quatrain:

> All cats are gray at midnight, when the moon
> Shines or when it doesn't, though morning soon
> Puts a stop to all that, until each cat's
> Too singularly like itself at noon.[9]

To be too much like oneself even at noon is the ultimate erasure of difference.

The Situationists (a group of rather unorthodox Marxists in Paris in the 1960s) borrowed this methodological metaphor (together with much else) from Hegel. Arguing that bureaucrats in the Soviet Union and in China had become identical state capitalists, class powers, even while each accused the other of not being sufficiently revolutionary, they went on to argue that "Ideology, pushed to its extreme, *shatters*. Its absolute use is also its absolute zero: the night in which all ideological cows are black."[10] Thus the Situationists argued that the competing ideologies were, like cows, all equally black in the shadow cast on all of them by the workers.[11]

Ernest Gellner added another twist when he used the same metaphor to tell a joke *against* Marxism, invoking the "cat" variant of the metaphor:

> There is an old East European joke concerning the differences between science, philosophy, and Marxism. What is science? It is trying to catch a very small black cat in a very large, entirely dark room. What is philosophy? It is trying to catch a very small black cat in a very large, entirely dark room, when it is not there. What is Marxism? It is trying to catch a very small black cat in a very large, entirely dark room when it is not there, and pretending that one has caught it and knows all about it.[12]

This is not, I think, a fair characterization of science, or philosophy (except, perhaps, Hegel's Schelling), or Marxism—though it does note their differences, but it is a not entirely inaccurate characterization of people who think that all Others (cows or cats) are alike.

The metaphor became so widespread that Dashiell Hammett, in *The Dain Curse*, let his tough private eye use it in a new variant; he refers to a "blind man in a dark room hunting for a black hat that wasn't there."[13] Has the cat become a hat? Is it a typo? Is it a joke? I wonder. David Shulman, in response to an early draft of this book, expanded the range of the metaphor to various religions: "Judaism is looking for a tiny black cat in a large dark room where there is no cat, while complaining loudly all the time that you have been badly and repeatedly scratched. Christianity is looking for a tiny black cat in a large dark room where there is no cat, while insisting that the one that used to be there has risen from the dead. Writing a doctorate is putting a tiny black cat in a large dark room and then coming back over and over to try to check if it is there."[14] And so forth and so on: like light bulb jokes, or, if you will, like myths, the metaphor of promiscuous sameness is itself promiscuous.

In a review of a violent movie, Terrence Rafferty complained: "When it's all over, and you've lit up your cigarette outside the theatre, you may have some trouble putting a name or a face to the movie that just had its way with you. 'Die Hard,' 'Lethal Weapon,' 'Goldfinger'—what's the difference? At a certain point, they all look the same in the dark."[15] Since this is at heart a sexual put-down,[16] it lends a masked obscenity to insults applied to nonsexual objects—even to films viewed in the darkness not of the bedroom but of the screening room.

Even without the metaphor of cats or cows in the dark, the assumption that all members of a class are alike has been used in many cultures to demean the sexual or racial Other. After all, the essence of prejudice has been defined as the assumption that an unknown individual has all the characteristics of the group to which he or she belongs. "People like you," or "They're all alike" is always an offensive phrase. Racism and sexism are alike in their practice of clouding the judgment so that the Other is beneath contempt, or at least beneath recognition; they dehumanize, deindividualize, the racially and sexually Other. "All Japanese look alike" is the racist counterpart to the sexist "In the dark, all cats are gray." The use of large numbers to obscure humanity, particularly political Others, is a well-known sexist trick, too: Mozart/Da Ponte's Don Giovanni boasted, famously, that he had seduced a thousand and three women in Spain.

Racism and sexism are often conflated not merely through peoples' shared attitude to the sameness of the sexual or racial Other, but in their *equation* of the sexual and racial Other. Often the woman herself is depicted as dark; or, to put it differently, the sexual Other—the woman—is conflated with the racial Other. Freud's use of the term "dark continent" to describe female sexuality has racial implications; he "borrowed the phrase from Victorian colonialist texts in which it was used to designate Africa,"[17] as Mary Ann Doane notes:

> The dark continent trope indicates the existence of an intricate historical articulation of the categories of racial difference and sexual difference. In it, there is an extraordinary condensation of motifs linking the white woman and the colonialist's notion of "blackness."[18]

Yet, as Eve Sedgwick points out, it behooves us to understand "*not* that all oppressions are congruent, but that they are *differently* structured."[19] That is, sexism and racism do not look precisely alike in the dark. In myth, as in life, knowledge of *difference* is the key to both sex and politics. Thus the nineteenth-century Sanskritist H. H. Wilson regarded the widely divergent, sometimes sexually deviant texts called Tantras as all "basically the same"; though he granted that they were "infinitely numerous," he remarked that a scholar need not read more than one or two Tantras to understand them all.[20] And what was done to texts was also done to people; or, to put it in what was more likely the causal sequence, what was done to people was also done to texts.

"Visible minorities" is the phrase used in Canada for people whose disabilities are not hidden (unlike those of some nationalities, presumably, or those with disabilities like deafness), but written on their faces (or on their bodies, if, for instance, they are in wheelchairs). Yet, as Ralph Ellison pointed out years ago, people of other races often become virtually invisible.[21] We speak of racial discrimination, but the myths teach us that the real problem is racial *in*discrimination—the unwillingness to discriminate between two different members of another race, the tendency to regard them all as doubles of one another. Niebuhr and Kant were part of an Enlightenment tradition that "expounded evil as the capacity to render invisible another human consciousness."[22]

One nineteenth-century writer asserted that "Tartar snouts all look the same, or Ethiopian ones all black, but when you look more carefully they are all different as well as alike. . . . [There are] some creatures which are so alike, as with flies, ants, worms, frogs, and many fish, that they cannot be told apart."[23] Carlo Ginzburg, who cites this text, remarks drily that "A Tartar architect, an Ethiopian unversed in architecture, or an ant would rank things differently." Indeed, the colonized return the compliment from time to time; an anthropologist friend of mine told me a story about another anthropologist, a short, fat, dark Jew, who was doing fieldwork in a town of 30,000 Chinese in which the only other non-Chinese was a tall, skinny, redheaded Lutheran minister. When the anthropologist complained that he kept getting the minister's mail, the Chinese postman apologized, saying, "Sorry, but you look so much alike."[24]

In order to continue to dominate these look-alikes, however, the powerful must be able to tell them apart. As Ginzburg puts it, "Every society needs to distinguish its members, but the ways of meeting this need vary with place and time."[25] Footprints in the ancient world[26] and fingerprints in the modern have been used to identify individuals. There is a political irony in the fact that the British learned the technique of fingerprinting from the Bengalis and then used it to control them (and other Indians). "In Bengal, as well as in China, there was a custom of imprinting letters and documents with a fingertip dipped in ink or tar; this was probably a consequence of knowledge derived from divinatory practice."[27] In 1860 Sir William Herschel, District Commissioner of Hooghly in Bengal, discovered this technique and decided to use it: "In India as in other British colonies, the natives were illiterate, disputatious, wily, deceitful, and to the eyes of a European all looked the same. . . . The imperial administrators had taken over the Bengalis' conjectural knowledge, and turned it against them." Even this technique, predicated upon the assumption that all "the natives" were *not* alike, however much they may have *seemed* to be so, was put to racist uses: "Galton . . . tried to trace racial characteristics in fingerprints, but did not succeed. He hoped, however, to pursue his research among some Indian tribes, expecting to find among them 'a more monkeylike pattern.' "[28]

It is this perverse use of the doctrine of sameness, applied to both texts and people, that the comparatist must overcome in order to argue for the very different humanistic uses of the same doctrine.

The Dog That Doesn't Bark

The metaphor of barking dogs has been used by historians of religions to describe various uses of comparison,[29] but like all good myths, it bears retelling in each new context and can always be used in new ways. Sherlock Holmes once solved a mystery, the case of Silver Blaze, a racehorse, by using a vital clue of omission. When Inspector Gregory asked Holmes whether he had noted any point to which he would draw the Inspector's attention, Holmes replied, "To the curious incident of the dog in the nighttime." "The dog did nothing in the night-time," objected the puzzled Inspector, the essential straight man for the Socratic sage. "That was the curious incident," remarked Sherlock Holmes. The fact that the dog did not bark when someone entered the house at night was evidence, in this case evidence that the criminal was someone familiar to the dog.[30] Dogs bark at *difference*—in this case, someone different from those with whom the dog was familiar.

We cannot, to borrow the Zen koan, hear the sound of one hand clapping; we cannot hear sameness. But through the comparative method we can see the blinkers that each culture constructs for its retellings of myths. Comparison makes it possible for us literally to *cross*-examine cultures, by using a myth from one culture to reveal to us what is *not* in a telling from another culture, to find out the things not "dreamt of in your philosophy" (as Hamlet said to Horatio).[31] Moreover, we can use comparative work to test theories about our own culture, by noting where our own dogs have not barked. Comparison defamiliarizes what we take for granted. We can only see the inflection of a particular telling when we see other variants.

The behavior of dogs offers another paradigm for the comparatist. Both the nature and the training of foxhounds make them use their noses, not their eyes (as sighthounds like Borzois do) to track the fox. A foxhunting colleague of mine, David Grene, once described his frustration on seeing a fox just yards away from young hounds who had their noses to the ground and insisted on following the scent off into the distance where the fox had been and back again to where he was now—but would not be for long. An older hound would have had the sense to look up.[32] Scholars bogged down in their rigid ways of scenting their prey are often forced by the comparative evidence to look up and see what is right in front of them, the more obvious (and invisible) human truths.

The comparative method also forces us to come to terms with the Other, the one both different from and the same as us. The challenge lies in choosing as the Other in whom we assume an initial likeness an Other as other as possible, as different from us as possible, perhaps one whom we don't like or understand at all at first and have to work hard to like or understand. The comparison that chooses an Other in which the initial likeness is more immediately apparent is more ethnocentric; it is easier, and ultimately it proves less.

But what aspects of the Other define Otherness? My colleague David Tracy, the Catholic theologian, is fond of engaging in dialogues with Buddhists; I used to chide him that he was taking the easy way out by choosing the reasonable, ethical Buddhists; to dialogue with Hindus would be the real test—all those gods, all those arms and heads. Not at all, he replied; Buddhists are far more Other than Hindus for a Catholic theologian since they have no god at all rather than too many gods, which is the Hindu challenge, mediated by the multiplicity of Catholic saints, the trinity, and so forth.[33] (Indeed, Catholicism and Hinduism have much in common, so much that a structuralist might suggest that Catholicism/Protestantism = Hinduism/Buddhism = South/North = multiplicity/unity = hot/cold = kitsch/aniconicism, and so on.) But Judaism, albeit monotheistic and hence on that level, at least, less Other than the atheism of Buddhism or the polytheism of Hinduism, turns out, for historical reasons, to pose even greater problems for a Catholic who wishes to engage in dialogue. Judaism has served as a projection for Catholics for so many years that the Jews are too close, too tangled with Catholic history, to be seen by some Catholics as they really are; unlike the Buddhists, the Jews must be retrieved from the Catholic projection and acknowledged in their reality, their real Otherness, before the conversation can begin.[34]

If we choose to use, for the Other in our comparison, a less dichoto-mizing word than "same," such as "similar," we might construct a contin-uum, as we did for verbal expressions in chapter 1; or better yet, we might make a Venn diagram: a set of categories that interlock like chain mail, with various degrees of resemblance or "family likenesses." In this way we can replace polarized grids with infinitely fluid continuums. But whatever word we choose to use for the same/like/similar/resembling pole of the comparison, we must come to terms with the other pole, the pole of dif-ference. And no matter what sort of an Other we choose at the start, from the initial assumption of likeness or sameness or similarity we must end up with difference.[35]

Moreover, similarity must not be allowed to be normative: to assume one's original stance, to begin by assuming the self in the Other on some level, to say that the Other is "like me" is to an extent inevitable. But it must immediately be qualified by both difference and the shift of center: one must go on to say, "I am like you," "I will be able to understand you because I am like you," and then, later, "I see ways in which you are in fact not like me." One must end by going over to the other side. For instance, if you know the Greek epic, the *Iliad*, you begin reading the Sanskrit epic, the *Ramayana*, by saying, "It's like the *Iliad*" (an epic). But then you must shift ground to notice how the *Iliad* is not like the *Ramayana*. It is natural but not good to be ethnocentric; acknowledging it is the first step but cannot be an excuse, a justification; you have to go on to see how the rest of the world is. There is no value-free comparison, but you do the best you can.

The initial, assumed comparison is always between us and the Other; this happens whenever we confront a single phenomenon from a culture not our own. Indeed, one of the arguments in favor of the comparative method is that even methods that pretend to be culturally specific are in fact comparative, when you take into account the fact that the scholar studying the one Other culture will always be making implicit judgments based upon implicit comparisons between the Other culture and the schol-ar's own. Moreover, particular tellings need comparative insight to prevent the interpreter from glossing that telling *only* in terms of the specific cul-tural context: a Cinderella tale in India, for instance, may very well be told in terms of the caste system (Cinderella treated as an Untouchable), but it cannot be explained *only* in those terms, once one knows that that story also occurs in other cultures that have no caste system.

When we go on from these initial, implicitly comparative assumptions to compare one Other with another Other, we are doing what is explicitly called comparison. But we are always pivoting upon our own understanding, which forms an invisible third side in the eternal triangle of the comparison of two other things. Deconstructionists see this subjectivity as inevitable in any interpretive position, and in a sense it is. But it is also a strength for anyone engaged in explicitly cross-cultural work: the observer, the one who compares the stories, stands at the intersection of cross-cultural paradigms and the unique events of history. By positioning herself on the plane of the various story lines, a scholar is able to triangulate and to construct a three-dimensional corpus of related stories. Of course, another person at another point of the triangle would construct a different corpus, but such structures are not competing for a single prize of Truth.

Jonathan Z. Smith has put it well: "In the case of the study of religion, as in any disciplined inquiry, comparison, in its strongest form, brings differences together within the space of the scholar's mind for the scholar's own intellectual reasons. It is the scholar who makes their cohabitation—their 'sameness'—possible, not 'natural' affinities or processes of history."[36] Taking up Charles Sanders Peirce's idea of the conceptual triad,[37] Smith points out that whenever we compare two things, we select and compare them with our own "intellectual reason," the third thing in the triangle of comparison.[38] But Peirce argued that that third thing had a kind of "semiotic realism" that was very real indeed.[39] I too argue for the reality of that third side.

For example, I am about to compare the story of Tamar and Judah from the Hebrew Bible (Genesis 38) and the story of Helena and Bertram from Shakespeare's *All's Well That Ends Well*. I selected them rather than other stories because both of them are implicitly compared in my mind with the subject on which I am writing a book, the sexual masquerade or bed trick:[40] in both stories, a woman whose husband refuses to sleep with her disguises herself as someone else and tricks him into bed. That third thing, the third side of the comparative triangle, is what makes them similar in my view: they both have a particular plot that interests me. To say that both the story of Tamar from the Hebrew Bible and the story of Helena from Shakespeare's *All's Well That Ends Well* have meaning for me, in America in 1997, speaks for a degree of generality: some problems that confronted Tamar and Helena are also being faced by contemporary American women. But it also means that a third construction has entered the field of play, and that my selection of these stories rather than others and my decision to highlight certain shared elements of them at the expense of other elements unique to each version is particular to me, not merely to my time and place. Claude Lévi-Strauss admitted that the themes that the mytholol" that the mythologist selects as the basis of the analysis "owe much to the analyst's subjectivity" and "have an impressionistic character."[41] But to say that they are subjective is not to say that they are entirely arbitrary. Their arbitrariness is limited by our responsibility to the data.

In comparing two myths, from two different cultures or within a single culture, we may use another myth (from that culture, or from another) to supplement our understanding of a given text. Such a supplement is needed in part, as Lévi-Strauss has demonstrated, because of the fragmentary nature of myths themselves (which must be supplemented by the fragments in other, related myths).[42] But the supplement is also needed because of the fragmentary nature of our *understanding* of myths, especially those embedded in ancient texts.

When myths tell us what happened, they do not always tell us why the people in the story did what they did or how they felt about what happened to them. To this extent, the myths remain open and transparent and can be retold within one culture or in several cultures with several very different meanings. Laconic texts leave us in the dark, where one thing looks much like another. Although well-told myths always have plenty of details to give them life and reality, they do not always have *psychological* details. Some myths are relatively brief because they are recited within rituals and liturgies that take place within clearly demarcated time periods; more secular genres, cut free of rituals, often add brilliant insights and artistic detail to the starker liturgical versions. I agree with the semioticist Yuri Lotman that "it no longer matters whether we use classical versions of myth or nineteenth-century novels as materials for our reconstruction of the mythological origins [I would say, meanings] of the text. Indeed, sometimes later texts provide more fruitful material for this kind of study."[43]

For example, when we read the Hebrew Bible story of Tamar and Judah, we might ask how it was that Judah was fooled, how he mistook Tamar for a strange prostitute.[44] Erich Auerbach noted long ago, in *Mimesis*, that the stark genre of the Hebrew Bible leaves silences, gaps, in stories that other traditions, such as the longer-winded, elaborated genre of the Greeks, tell in greater detail; in comparison with Homer, the Hebrew Bible externalizes "only so much of the phenomena as is necessary for the purpose of the narrative, all else left in obscurity; the decisive points of the narrative alone are emphasized, what lies in between is nonexistent; time and place are undefined and call for interpretation; thoughts and feelings remain unexpressed, are only suggested by the silence and the fragmentary speeches."[45] In the story of Tamar and Judah, the narrative background remains opaque and the reader is left with insoluble riddles. As Robert Alter says, "No response on the part of Tamar is recorded. This may suggest silent submission, or at least her lack of any legal options as a childless young widow, and it certainly leaves us wondering about what she is feeling—something which her actions will presently elucidate."[46] In fact, her actions do not elucidate a great deal.

Within this particular tradition, the Jewish tradition, later commentaries were troubled by Judah's failure to recognize Tamar and argued about it and attempted to grapple with it. (They suggested that Judah was drunk,[47] or had never seen Tamar *unveiled*,[48] and so forth).[49] These commentaries force us to face several interesting questions of interpretation. First of all, from the standpoint of genre, we may ask whether it is kosher, as it were, to cite successive commentaries on a text as an interpretation of that text, or whether it would be wiser to view the new interpretation as a totally different version, and then deal with the question of why this new insight was drawn from the old text. And what do you do when you think the commentaries are misreading the text? Our response to these questions may be qualified by our awareness of the status of the commentary in each particular tradition; some are more closely tied to the text than others. (Here the comparison of commentaries tells us something about what each one barks at, as it were, that we would not notice by looking at each commentary by itself). But regardless of our confidence, or lack of confidence, in the commentarial tradition, we must grant that the culture, through its commentaries, opens up the text for us, makes a space within which we too may endeavor to construct our own meanings[50]—sometimes, indeed, to appropriate the text for our own purposes.

We can, however, also seek unofficial commentaries outside the tradition of the original text. It might well be argued that Shakespeare's *All's Well That Ends Well* offers many wise answers to the questions left open by the Hebrew Bible story of Tamar and Judah, insights into the psychology of sexual rejection, for example, answers that the rabbis did not think of (or did not choose to record) as well as different answers to questions that they did think of. Some postmodern scholars create their own fictions, blatantly imagining what the author might have had in mind but neglected to put into the text, and all creative analysts of myth must do this to some extent. Tom Stoppard did to Shakespeare what, I am arguing, Shakespeare did to the Bible when Stoppard wrote *Rosencrantz and Guildenstern Are Dead*, creating dialogue to fill in the gaps that Shakespeare had left between the two characters' relatively brief appearances on stage in *Hamlet*.

Gary Saul Morson has illuminated a similar process in the ways in which certain novelists, particularly Dostoyevski and Tolstoi, imagine and vividly depict alternative events that allow us to see what might have been. He argues that essentially the same device is also "found in popular culture, in religion, and in other forms of low and high literature, such as the form I call the *paraque*"—a term he has coined to describe the process by which "one author continues or fills in the gaps in a well-known classic by another."[51] The realm of myth is the realm of Morson's *paraque*, par excellence.

Hilary Mantel argued against this sort of creative expansion by scholars, as opposed to novelists, in his review of a book by John Demos about captivity narratives:

> One might argue that in his new book Demos has done the risky, the necessary thing. He has embraced imagination, and yielded—in a controlled and chary way—to its delights. So he has written certain interposed passages of reconstruction, or supposition, or—let us spit the word out—fiction.[52]

But the comparatist can sidestep the dangers of fiction and take the more reasonable, if relatively cowardly, option of using the speculations found in similar stories told in other cultures to fill in what is not said in the text under consideration. From Lévi-Strauss we learn that within a culture, the best gloss on a myth is another myth within that culture; from Mircea Eliade we learn that outside a culture, the best gloss on a myth is a myth from another culture. And we can enlarge the arena of meaning more and more, leaping from myth to myth as if they were stepping-stones over the gulf that seems to separate cultures. In this way the comparatist may use Shakespeare to discipline his or her own imagination of what might have been in the minds of Tamar and Judah. Zwi Jagendorf, speaking of the trick that Leah plays on Jacob (a sexual substitution both like and unlike the trick that Tamar plays on Judah), agrees that "Shakespeare makes us understand in Helena's words what Leah might have thought in Jacob's arms."[53] And this is a two-way flow: questions about Shakespeare might be resolved by looking back (or sideways) at myths, "the same sort of myths out of which many of [Shakespeare's] plays develop."[54]

For example, one suggestion, not in any Jewish commentary that I know, is made by a variant of the myth of Tamar from yet another tradition, which reverses the gender of the trickster and the stated reason for the trick but retains the central problem of recognizing, or not recognizing, one's spouse in bed. This is the story of the return of Martin Guerre, as documented by Nathalie Zemon Davis, in which an imposter did or did not fool Martin Guerre's wife in bed.[55] From the French incident we learn that the "duped" person may well not be duped at all, but may have reasons to pretend to have been duped—an insight that makes a lot of sense if we read it back into the story of Tamar and Judah. Going outside the tradition allows us to note that in the Hebrew Bible the dog does not bark at the problem of Judah's possible self-delusion.[56] But that silence, which we only notice from the noise of variant stories, cannot simply be filled in by speculations offered by other traditions; we must also note the fact that the Hebrew Bible *chooses* to be silent, that it doesn't care to consider the question of Judah's possible complicity in his own delusion. It is also evident that the Bible did not care to tell us what Tamar felt like when she slept with Judah. But we can answer some of our own questions about the Bible by reading Shakespeare; we can imagine what a woman in Tamar's situation might have felt, and imagine a woman's voice in the Bible asking that, and being suppressed. Silence too is a statement, but one that we can only hear when we compare it with other sounds.

The comparative method suggests that we might, with caution, read into the story of Tamar and Judah some of the answers suggested by non-Jewish texts. So much has been written about the story of Tamar by biblical scholars that I could never hope to rush in where Talmudists fear to tread, to contribute to their conversation. But I might, I hope, bring the story into another sort of conversation, about the meanings of such stories not merely in the historical context of ancient Judaism but in the broader context of the human religious imagination and even beyond, in the context of human experience. And I would hope that scholars of the Bible might come to read *All's Well That Ends Well* for new insights into the story of Tamar, and that Shakespearean scholars might look again at the Bible.

But then a still small voice of caution is heard: Would the author of the story of Tamar have felt like Shakespeare about such things as sexual rejection? And a related question: How do we know our questions are not projections? To some extent, of course, they are; we cannot know what was in the mind of an author. But projecting other texts, rather than or in addition to our own ideas, into the text in question at least makes the projection more subtle, and argues for an imaginary line drawn not just between our heads and the Bible but between Shakespeare's head and the Bible. This method puts the texts themselves in conversation with each other,[57] sometimes even in the intimate pillow talk of textual intercourse.

The key to the game of cross-cultural comparison lies in selecting the sorts of questions that might transcend any particular culture. Some people think that there are no such questions, but some think, as I do, that worthwhile cross-cultural questions can be asked. Marliss C. Desens assumes a commensurability in audience response to the tales of the trick played by Tamar in Genesis and Helena in Shakespeare: "It may be that some of our contemporary responses to the bed-trick belong to our own cultural context, and we should not ignore such responses [I would say, we should not assume that the first audiences shared them], but we might also pause to examine whether we have some common bond with those first audiences."[58]

Lévi-Strauss himself said it best and most boldly: "In proposing the study of mankind, anthropology frees me from doubt, since it examines those *differences and changes* in mankind which have a meaning for all men, and excludes those peculiar to a single civilization, which dissolve into nothingness under the gaze of the outside observer."[59] Thus difference itself becomes a basis for comparison—a comparison made possible only by the assumption that difference has "a meaning for all men" (and, presumably, for all women). In other words, one of the ways in which we are all alike is our shared interest in our differences.

The collecting of variants reconstructs a narrative pattern that becomes clearer as stories are added to it, like "the assembling of a jigsaw puzzle when no box cover exists to reveal what the completed picture should look like. . . . Puzzle pieces are constructed so that a single one of them links more than one other."[60] There is a Midrash on Psalm 85:11 ("Love and truth fought together") about an argument between Love and Truth in which, to break the tie, God hurled Truth to the ground (Daniel 8:12), smashing it to smithereens.[61] Later tradition continues the story: "From then on truth was splintered all over in fragments, like a jigsaw puzzle, and while a person might find a piece, it had little meaning until he could find others who had different pieces of the puzzle, and thus slowly they could try to fit their pieces of Truth together to make some sense of things."[62] But when we choose to juxtapose one piece of the puzzle, one variant of a myth, with another piece, another myth, we assume that there *is* a puzzle, even though there never has been a box with the picture; moreover, we are assuming that the two pieces are parts of "the same" puzzle rather than two different puzzles, that they are variants on "the same" theme—and we must say what we mean by "the same." This is not so easy as might at first appear.

The Same Old Story

What do we mean when we say that the story of Tamar and the story of Helena are variants of "the same" myth? No two retellings of the same story are quite alike. Even two variants of a story composed by one person at different moments, or two identical recitations of one variant heard by the same person at different moments, may be very different. Because we have lived through more of our own personal histories each time we hear the story, we hear it differently even if not a word is changed. The same story is not the same story. This is what the French philosopher Jean-Pierre Joshua had in mind when he remarked that he re-read Proust every ten years to see how *he* had changed.[63] Woody Allen satirized this difference in re-readings of "the same" story in a short story in which a Jewish businessman from New York got into Flaubert's novel *Madame Bovary* and had an affair with Emma, so that anyone who read the book read about the businessman. A Stanford professor, noting with surprise that this new character had entered the text, explained to his class, "Well, I guess the mark of a classic is that you can reread it a thousand times and always find something new."[64]

Hamlet's mother, referring to the death of his father, insisted, "Thou know'st 'tis common. . . . Why seems it so particular with thee?" to which Hamlet replied, "Seems madam? Nay, it is. I know not 'seems.'"[65] Myths too, though "common," always become "particular." They are not really "the same" when they are transposed from one cultural context to another. The signifiers translate from Sanskrit to English, but what is signified may be very different indeed. And since the meanings given to those structures even within a single culture often differ dramatically, we can expect even wider variations when we cross the boundary into another culture. The myth that is reassembled from "the same" parts, even a variant that presents "the same" parts in "the same" order, may take on a new meaning and become a different myth within a single culture, let alone when it is translated into another.

For instance, the Hindu story of the creation of a double of Sita to save her from being raped by the demon Ravana and the Greek story of the creation of a double of Helen to save her from being seduced by Paris are only superficially the same; the shadow Sita was constructed to keep Sita pure when she was elevated to divinity between the earlier telling by Valmiki and the later telling by Tulsi Das, while the phantom Helen was constructed by Plato, Herodotus, and Euripides to mock the vain futility of the Trojan war (and, by implication, the Peloponnesian war), since the Trojan war was fought (according to them) for a whore who wasn't even there. In both cases there are significant differences not only between one culture and another (Hindu and Greek), but between different retellings in a single culture (from Valmiki to Tulsi and from Homer to Euripides).[66]

Within the storytelling tradition itself, the dangers of regarding the stories of two different people as "the same" have been well explored. In Anthony Trollope's novel *Kept in the Dark*, a man and a woman meet; he tells her his story, that he was jilted by his fiancée; she, it happens, has just jilted her own fiancé, and hesitates to tell him this because, she reasons, her story is the same as his story and he will think that she is mocking him, throwing his own story back in his face. She keeps the secret of her previous engagement even after she eventually marries him. When he finds out, he is deeply troubled—not by the similarity, but by the difference: her fiancé was a cad and a bounder, unlike him; and his fiancée was a silly little girl, unlike her. And even if their stories *were* in essence the same, why did she assume that this would estrange them rather than draw them even closer together (as, in the end, it does)?

The Context

Attention to cultural specificity is part of the Hippocratic oath of historians of religions, including mythologists. The need for historical, in addition to cultural, specificity demands even more rigor, for it requires that the phenomenon (in my case, the myth) be contextualized not only in space (the bounds of the culture) but also in time (the particular moment in that culture when the myth was told). This demand is one that many historians of religions regard as even more essential to their work than the demand for cultural specificity.

Texts have contexts, are determined by their contexts; the context in which "the same" story is told may totally transform its meaning, like the glass of water in the old toast to the exiled kings: when James II and James III were in exile in France, their supporters in England, forced to toast the reigning kings whom they did not recognize, would raise their wine glasses and say, "To the king"—but they would hold their wine glasses over their water glasses, so that they were in fact toasting "the king over the water." Exponents of the myth-and-ritual school argue that the ritual (the equivalent of the gesture with the wine glass) holds the key to the meaning of the myth (the equivalent of the words of the toast). With myths such as the story of Eden, which we will consider in chapter 4, the particular point in time and space in which the myth is told may serve, like the glass of water in the toast, to turn the meaning on its head. Even if we acknowledge that the myth in all of its widely distributed forms carries some cross-cultural human meaning, what it *says about* this basic meaning differs not only from culture to culture but within individual cultures. And when one culture borrows a plot or a theme from another, it becomes a different plot; it is not "the same" story anymore.

Context is the key to the answer offered by Laura Bohannan to a question we considered above—Would the author of a story in the Hebrew Bible have felt like Shakespeare about such things as sexual rejection? Bohannan documented, hilariously, the ways in which the plot of *Hamlet* became very different once she had heard it explained by the Africans among whom she did her fieldwork: Hamlet became the villain, Claudius the hero. This narrative debacle arose when an Englishman challenged Bohannan, an American, saying, "You Americans often have difficulty with Shakespeare. He was, after all, a very English poet, and one can easily misinterpret the universal by misunderstanding the particular." Bohannan protested "that human nature is pretty much the same the whole world over; at least the general plot and motivation of the greater tragedies would always be clear—everywhere—although some details of translation might produce other slight changes."[67] The uproarious Hamlet revision seriously challenged this belief in Bohannan—though not, I must admit, in me.

Yet I would be the first to grant that a story told in a different context can become a very different story. Jorge Luis Borges writes about the difference between two tellings of a story that are literally the same, word for word, in his tale of Pierre Menard, who personally reinvented Cervantes' story of *Don Quixote*:

> It is a revelation to compare Menard's *Don Quixote* with Cervantes.' The latter, for example, wrote (part one, chapter nine):
>
> . . . truth, whose mother is history, rival of time, depository of deeds, witness of the past, exemplar and adviser to the present, and the future's counselor.
>
> Written in the seventeenth century, written by the "lay genius" Cervantes, this enumeration is a mere rhetorical praise of history. Menard, on the other hand, writes:
>
> . . . truth, whose mother is history, rival of time, depository of deeds, witness of the past, exemplar and adviser to the present, and the future's counselor.
>
> History, the *mother* of truth: the idea is astounding. Menard, a contemporary of William James, does not define history as an inquiry into reality but as its origin. Historical truth, for him, is not what has happened; it is what we judge to have happened. The final phrases . . . are brazenly pragmatic.[68]

The same words take on entirely different meanings for us because of our understanding of what has happened in history between the two moments of their composition. The content of the piece is not insignificant, either: if history is truth, then when the same words move forward in history, they are no longer the same words.

Wherever possible, it is important to note the context: who is telling the story and why. Even when we do not know the answers to these questions (as is usually the case, especially with ancient texts), it is still useful at least to hazard an educated guess (a guess I will try to make about women's voices). Even though we cannot know the context of the readers (let alone the authors) of many of our ancient texts, we ourselves, as readers, are a context, sometimes the only one to which we have access: we can always know (and sometimes only know) what the texts mean to us. And when we do not know the true voice of the tellers, the original authors and audiences, we must, *faute de mieux*, listen to the voices in the text.

But even when we do know the author, the text's embeddedness in its culture makes it extend beyond its "author." Texts may be not only androgynous but also, ultimately, nonsectarian. Their authors may not be anonymous, but they are collective. And that collectivity extends beyond the bounds of culture to other cultures that may share many of the same plots and agendas, despite their different historical experiences. Moreover, the contexts themselves are embedded in the texts if we know how to look for them, in the unique details that each text takes from its context.

Clearly we lose a great deal when we lose context. But comparative work need not be contextualized to be rigorous, and concern for context can become hypertrophied. Of course, it is essential for the comparatist to *know* the general context in order to have data against which to test any interpretation (this means learning languages, reading commentaries, and so forth). But it is not essential for this thick cultural description to be a part of the interpretation ultimately presented to the reader as a basis of comparison. Though something precious is lost when context is lost, something else, also precious, is gained.

The argument for comparison must justify taking myths out of their historical context and supplying instead the context of other myths, other related ideas, as Lévi-Strauss argued long ago.[69] And, as he has not explicitly argued but as his own writings seem to imply,[70] these other myths may be taken from other cultures. Often the best way to understand a myth is by understanding how it differs from other myths in the same culture as well as from variants in other cultures.

We might also compare the contexts themselves, and some people do. We can, for instance, compare performative contexts, asking in each case, What makes a teller choose to tell that story then? What else is going on? We can also compare the relations between text and context in two parallel situations. Milman Parry and Albert Lord compared the contexts, the oral performances, of observable tellers of tales in contemporary Yugoslavia with what they extrapolated from the unobservable situation of Homer in ancient Greece (as I would consider certain aspects of the expanded myth in Shakespeare in relation to the unavailable psychological context of the Hebrew Bible); this has led to a new, albeit disputed, reading of Homer.[71] Discussing myths of transsexuality in India, the Indologist Robert P.

Goldman argues on the one hand that they are generated by "a powerful complex of anxieties that is generated by specific features of traditional South Asian family and social life," and on the other that "The kinds of myths, legends, and fantasies cited in this paper, and the social, psychological, and political realities of which they are expressions are by no means restricted to South Asia. . . . Innumerable examples of this can be adduced from European, East Asian, Islamic, and other traditions."[72] In other words, the myths *and the contexts* that, in this view, explain them are shared across "European, East Asian, Islamic, and other traditions."

Comparing contexts—more precisely, comparing the relations of texts to their contexts—might allow us to advance the comparative enterprise without lapsing into the follies of universalism, by taking a kind of middle ground. If we construct another continuum, this time one of the individual, the group/culture, and the human race, we might focus on one relatively solid intermediary path between the two extremes: cultural morphology, or the morphology of cultural types. For groups or societies that have the same sorts of structures and practices may tell the same sorts of myths. Perhaps it is best to look for parallels not within a single culture (treating men and women, rich and poor, as the same, overlooking the differences between kings and peasants, men and women), let alone across cultures, but between the same sorts of people in different cultures (Chinese peasant women and Indian peasant women).[73] This project would take account of differences between men and women as storytellers, and also between rich and poor, dominant and oppressed, through the comparison of contexts. The morphological approach somewhat resembles the project suggested by Milan Kundera: "Insofar as it is possible to divide people into categories, the surest criterion is the deep-seated desires that orient them to one or another life-long activity. Every Frenchman is different. But all actors the world over are similar—in Paris, Prague, or the back of beyond."[74]

The morphological approach also allows us to acknowledge what the historicizing approach often obscures, that the negative aspects of other peoples' prejudices (such as their attitudes to women) are also shared (a sexist stance that might be called politically erect). When cultural studies silences the cross-cultural critique, as it sometimes does, it may back into another political problem by implicitly validating injustices committed within another culture—just as cultural relativism often does, though coming from another direction. Cultural morphology could tackle these injustices in a new way. But comparing the contexts threatens to take them out of context, and thus to land us in an infinite regress (are all peasants alike? all women?). Moreover, a telling embedded in its context requires a lot of space, and thus limits the comparison.

I have argued for what is gained by comparison, why it is worth doing; and I have acknowledged what is lost when we ignore context. Brent D. Shaw, reviewing Caroline Walker Bynum's *The Resurrection of the Body* (a book first presented in a previous American Lectures on the History of Religions series), argued:

> The social forces that were particular to a given historical epoch of-fer a better explanatory context, for concepts of self and embodi-ment in the hereafter, than a generalized, ahistorical, long-term fear. If the relation of body to soul in the late middle ages was de-scribed in the imagery of lovers, then this must be related to the increasing importance of new ideas of secular love in the period; and those new ideas, in turn, must be related to the emergence of new economic individuals.[75]

Why *must* new ideas of secular love be "related to the emergence of new economic individuals"? The analysis that Shaw is calling for would give a certain sort of answer, grounded in one moment; Caroline Bynum asks different questions and offers different answers that extend beyond that moment.

There are ways in which to make the comparative project responsibly aware of the complementary (I refuse to regard it as competing) project of historical contextualization. It is not my intention to privilege the com-paratist over either the authors within the culture or other scholars who contextualize the myths within the culture: the cross-cultural view is not an overview that subsumes the contextualized view, but an alternative view that slices the problem in a different way, that sees sideways, hori-zontally, instead of vertically. Nor do I mean to imply that the historical contexts in which the cross-culturalist finds her stories are not themselves cross-cultural, multicultural; the original context is itself complex, the product of many cultural interactions, and the cross-culturalist simply substitutes for them other (multi)cultures. Sir Isaiah Berlin took the title of his famous essay on history, *The Hedgehog and the Fox*, from a line of Archilocus: "The fox knows many things, and the hedgehog knows one big thing." It could be argued that comparatists are foxes, contextualists hedgehogs; scholarship needs them both.

The Whole and the Parts: Chariots and Knives

Given the change that inevitably takes place when a myth is moved from one culture to another, how can one argue for the continuing identity of one story in many variants, or the essential unity in cross-cultural variants of a story? One might adapt to this case the argument that was made by William James about Sir John Cutler, who had a pair of black worsted stockings that had been darned so often with silk thread that they had no trace of the original thread. "If they had been endowed with consciousness through the darning, they would at the end have thought themselves as still a pair of worsted stockings, though not a thread of the original material was left."[76]

David Hume argued along the same (or similar) lines for the continuing identity of one person in many different forms:

> A ship, of which a considerable part has been chang'd by frequent reparations, is still consider'd as the same; nor does the difference of the materials hinder us from ascribing an identity to it. . . . This is the case with all animals and vegetables; where not only the several parts have a reference to some general purpose, but also a mutual dependance on, and connexion with each other. The effect of so strong a relation is, that tho' every one must allow, that in a very few years both vegetables and animals endure a *total* change, yet we still attribute identity to them, while their form, size, and substance are entirely alter'd. An oak, that grows from a small plant to a large tree, is still the same oak; tho' there be not one particle of matter, or figure of its parts the same. An infant becomes a man, and is sometimes fat, sometimes lean, without any change in his identity.[77]

The Tin Woodman of Oz, after all, had replaced every part of his body but still remained somehow himself (though significantly, he *thought*, wrongly, that he lacked a heart). And scientists tell us that our bodies are entirely regenerated, cell by cell, every seven years (the period also traditionally regarded as the limit for sexual fidelity, the so-called "Seven Year Itch," perhaps not a coincidence).

Ernest Gellner has argued that Hume's Enlightenment metaphor of the ship was designed to prevent a kind of Manichean splitting:

> [Hume's] *Treatise on Human Nature* gave a profoundly *un*-dualistic account of man, and one continuous with nature. . . . So duality was overcome: the old cohabitation of Angel and Beast was replaced by Hume's famous "Bundle of Perceptions." The elements from which this bundle was assembled were exactly the same as those of any other object of nature, and were simply accumulated by the senses. So there was no further reason to assume special, extra-territorial status for humankind within nature. That creature, assembled from such fragmented, transparent and hence basically innocuous elements, I shall on occasion call the "Bundleman."[78]

Hume's is therefore not a fragmenting, but on the contrary an integrating, construction of the self.

But the same/similar image (in this case, a chariot rather than a ship) was invoked by an ancient Buddhist text to argue *against* the continuing identity of one person in many different forms. The Buddhist text is in itself a fine example of cross-cultural understanding: it is *The Questions of Milinda*, which purports to record a conversation that took place between the Greek king Menander, who ruled in northwestern India about the middle of the second century B.C.E. (though the text is later by some centuries), and the Buddhist sage Nagasena, who converted the king to Buddhism. Here is a somewhat condensed version of their conversation, another version of the sage-and-stooge routine that we first encountered in the tale of Sherlock Holmes (with the added Socratic twist: "Read my mind"):

> King Menander asked, "How are you known, and what is your name?" and Nagasena replied, "I'm known as Nagasena, your Majesty; that's what my fellow monks call me. But though my parents may have given me such a name, it does not imply that there is a permanent individual." The king said, "If your fellow monks call you Nagasena, what is Nagasena? Is it your hair?" "No, your Majesty." "Or your nails, teeth, skin, or other parts of your body, or the outward form, or sensation, or perception, or the psychic constructions, or consciousness? Are any of these Nagasena?" "No, your Majesty." "Then for all my asking I find no Nagasena. Nagasena is a mere sound! Surely what your Reverence has said is false."
>
> Then the Venerable Nagasena addressed the King. "Your Majesty, how did you come here—on foot, or in a vehicle?" "In a chariot." "Then tell me what is the chariot? Is the pole the chariot?" "No, your reverence." "Or the axle, wheels, frame, reins, yoke, spokes, or goad?" "None of these things is the chariot." "Then all these separate parts taken together are the chariot?" "No, your Reverence." "Then is the chariot something other than the separate parts?" "No, your Reverence." "Then for all my asking, your Majesty, I can find no chariot. The chariot is a mere sound. What then is the chariot? Surely what your Majesty has said is false! There is no chariot!" "What I said was not false," replied the king. "It's on account of these various components, the pole, axle, wheels, and so on, that the vehicle is called a chariot. It's just a generally understood term, a practical designation." "Well said, your Majesty! You know what the word 'chariot' means! And it's just the same with me. It's on account of the various components of my being that I'm known by the generally understood term, the practical designation Nagasena!"[79]

Thus there is nothing but a convention, a name. That both Hume and the Buddhist chose the same/similar image (of the construction of a chariot or a ship) to explain the same/similar process (of the continuous de- and re-construction of the human body) is an example of form mirroring content (the similarity of the minds of the authors writing about the sameness of the successive bodies); that they used it for diametrically opposed arguments (one that the body *was*, the other that the body *was not*, the same) is an example of the transparency of such images, of their ability to support polarized meanings, and of the importance of historical context. Together, the two cross-cultural uses of this image provide a parable of the similar-in-the-different.

A. K. Ramanujan made a good case against Hume and for Nagasena, using a folk metaphor for the way that different histories make the "same" symbol different: A bird had golden feathers, and plucked them out one by one to help her friends. Each time a feather came off, a black feather came to take its place. Eventually the bird had nothing but black feathers; but it was not the "same" as a bird who had always had nothing but black feathers.[80] There is also the story of the knife:

> In a story told about Aristotle in Europe, and about an Indian philosopher in India, the philosopher meets a village carpenter who has a beautiful old knife and asks him, "How long have you had this knife?" The carpenter answers, "Oh, the knife has been in our family for generations. We have changed the handle a few times and the blade a few times, but it is the same knife." Similarly, in a folktale that goes on changing from teller to teller, the structure of the tale may remain constant while all the cultural details change. Parts of different tales are combined to make a new tale which expresses a new aesthetic and moral form characteristic of the culture. When the same tale is told again in a different time or place, it may come to say fresh and appropriate things, often without any change in the story line. Any fixity, any reconstructed archetype, is a fiction, a label, a convenience.[81]

This "fiction" is the shared core of meaning that I have argued for. But a fiction is a very real thing, and I think that the carpenter and Hume were right: it *is* the same knife in a sense worth talking about—formal, perhaps even historical, but not material. It is also significant that this story had meaning for the followers of both Aristotle and "an Indian philosopher," to say nothing of Hume and the ancient Buddhists. Indeed, I know of other American examples: a friend of mine once saw, in a museum, a hatchet said to be the one with which George Washington had chopped down the cherry tree; the label noted that the handle had been replaced many times, and so had the blade, but it was still George Washington's hatchet.[82] So, too, for legal reasons, a friend restoring a historically significant but totally decayed house in Key West had to do it one wall at a time, so that the original structure always remained in place.[83] A scholar arguing for cultural distinctiveness would take the texts from Hume and argue that the Buddhist myth is different from Hume's metaphor; indeed, no one variant of the Buddhist myth is like another; indeed, no one Buddhist is like another Buddhist. But a cross-culturalist would argue that many myths say that the whole survives—or, as the case may be, does not survive—even when all the parts change. We might say that Milinda's chariot was replaced by Aristotle's knife, which was replaced by the Indian knife, and that by Washington's hatchet, and that by Hume's ship, and that by the house that Jack built in Key West. But this certainly does not mean that we cannot take an equal interest in the moments when the blade or the handle was replaced, the moments of cross-cultural translation.

The same Buddhist text that discussed the chariot provides us with another image, of the lamp and the flame, closer to that of the knife's blade and handle. This image is embedded in an explanation of the mechanism by which rebirth can take place despite the fact that there is no soul to transmigrate, but we might adapt it to the argument for the transmigration of certain mythic themes despite the fact that there is no archetype to hand on. King Menander asks, "When a man is born does he remain the same [being] or become another?" to which Nagasena replies, predictably, "He neither remains the same nor becomes another." When the king asks for an example, Nagasena argues that, just as the flame that burns in a lamp is different at every moment, yet "The same lamp gives light through all the night. . . . Similarly, one person comes into existence, another passes away, and the sequence runs continuously without self-conscious existence, neither the same nor yet another." And just as when a man lights one lamp from another, one lamp does not transmigrate to the other, so too "There is rebirth without anything transmigrating."[84] So too, we may say, there is a connection between the different variants of these stories in different cultures even though there is no single thing that is always carried across the cultural boundary.

Despite the usefulness, for the comparative enterprise, of the Enlightenment concept of the Bundleman and the role of Enlightenment thinkers in advancing the doctrine of human universals, the Enlightenment is in some ways the villain of this piece. Its rationalism brought a resurgence of a strain of Euhemerism, the belief (named after an ancient Sicilian named Euhemerus, who demythologized the Greek gods) that myths and fairy tales are not only based on true stories about real people, but that they were originally *told* as stories about specific real people. I argue that even if this were so, these stories were, from the start, also about human problems that extended beyond the particular individuals in the first telling.

The Euhemerist emphasis on social conditions (even on social conditions shared by more than one particular culture) snatches the (lived) cross-cultural experience from the jaws of the (fantasized) archetype. This is well and good. But to defend social context over ahistorical structures is to choose empiricism over imagination. Lawrence Sullivan provides a useful corrective to Jonathan Z. Smith's useful corrective to Mircea Eliade's lack of historicism when he reminds us that the social sciences, of which history is one, were utilized as a defense and distraction against the powerful worldviews of colonized peoples emerging into Western consciousness. To insist on historical context is therefore to deny the power of the mythic or imaginal consciousness; it is yet another way to deny difference, to remain unmoved and in control.[85] This insistence, this denial, if carried out to the letter, would be the death of the study of cross-cultural mythology.

Chapter 3

Implied Spiders and the Politics
of Individualism

Universalist Problems

What do we mean by saying that a story is "the same as" or even "similar to" another story while acknowledging that the context is different? We often feel that the various tellings of a much-retold myth are the same, at least in the sense that they do not disappoint us by omitting what we regard as essential parts of the myth, without which it would lose at the very least some of its charm, and at the most its meaning. When we say that two myths from two different cultures are "the same" we mean that there are certain plots that come up again and again, revealing a set of human concerns that transcend any cultural barriers, experiences that we might call cross-cultural or transcultural. As Marina Warner puts it,

> Of course there are fairy tales unique to a single place, which have not been passed on. But there are few really compelling ones that do not turn out to be wearing seven-league boots. The possibility of holding a storehouse of narrative in common could act to enhance our reciprocal relations, to communicate across spaces and barricades of national self-interest and pride. We share more than we perhaps admit or know, and have done so for a very long time.[1]

We share, for instance, the realization that we are separate from our parents, the knowledge that they will die ("Thou know'st 'tis common"), that we will die. And we share the experiences of joy: sex, food, singing, dancing, sunrise, sunset, moonlight, puppies, going to the seashore. People all over the world fall in love and have babies; stories about these experiences must have *something* in common. As C. S. Lewis put it, "Myth is the isthmus which connects the peninsular world of thought with the vast continent we really belong to."[2] We share certain dispositions and predilections, and that's why coffee and tea catch on everywhere once they are brought from the Orient[3] — and why certain myths catch on when they are brought from the Orient.

And certain questions recur in myths, which I would call religious questions: Why are we here? What happens to us when we die? Is there a God? How did men come to be different from women? Questions such as these, which are the driving force behind myths, have no empirical answers, and there is much disagreement about the nonempirical answers that have been advanced. Different cultures predispose their members to perceive shared experiences differently and to ask shared questions differently. Cross-cultural comparisons therefore have much to contribute to the insoluble chicken-and-egg paradox of nature vs. nurture: if we suspect that certain things are culturally constructed but several different cultures construct them in the same way, that sameness strikes a blow on the side of nature.

The themes held in common with other texts may not constitute the most important aspect of a myth, but they do make a useful base from which to ask questions about differences. Some of the questions posed by myths and some of the images and the naked outlines of a narrative are cross-cultural, but the shared images and ideas are structured in a narrative in different ways, so as to give very different answers and sometimes to ask different questions. Onto the shared base, each telling adds something unique, sometimes transformingly unique. And a shared meaning need not be an identical meaning. Jonathan Z. Smith has rightly faulted comparatists for assuming that they must "assert either identity or uniqueness."[4] Indeed, perhaps the claim of the comparatist should be not that two stories are identical but merely that they share some meanings.

Accounting for mythological themes that appear in different cultures by assuming that they derive from certain shared human experiences frees us from the obligation of specifying a mechanism (such as C. G. Jung's collective unconscious, or, more respectably — but no more convincingly — historical diffusion) by which a universal theme might be perpetrated. All we need point out is that the same forms do appear in many different places, in response to human experiences that appear to be similar on at least one level, and that they take on different meanings to the extent that those experiences turn out to be dissimilar on other levels.

As Shylock said in defense of one minority group, "Hath not a Jew eyes? Hath not a Jew hands, organs, dimensions, senses, affections, passions? If you prick us, do we not bleed? If you tickle us, do we not laugh? If you poison us, do we not die? And if you wrong us, shall we not revenge?"[5] Note the different sorts of things that he implicitly holds up for comparison: physical organs and physiological processes, which most of us would agree are universal; but also affections and passions, laughter and revenge, which some of us would regard as far more culturally constructed. President John F. Kennedy, in his epoch-making speech at the American University in 1963, trying to end the cold war, named what he regarded as "our most common link": "We all inhabit this small planet, we all breathe the same air, we all cherish our children's futures, and we are all mortal." The arguments of Shylock and Kennedy arose out of political rather than academic debates, but their point is also useful in a more general humanistic argument. Indeed, we might even aspire to generalize beyond human commonality and include animals among those who share our experiences—they too, after all, breath air, care for their young, and are mortal—though it is unlikely that they share with Shylock and Kennedy the awareness of their own mortality.[6]

Plato discussed the relationship between such shared experiences and the myths that refract them in a discussion of myths about the change in the direction of the sun and moon:

> Every one of these stories comes from the very same experience (*pathos*), and in addition to these thousands of others even more amazing (*thaumastotera*), but in the course of time some of them have been lost and others have been scattered in diaspora (*diesparmena*) and are told each one separated from the others. But the thing that is the cause (*aition*) of all of these, the experience, no one has told.[7]

Plato's single, seminal experience is a cosmic one that occurred only once: the withdrawal of the creator from the universe after he had created it. My single, seminal experience (for each myth) is a human one that occurs again and again, such as the withdrawal of a mother at the moment of inevitable separation. The parallelism between these two events is obvious: both are about the loss of a creator, though Plato's loss occurs on what I would call the level of the telescope, mine on the level of the microscope. I would take from Plato not the specific content of his theory but the outlines of the process that he specifies: the fragmentation of myths from a single experience.

Behind a narrative is an experience, real or imagined: something has happened—not once, like a historical event, but many times, like a personal habit. Narrative does not receive raw experience and then impose a form upon it. Human experience is inherently narrative; this is our primary way of organizing and giving coherence to our lives. But we can never give an exact account of an experience, any more than we can retrieve a dream without any secondary revisions or elaborations. However close we get, we can never reach it, as in Zeno's paradox of Achilles and the tortoise—we get halfway there, and half the remaining distance, and so on, but never all the way.[8] There must be an experience for all the retellings to refract it as they do, but all we have are the refractions (some closer to the experience, some farther), the tellings, which are culturally specific, indeed, specific to each individual within the culture. And we can get close (as close as Achilles got) to this ideal raw experience by extrapolating from what all the myths have in common, modified in the light of what we can simply observe about the human situation in different cultures.

A parallel to the Platonic experience behind the myth may be seen in linguistics (an area from which other mythologists, notably F. Max Müller[9] and Claude Lévi-Strauss, have drawn their inspirations). Certain words are strikingly similar in a number of Indo-European languages: *foot* (English), *pied* (French), *fuss* (German), *ped* (Latin), *pada* (Sanskrit), etc. Following linguistic rules such as Grimm's Law, which tell us how sounds change through time, it is possible to construct the one *proto-Indo-European word that could have given rise to all the words in the group. That word does not exist; the asterisk that precedes it marks it as a purely theoretical construct. Yet the hypothesis of its existence solves the riddle of the relationship among all the other words. One cannot follow this method too slavishly; the fact that there is no common Indo-European word for *hand* might lead to the conclusion that the *proto-Indo-Europeans had feet but no hands. Nor can one trace Indo-European myths back to a theoretical origin as easily as one can trace Indo-European words; Max Müller and Georges Dumézil tried, with varying degrees of success, but it remains highly problematic.[10]

The linguistic analogy is nevertheless appropriate, because one thing that these myths have in common to one degree or another is language. That is, although language is often thought (by people like the Pumpkinhead of Oz, whom we met in the introduction) to be an uncrossable barrier bewveen people, some people think, as I do, that it is one of the great things that humans share, and that it offers a way across all barriers. Michael D. Coe describes both ends of the continuum between universal and culturally specific linguistic characteristics. First he speaks of cultural specificity: "It seems that the unborn fetus must already react to language, for experiments with four-day-old French infants show that they suck much harder while hearing French than while hearing Russian." (I wonder if the babies listening to French also called for wine instead of milk, and corrected the experimenter's accent.) Other experimenters have reported that Chinese babies babble single syllables with different tones.[11] Mr. Coe's experiments are somewhat reminiscent of one that Herodotus reported over two thousand years ago, in which the Egyptians isolated infants at birth to see what language they would "naturally" speak (it turned out to be *bekos*, the Phrygian word for "bread").[12] But then Mr. Coe speaks of universality: "Even though there are 4,000 to 6,000 languages today, they are all sufficiently alike to be considered one language by an extraterrestrial observer. In other words, most of the diversity of the world's cultures, so beloved to anthropologists, is superficial and minor compared to the similarities. Racial differences are literally only 'skin deep.' The fundamental unity of humanity is the theme of Mr. Chomsky's universal grammar."[13] Noam Chomsky's grammar is hardwired for all of human nature (and even applies to some primates, as is evident from the study of a talented chimp named, appropriately, Nim Chimpsky).[14] Coe's basic point—or rather, his basic two points, for difference and for sameness—are well taken.

Elaine Scarry has argued similarly for the universality of the relationship between language and pain:

> Even if one were to enumerate many additional examples, such cultural differences, taken collectively, would themselves constitute only a very narrow margin of variation and would thus in the end work to expose and confirm the universal sameness of the central problem, a problem that originates much less in the inflexibility of any one language or in the shyness of any one culture than in the utter rigidity of pain itself: its resistance to language is not simply one of its incidental or accidental attributes but is essential to what it is.[15]

There is therefore a level of human experience—pain is a vivid example— that precedes and even resists any language, including the language in which myths are told; yet that very experience that resists language is something that binds us to one another. The universality of pain, even in its wordlessness, is an example of the experience behind the narrative, before language, that both deconstructionists (like Mark Taylor) and post-Freudian feminists (like Julia Kristeva, following and modifying Lacan) have tried to reach in very different ways. So too, the many languages in which myths are told, despite their enormous variations, have in common their very inability ever to express those experiences, and their continuing, quixotic attempts to do so.

Clifford Geertz has argued that "People, as people, are doubtless much the same everywhere. That is what you commit yourself to in calling them people, rather than Egyptians, Buddhists, or speakers of Turkish. But the parts they play, the parts available for them to play, are not."[16] Thomas Laqueur makes vivid both sides of the argument between difference and sameness. First he states that context is essential to our understanding of the meaning of a myth, in his case the myth that male and female bodies are of one sex: "Sex, like being human, is contextual. Attempts to isolate it from its discursive, socially determined milieu are as doomed to failure as the *philosophe*'s search for a truly wild child or the modern anthropologist's efforts to filter out the cultural so as to leave a residue of essential human- ity."[17] But then he argues for the survival of something important inde- pendent of context, something very like "a residue of essential humanity": "The one-sex model . . . seems to have persisted over millennia during which social, political, and cultural life changed dramatically."[18] And this something cannot be explained in terms of any particular "social, political, and cultural" context.

Jungians would argue that the basic theme was always available every- where, like a kind of underground ocean of story flowing everywhere on the planet—another useful metaphor for the historian of religions. They would argue that we're all hot-wired (or hardwired) with myths from this pool, and that from time to time and from continent to continent, a story- teller sinks a well and taps into it. They would argue that the author of the story of Tamar and Judah, for example, drew from a particular pool in that ocean, and that Shakespeare drew from the same pool when he wrote the story of Helena and Bertram in *All's Well That Ends Well*. A. K. Ramanu- jan used a similar metaphor in referring to the recycling of themes *with- in a particular culture*: "The cultural area in which *Ramayanas* are en- demic has a pool of signifiers (like a gene pool), signifiers that include plots, characters, names, geography, incidents, and relationships. . . . Every author, if one may hazard a metaphor, dips into it and brings out a unique crystallization, a new text with a unique texture and a fresh con- text."[19] His statement is meant to apply to cultural diffusion and specific contexts within a single culture, and certainly names and geography would be culturally specific. But I believe that the metaphor of the pool can be extended to cross-cultural diffusion as well, where plots, charac- ters, incidents, and relationships may draw us out into the deeper waters of a much larger pool.

As Lévi-Strauss put it with uncharacteristic naïveté, "How are we going to explain the fact that myths throughout the world are so similar?"[20] And, more subtly:

Mythic stories are, or seem, arbitrary, meaningless, absurd, yet nevertheless they seem to re-appear all over the world. A "fanciful" creation of the mind in one place would be unique—you would not find the same creation in a completely different place. . . . If this represents a basic need for order in the human mind and since, after all, the human mind is only part of the universe, the need probably exists because there is some order in the universe and the universe is not a chaos.[21]

If one did not know that the author of this remarkable credo was the great French structuralist, one might have mistaken him, in the dark, for Jung.

Cross-Cultural Solutions

Demonstrating that a particular myth does in fact occur in every known culture is theoretically impossible, since stories are being forgotten and cultures created all the time. Moreover, this task is, in practice, unlikely to be achieved even in approximation. But even if we were able to prove that a certain myth was universal, we would have to explain its universality in terms of some universalist theory (Jungian, Freudian, Eliadean, or at least diffusionist), a daunting proposition. On the other hand, to assert that a myth occurs cross-culturally is merely to show that its meanings are not bounded by any one particular culture, a far less ambitious task (though no sinecure, either).

The universalism of most systems of comparison can, I think, be avoided. The great universalist theories were constructed from the top down: that is, they assumed certain continuities about broad concepts such as sacrifice, or a High God, or an Oedipal complex; but these continuities necessarily involved cognitive and cultural factors that, it seems to me, are the least likely places in which to look for cross-cultural continuities. The method that I am advocating is, by contrast, constructed from the bottom up. It assumes certain continuities not about overarching human universals but about particular narrative details concerning the body, sexual desire, procreation, parenting, pain, and death, details which, though unable to avoid mediation by culture entirely, are at least *less* culturally mediated than the broader conceptual categories of the universalists. Elaine Scarry argued this well:

The concepts of body and voice . . . though not themselves prior to cultures and artifice, are perhaps as close to prior as is possible, for they appear to emerge as explanatory rubrics in early moments of creating, or when there is some problem in the relation between maker and made things that carries us back to the original moment of making. At the same time, they do not, once made culture has been fully entered, cease to be analytically useful, in part because they are at all times immediately recognizable. They continue to be in the end our best as at the beginning our only, companions.[22]

So too, Judith Butler has argued that the body can only be conceived of through language, but it exists outside of language.[23]

A scholar working from the bottom up leans more heavily on data, informed, even inspired, though she may be by theory; she begins with a thorough historical study and then goes on to make it comparative. A scholar's experiences of real life and texts form her tastes and interests, the ingredients of the third side, the motivating idea; but that idea then leads her back to her texts, where she may find unexpected details that will in turn modify the idea of what she is looking for. Working from the bottom up forces a scholar to take into consideration many variants, many examples to induce a generalization, for the bottom-up argument is more numerological than logical, more inductive than deductive: it seeks to persuade by the sheer volume of its data rather than by the inevitability (or falsifiability) of the sequence of its assertions.[24] Induction, which is always a bootstraps operation, must be at the very least bolstered by meticulous, painstaking, fastidious scholarship.

Working from the bottom up also encourages a scholar to build an argument like an Irish wall: a good Irish wall needs no mortar, for if the stones are selected carefully and arranged so that they fit together tightly, they will hold one another up and the wall will stand. So too, if a scholar selects her texts carefully and places them in a sequence that tells the story she wants to tell, she will need relatively little theory to explain why they belong together and what sort of an argument they imply together.

The Implied Spider

Geertz is wary of certain assumptions about the nature of what is "the same" in different cultures: "When ingeniously juxtaposed, these fields can shed a certain amount of light on one another; but they are neither variants of one another nor expressions of some superfield that transcends them both."[25] Instead of a "superfield that transcends them," I would suggest that they are expressions of an experience that precedes them, without which one would not "ingeniously juxtapose" them at all, or come into the light that such a juxtaposition can shed. In another famous essay, Geertz speaks of humans as animals suspended in webs of significance that they themselves have spun, webs of culture.[26] Gananath Obeyesekere takes up the metaphor, remarking that "In reading Geertz I see webs everywhere but never the spider at work."[27] Obeyesekere goes on to cite the Upanishadic metaphor of God as a spider emitting the world from inside himself (which we will soon consider) and remarks: "But the anthropologist is not god; he must create the world out of the world and not out of his own navel. . . . [He spins] webs of significance—but out of what?"[28]

This is a useful metaphor for the comparatist if we take the spider to be, not as in Obeyesekere's usage the maker of culture (or the anthropologist) who spins the web of the myth (or the ethnography), but the shared humanity, the shared life experience, that supplies the web-building material, the raw material of narrative to countless human webmakers, authors, including human anthropologists and human comparatists. These human storytellers gather up the strands that the spider emits, like silk workers harvesting the cocoons of silkworms, to weave their own individual cultural artifacts, their own Venn-diagram webs of shared themes all newly and differently interconnected. My image of what I want to call the implied spider draws upon Wayne Booth's useful concept of the "implied author" (which itself builds upon Wolfgang Iser's concept of the "implied reader"),[29] the author implied by the individual passions revealed in his writing.[30] The implied spider generates, and is therefore implied by, the stuff that myths are made on; this is my answer to Obeyesekere's question, "out of what?" I argue that we must believe in the existence of the spider, the experience behind the myth, though it is indeed true that we can never see this sort of spider at work; we can only find the webs, the myths that human authors weave.

Indeed, if we think there is no spider, there is no spider; only our belief makes it (like Tinker Bell) real, as Shakespeare's Leontes once pointed out:

There may be in the cup
A spider steeped, and one may drink, depart,
And yet partake no venom, for his knowledge
Is not infected; but if one present
Th'abhorred ingredient to his eye, make known
How he hath drunk, he cracks his gorge, his sides,
With violent hefts—I have drunk, and seen the spider.[31]

And if we think there *is* a spider, there is a spider.

The fact that we cannot recover the experience, or the implied spider, does not mean that they do not exist. We cannot see the wind either, but we can watch it move, carving a path in a field of long grass. Where Geertz and Obeyesekere were talking about the elusiveness of culture, theologians apply the spider argument to proofs of the existence of God. And there are many myths about the survival of an invisible lover or god in visible forms like shadows and footprints.[32] Of course, this is not a foolproof proof: in nineteenth-century literature, people would "know" that ghosts were present because chairs moved; the presence of the absent lover or god is verifiable only psychologically, not physically. Sometimes there is smoke without fire. But the wind, the author, the dream, the web (and, in a psychological sense, the ghost and the lover)—above all, the experience must have existed to leave the tracks that we see, the bent stalks, the text, the secondary revision, the web (and the shadows and the footprints)—the narrative. And they are essential points from which we orient (or, for most people, occident) the materials that we *can* get back to, the materials of the narrative.

The metaphor of the web of the mythological spider bridges several different cultures. The mystical Hebrew text, the *Zohar*, likens God to a silkworm that "wraps itself within and makes itself a palace," which the translator glosses to mean that the silkworm "spins a cocoon out of its own substance," an image that he then compares to the Upanishadic image of the spider.[33] But where I am using the image of the spider to explain the migration of myths, the Upanishads, composed in Sanskrit around the sixth century before the common era, use it as Nagasena used the metaphor of the flame, to explain the transmigration of the soul:

> As a spider might come out with his thread, as small sparks come forth from the fire, even so from this Soul come forth all vital breaths, all worlds, all gods, all beings.[34] As a spider emits and draws in [its thread], as grasses arise on the earth, as the hairs of the head and body from a living person, so from the Imperishable arises everything here.[35] The one God covers himself, like a spider, with threads produced from primary matter.[36]

The essence of the spider was well captured by Walt Whitman:

> A noiseless patient spider,
> I mark'd where on a little promontory it stood isolated,
> Mark'd how to explore the vacant vast surrounding,
> It launch'd forth filament, filament, filament, out of
>   itself,
> Ever unreeling them, ever tirelessly speeding them.
> And you O my soul where you stand,
> Surrounded, detached, in measureless oceans of space,
> Ceaselessly musing, venturing, throwing, seeking the spheres
>   to connect them,

Till the bridge you will need be form'd, till the ductile
    anchor hold,
Till the gossamer thread you fling catch somewhere, O my
    soul.[37]

Like the spider in Whitman's poem and the author of the myths, we must fling the thread of our thoughts ahead of us until it catches somewhere, in the product of the imagination of some other human being, to build the bridge between myths. Performers in oral traditions believe in the totality of the text, even though each performs only fragments, never the whole text. In a similar sense, what we call the *Iliad* is a spider, and so is *Hamlet*: there is no single text, merely variants used in various performances; yet we know there is an *Iliad*, and a *Hamlet*.[38]

Kierkegaard wrote eloquently about the spider's courage in leaping into the unknown, in a book called, significantly, *Either/Or*:

> What portends? What will the future bring? I do not know, I have no presentiment. When a spider hurls itself down from some fixed point, consistently with its nature, it always sees before it only an empty space wherein it can find no foothold however much it sprawls. And so it is with me: always before me an empty space; what drives me forward is a consistency which lies behind me. This life is topsy-turvy and terrible, not to be endured.[39]

Again the spider is used as a metaphor for blind faith in the future. But we can use it as a metaphor for blind faith in the existence of spiders—or authors, or shared human experience, or the text.

Recently, Joan Aitchison used the metaphor of the spider and the web to describe the universality of human language in terms not inconsistent with our earlier discussion of Chomskian grammar:

> Webs, especially cobwebs, may entangle. Yet webs themselves are not a tangle. They have a preordained overall pattern, though every one is different in its details. Nature forces humans to weave the language web in a particular way, whatever language they speak. We are free only within a preset framework. . . . But humans, unlike spiders, can think about the webs they have woven. This sometimes gives rise to a superfluous cobweb of worries. . . . We humans are like spiders who get accustomed to moving along some strands of our web, and not others. . . . The brain is turning out to be like a massive spider's web with its numerous circuits and multiple interconnections.[40]

The "preordained overall pattern" of the web contains the human universals, indeed (as Lévi-Strauss argues) the structures of the human mind (rather than the brain) and perhaps of the universe. The details, and the superfluous cobwebs, vary from culture to culture and from individual to individual. But the mind itself, the basis of language and myth, is part of what could truly be called a World Wide Web.

The Postcolonial and Postmodern Critique of Comparison

I have been arguing for the uses of comparison despite the problems that it poses. But in the discipline of the history of religions, scholars have, by and large, abandoned universalist comparative studies of the sort that Mircea Eliade made so popular, as had the triumvirate of Frazer, Freud, and Jung before him. Many people think that such studies cannot be done at all, while others think that they should not be done at all. So far in this chapter, I have tried to tackle the question of whether they *can* be done; now let us consider whether they *should* be done (and postpone, until the next chapter, *how* they can be done).

The most common arguments against extant works of comparison are that they lack rigor; that they advance unfalsifiable universalist hypotheses; and that they are politically unhealthy. I will take up these three challenges one by one.

As for the lack of rigor, it is certainly true that there is a great deal of shoddy and superficial comparative work flying about; the less talented acolytes of the great comparatists of the early twentieth century have fallen into many of the pits I have described above as well as others that we will consider below, and given comparison a bad name. One of the reasons I lost my temper with Joseph Campbell was because he did it wrong and made it harder for me to persuade people that it was possible to do it right;[41] his static monomyth is the very antithesis of the ceaselessly engaged and always subject-filled approach that I argue for here. Many comparatists suffer from what has been called "Fluellenism,"[42] after Captain Fluellen, Shakespeare's Welshman who insisted on comparing Alexander the Great and the young Henry V; when others tried to point out the differences between the two men, Fluellen insisted, "There is a river in Macedon, and there is also moreover a river at Monmouth. . . . 'Tis alike as my fingers is to my fingers. . . . I speak but in the figures and comparisons of it."[43] Fluellens are always seduced by superficial convergences, which may be coincidental or otherwise meaningless. What does it mean, for instance, that the same sentence means "The train has arrived," in Finnish and in Hungarian, but the part of the sentence that means "the train" in Finnish means "has arrived" in Hungarian, and vice versa? When confronted by such data, the responsible comparatist must cry out, "Get thee behind me, Satan."

But when more specific, consistent, and meaningful analogies are sought, comparison *can* be done responsibly; Carlo Ginzburg,[44] J. Z. Smith,[45] Bruce Lincoln,[46] and Lawrence Sullivan[47] do it well, in my opinion. One way to stay on the right side of the line of responsible comparison is to observe the distinction (not the dichotomy) that Clifford Geertz has made between fruitful differences and sterile dichotomies:

> There is a difference between a difference and a dichotomy. The first is a comparison and it relates; the second is a severance and it isolates. . . . The dissimilitudes of Morocco and Indonesia do not separate them into absolute types, the sociological equivalent of natural kinds; they reflect back and forth upon one another, mutually framing, reciprocally clarifying.[48]

Clearly I am calling for a comparison that relates, that frames, that clarifies. I would also insist that the comparatist have a knowledge of the language of the primary texts of at least one of the traditions in question, which would then inspire a proper sense of caution and limited ambitions in the inevitable dealings with translations of texts from other traditions, an understanding of what one can and cannot do with translations. And the comparatist must *know* the context—at the very least, have read a good book by someone who *really* knows the context—in order to know the meaning of the text, even though she may not use the context in the comparison. I hesitate to say any more in the abstract about rigor other than that, like pornography, *lack* of rigor is something I always know when I see it. Rigor for me comes out of practice, out of being aware of the sorts of problems and assumptions that are addressed in this book; and out of adhering carefully to a step-by-step method like the one that I am about to describe. So much for rigor.

As for unfalsifiable theories, few conceptually bold studies in any field can avoid them entirely, but their harm can be minimized if they are not followed unconsciously or reductionistically but are invoked explicitly and in groups; in this way the comparatist drawing upon more than one theory might allow their shortcomings to hold one another up like two drunks, or cancel one another out, if not kill one another off like the cats of Kilkenny in the limerick ("and instead of two cats, there weren't any").[49] (This means eclecticism.) And hypotheses about patterns of meaning in any group of stories may be, if not falsified, at least tried in the field of many, many stories from many, many cultures, retold with attention to many, many details, or tested for anachronism, incoherence of explanation, and so forth.

The question of the politics of myth is more complex. There is, I think, some irony in the fact that the modern comparative study of religion was in large part designed in the pious hope of teaching our own people that "alien" religions were like "ours" in many ways. (By "ours" we usually meant Protestantism, as do scholars who mean, but never say, what is said by Mr Thwackum in Fielding's *Tom Jones*: "When I mention religion, I mean the Christian religion; and not only the Christian religion, but the Protestant religion; and not only the Protestant religion, but the Church of England.")[50] The hope was that if we learned about other religions, we would no longer hate and kill their followers; that "to know them is to love them." Emmanuel Levinas argues that the face of the other says, "Don't kill me";[51] this is the face that the comparative enterprise strives to illuminate. A glance at any newspaper should tell us that this goal has yet to be fulfilled in the world at large.

But the academic world, having gone beyond this simplistic paradigm, now suffers from a post-postcolonial backlash. In this age of multinationalism and the politics of individual ethnic and religious groups, of identity politics and minority politics, to assume that two phenomena from different cultures are "the same" in any significant way is regarded as demeaning to the individualism of each, a reflection of the old racist attitude that "all wogs look alike." In our day too, and at the other end of the anticolonial continuum, seeing correspondences between cultures has come to be regarded as politically retrograde for different reasons. As Annie Dillard discovered in China in 1983, "Mao said that there is no such thing as 'human nature'; there is only class nature. To talk about human nature is, then, to undermine the theoretical basis of socialism. . . . That people, despite differences in culture, have feelings in common . . . was, as recently as four months ago, a somewhat risky statement in China."[52]

Moreover, in the present climate of anti-Orientalism, it is regarded as imperialist of a scholar who studies India, for instance, to stand outside (presumably, above) phenomena from different cultures and to equate them. Merely by emphasizing their commonalities, we are implicated in what Rolena Adorno has called "the process of fixing 'otherness' by grasping onto similarities." Other evil effects of simplistic comparison have already taken their toll in some of the social sciences today (particularly political science and economics), where dominant theories like that of "rational choice," supposedly the same for everyone, have driven out the more particularized disciplines of area studies. Psychologists also have, until quite recently, too often assumed a universal biological, cognitive, and affective base for human behavior, neglecting cultural factors.

But we must beware of leaping from the frying pan of universalism into the fire of another sort of essentialism that can result from contextualizing a myth in one cultural group. In this Kali Yuga of cultural essentialism, we must search for something that is essential but not essentialist. Indeed, I might formulate the basic problem addressed in this chapter as the problem of competing essentialisms. And by essentialism I mean hypotheses about the unity of a group that a scholar holds on to even when they have destructive results, like a monkey who traps himself by refusing to let go of a banana in his fist inside a cage whose opening is big enough for his fist but not for the banana. I mean a priori prejudices (and, as I have argued, any scholarly hypothesis must begin with something like such a prejudice) that are not dropped or modified when members of the target groups turn out to be different. I want to say to all the reductionists I know: "Let go of the banana." Paul Feyerabend once wrote a book entitled *Against Method*; my method could be called, "Against Reductionism."

The emphasis on individual cultures, when reduced to the absurd (as it too often is), may lead to problems of infinite regress, first, as we have just seen, in the ever-broadening comparisons of contexts and ultimately, in the ever-narrowing contexts themselves. This emphasis tends to generate a smaller and smaller focus until it is impossible to generalize even from one moment to the next: nothing has enough in common with anything else to be compared with it even for the purpose of illuminating its distinctiveness; each event is unique, like William James's crab, himself alone, not just a crustacean.[53] The radical particularizing of much recent theory in cultural anthropology, for instance, seems to deny any shared base to members of the same culture, much less to humanity as a whole.[54] But any discussion of difference must begin from an assumption of sameness; Wilhelm Dilthey has said that "Interpretation would be impossible if expressions of life were completely strange. It would be unnecessary if nothing strange were in them."[55] If we start with the assumption of absolute difference there can be no conversation, and we find ourselves trapped in the self-reflexive garden of a Looking-Glass ghetto, forever meeting ourselves walking back in through the cultural door through which we were trying to escape.[56]

Even the most relentless of French deconstructionists could not, I think, compare the text of a Greek tragedy and, say, the text of an instruction manual for *WordPerfect Windows*, 1995; there is no common ground, no sameness. But any comparatist worth her pay could compare that Greek tragedy with many a story from *The New York Times* in 1995. If all stories on a given theme were the same, any study of them would make a very short book: one text and a *very* long footnote. But if they were all *entirely* different, incomparably, incommensurably different, not only would there be nothing to compare, but also we would never be able to understand any story but our own. We must strive to "keep an exquisite balance between the Platonist drive to unity and the nominalist drive to the irreducibly particular. If we go to bed with Plato, we might better wake up with Aristotle."[57] Maintaining this balance is particularly difficult in an age like ours when the extremes of globalization and diversification have come to power simultaneously and continue to egg each other on.

But similarity and difference are not equal, not comparable; they have different uses. We look to similarity for stability, to build political bridges, to anchor our own society, while we spin narratives to deal with our uneasiness at the threat of difference. Either similarity or difference may lead to a form of paralyzing reductionism and demeaning essentialism, and thence into an area where "difference" itself can be politically harmful. For where extreme universalism means that the other is exactly like you, extreme nominalism means that the other may not be human at all.[58] Many of the people who argued (and continue to argue) that Jews or blacks or any other group defined as "wogs" were all alike (that is, like one another) went on to argue (or, more often, to assume) that they were all different (that is, different from us white people, us Protestants), and this latter argument easily led to the assertion that such people did not deserve certain rights like the rest of us. Essentialized difference can become an instrument of dominance; European colonialism was supported by a discourse of difference.

I have argued that the members of a single cultural "group" may be very different, and it is just as insulting to say that all Japanese are alike as to say that the Japanese are just like the French. (The same goes for *fin de siècle* types: the essentialism of time can be just as harmful as the essentialism of place.) I applaud the art historian Sir Ernst Gombrich, who resists categories like "Renaissance man" or "Romantic psychology" as one would resist claims for "Aryan man" or "German physics."[59] The culturally essentialized position is in itself both indefensible and politically dangerous. Yet it is often assumed in "culturally contextualized" and historically specific studies: "Let me tell you how everyone felt at the *fin de siècle* in Europe and America." The focus on the class or ethnic group, if monolithic, can become not only boring but also racist.

My aim is an expansive, humanistic outlook on inquiry that enhances our humanity in both its peculiarity and its commonality. I am unwilling to close the comparatist shop just because it is being picketed by people whose views I happen, by and large, to share. I have become sensitized to the political issues, but I do not think that they ultimately damn the comparative enterprise. I want to salvage the broad comparative agenda even if I acquiesce, or even participate, in the savaging of certain of its elements. I refuse to submit to what Umberto Eco has nicely termed "textual harrassment" and Velcheru Narayana Rao calls (in Sanskrit) *bhava-hatya*, literally "ideacide" but in actuality a good translation for "ideology": murder by idea, as well as the murder of ideas (Sanskrit compounds, like myths, can swing both ways like that). I am not now, and have never been, a card-carrying member of the British Raj. But I refuse to stop reading and translating texts edited by people who were. There is much in the colonial scholarship on India that is worth keeping; I am unwilling to throw out the baby with the bathwater. As the irrepressible Lee Siegel put it recently, "Those hegemonic, imperialist, Eurocentric colonialists were such amazing writers and they knew so much more about India than all of us. They could ride horses, too."[60]

But there is also much in the postcolonial critique that is worth keeping; indeed, we can no longer think without it. We are aware, willy-nilly, of how our texts have come to us; they now say to us, like third-world immigrants in England, "We're here because you were there." Colonialism is no longer the political force it once was, but it is still there, especially if we use a word like imperialism instead of colonialism and bear in mind the aspects of our scholarship that still invade the countries we study, like the Coke bottle that intrudes into the lives of The Natives in the (racist) film *The Gods Must Be Crazy*.[61] In particular, the postcolonial critique has made us aware of how deeply evolutionist ideas are embedded in the history of comparison, and how hard we must work to overcome them. The joke about the caveperson and the tiger rests upon evolutionist ideas, as does, ultimately, the idea of a common humanity.

But we *can* overcome the negative fallout from evolutionism; we don't have to go on doing it like that. The very fact that we have been made aware of these problems should make it possible for us to avoid them, at least to some extent. There are sharks in the waters of comparison, but now that we know they're there we can still swim—a bit more cautiously, perhaps. We now realize, for instance, that the cultures we are comparing have compared, too; that they are subjects, like us, as well as the objects of our study. Herodotus compared his ancient Greeks with the Egyptians; a number of recent studies have documented the attitudes of the ancient Chinese, Hindus, and others toward the Others on their borders.[62] In this way we can switch focus: the text you look *at* becomes a text you look *through*; the mirror becomes a window.

We now know how the early Christians strove to understand, and to justify, the stunning resemblances between their religion and that of the pagans they so despised. Justin insisted, "It is not we who think like the others, but all of them who imitate us in what they say," and Clement of Alexandria accused the Greeks of stealing from the Christians.[63] Still unsatisfied, Clement initiated "The Thesis of Demonic Imitation," later advanced by Tertullian and Justin, which argued the case most Jesuitically (if I may be anachronistic):

> In [Justin's] eyes, demons find a choice ground for their manipulations in particular pages of the Scriptures: in the Messianic prophecies, inspired visionaries mysteriously described the Savior long before his coming. So the demons, in order to deceive and mislead the human race, took the offensive and suggested to the poets who created [Greek] myths that they give Zeus many sons and attribute monstrous adventures to them, in the hope that this would make the story of Christ appear to be a fable of the same sort, when it came.[64]

This Christian comparative apologetic, in a twisted form, was the driving force behind that great nineteenth-century comparatist, Sir James George Frazer, too: what to do about the similarities between Christianity and "paganism."[65]

More generally, Protestant scholars in the nineteenth century renewed the ancient Christian imperial comparative project, now adding an anti-Catholic bias, producing an agenda that has continued to pollute the scholarship on comparison even in our day.[66] This history of the ways in which Others have compared their own Others shows not only that our colonialism was not the first colonialism, but also that comparison has long been an imperial enterprise. We need to know this so we can stop doing it the way they did it and start doing it the way we do it. This is, by the way, another instance of the uses of comparison to defamiliarize our own methods: when we compare ourselves as comparatists with the ancient comparatists, we notice things about ourselves that we had overlooked.

In pursuing the multivocal, multicultural agenda, we must face the implications of the fact that we use other peoples' stories for our purposes. The political problem inheres in the asymmetry of power between the appropriating culture and the appropriated. Thus, if Europe has dominated India, it is deemed wrong for a European to make use of an Indian myth. But it seems to me that there are very different ways of using other peoples' myths, some of them fairly innocuous,[67] and that the usual alternative to appropriating a foreign text (however inadequate or exploitative or projective that appropriation may be) can be even worse: ignoring it or scorning it. Moreover, the European appropriation need not supplant the Indian version; the native voice can be heard even above the academic clamor of the foreign voice.

The gift that the postcolonial critique has given us is a heightened awareness of what we are doing, why, and the dangers involved. But the gift sours when the giver takes it back by arguing that these dangers are so great that we cannot do it at all. We should use the postcolonial consciousness not to exclude Western scholars from the study of non-Western myths, which merely contributes to the ghettoization of the Western world of ideas, but to show how myths (and the comparative study of myths) can be used as ghetto-blasters in our own society as well as in the world at large—that is, to blast apart the ghettoes of ideology. Surely it is possible to bring into a single (if not necessarily harmonious) conversation the genuinely different approaches that several cultures have made to similar (if not the same) human problems. To return to the image of the lens, We must supplement the tunnel vision of identity politics with the wide screen of cross-cultural studies.

The postcolonial agenda is compatible with some agendas of postmodernism, the age that rejects metanarratives and argues for the infinite proliferation of images.[68] For postmodernism, sameness is the devil, difference the angel; the mere addition of an *accent aigu* transforms the modest English word into the magic buzzword for everything that right-thinking (or, as the case may be, left-thinking) men and women care about: *différence* (or, buzzier yet, *différance*). From Paris the new battle cry rings out: *Vive la différance!* The deconstructionist myth of Difference is what Joel Fineman, citing René Girard, has called "a story, always a story, by means of which societies resolve and ward off a catastrophe of order that Girard labels the crisis of 'No Difference' and that he defines as a loss of cultural distinctions so profound as to spell cultural suicide."[69]

But the postmodern critique has not solved the problem of cultural difference, as Eve Sedgwick has pointed out:

> Every single theoretically or politically interesting project of postwar thought has finally had the effect of delegitimating our space for asking or thinking in detail about the multiple, unstable ways in which people may be like or different from each other. This project is not rendered otiose by any demonstration of how fully people may differ also from themselves. Deconstruction, founded as a very science of *diffEr(e/a)nce*, has both so fetishized the idea of difference and so vaporized its possible embodiments that its most thoroughgoing practitioners are the last people to whom one would now look for help in thinking about particular differences.[70]

Yet there is a crucial difference between premodern constructions of difference and postmodern *différance*.[71] Deconstructionism, in particular, has promoted the concepts of multivocality and multiple interpretations that are essential to the method for which I will argue in chapters 4 through 6. And it has sharpened our awareness of our unexamined assumptions about individual authors, a subject to which I wish now to turn.

The Problem of Individualism

We may apply to our anonymous myths contemporary literary critics' insights into both the products of popular culture and canonical works of literature. Though both of these narrative forms have, as some of our ancient myths do not have, known social contexts, some works of popular culture (particularly, but not only, those from nonliterate cultures) share with many myths the lack of known or individual authors and hence come within the mythologists' camp. Films, for instance, like camels in the old joke, are often created by committees. So too the hermeneutics of suspicion renders irrelevant the problem of the intention of the individual author of a great work of literature, making that work fair game for mythologists. For in order to know what Shakespeare "meant," we would need to know a great deal about Elizabethan England; but if excavating author intention is no longer regarded as a realistic goal, we do not need to know Shakespeare's social context in order to compare his stories, and his unique way of telling them, with those from other cultures.

The postmodern critique thus helps us to avoid some of the distortions that result from a certain kind of concentration on individual authors. Hilary Mantel, in his discussion of John Demos's book, noted the flaws in a different kind of attempt to solve these problems:

> In [a previous] book Demos was careful not to focus on invididuals; he wanted to improve on the anecdotal method. He made an aggregation of the settlers' lives, for the sake of a wide and general picture which is not distorted by the idiosyncrasies of personal predilection and personal fate. This is valuable work, and his book is a swift, informative read. . . . But it is easy to see why the generalising method seems deficient to a man of imagination. What is true of everybody is true of nobody.[72]

There is a danger of losing human meaning if you select only what is in the common core. To avoid this universalizing trap, we might try to move in the other direction, to take explicit account of the "personal predilections" of many different individuals.

For each telling adds something unique, sometimes transformingly unique, to the shared base, and we must ask of each telling the Passover question: Why is this variant different from all other variants? What particular contribution does this retelling make? We might do better, therefore, to anchor our cross-cultural paradigms in the unique insights of particular tellings of our cross-cultural themes. This is one way of steering between the Scylla of universalism and the Charybdis of cultural essentialism: by concentrating on the insights from individual myths, we need not assume that all Hindus are alike, or all Jews. A telling of a myth from one country is as likely to share *some* things with a telling from another as with a telling from elsewhere in the same country. Just as our awareness of the individual scholar making the analysis, the third side of the triangle, provides an anti-essentialist anchor, so too does our awareness of the individual contribution of the text's author. This focus takes the call for difference very seriously indeed and follows it to the ultimate case, that of the individual whose insights transcend her particular moment and speak to us across time and space. The emphasis on the individual balances the move outward, from culture to cross-culture, with a move inward, from culture to the individual author. It balances the focus on the individual with a focus on the human on the other end of the continuum—the microscope and then the telescope, thus opening up a second front in the battle against the constricting category of culture.

This method argues that *All's Well That Ends Well* must be read not merely as a typical (or even atypical) story of a man who rejects his wife, nor merely in the context of Elizabethan England (an approach that assumes that Shakespeare can be "explained" by nothing but the same influences that formed all other Elizabethans—an extension of the statement by Laura Bohannan's British challenger that Shakespeare is a "very English poet"). Instead, this method would treat that text as the peculiar insight of one Elizabethan Englishman who was in many ways different from all others. The focus on individual insight leads us to a variety of what Paul Ricoeur called a second naïveté, positing a "sameness" that only superficially resembles a quasi-Jungian universalism but is actually based on a *pointillism* formed from the individual points of individual authors. Annie Dillard argued for this in her book about Chinese writers:

> The truth about China I leave to the experts. I intend only to tell some small stories, and to depict precise moments precisely, in the hope that a collection of such moments might give an impression of many sharp points going in different directions—might give a vivid sense of complexity. The narratives and analyses in this section are not value-free, of course, but they yield, I hope, contradictory impressions.[73]

"Contradictory impressions" are precisely what I hope to yield by my method. This emphasis upon real people, arguing from the bottom up, obviates the sorts of problems that arise when we argue from the top down and posit a transcendental agent as the source of cross-cultural congruences. And these real people are not merely political agents; they are the authors of texts with many different agendas.

Joan Scott has described the uses of individual names in furthering the apparently opposite feminist wish to designate groups by name in the construction of various sorts of histories:

> We insisted that the names of individual women be added to the lists of scientists, inventors, politicans and artists. It was, in fact, the individualizing of women that offered the best way out of the ahistorical category of the group. It was an uncomfortable strategy to me at first, for it seemed to bow to the conservative critique that rejects all group categorization as antithetical to individuality. I finally decided that this was not the case because the inclusion of differently marked individuals deprived the abstract individual of his singularity and universality.[74]

That is, the inclusion of *a number* of individuals prevents the concept of the ideal individual (male and white, in the case that Joan Scott is arguing) from becoming the standard.

What do we lose by this emphasis on the individual text? We lose the sort of big picture that is suggested by statistical analyses, a rough tabulation that is useful for cultural studies (x is a central and recurrent Hindu text, there are more versions of x than of y, more women do x than y; and — within limited parameters — there's none of x [when we might expect x, since we know it from elsewhere: the dog that doesn't bark]). Yet we do get a big picture, of a different sort, by putting all the individual texts together.

Those who would regard universalism as a colonialist debasement of the integrity of the ethnic unit might also regard such an emphasis upon individual creativity as an élitist debasement of the democratic unit. But surely this need not be the case. It is just as foolish to assume that an emphasis on the individual will be élitist as it is to assume that the opposite emphasis, on the entire human race, will be fascist. The emphasis on individual storytellers is élite only in the very narrow sense of the word — that some are "chosen" out of the group — but not in its broader implications — that those who are chosen have a particular social or cultural advantage. It acknowledges the unequal distribution of talent (in this case, storytelling talent), but does not assume that talent will be found in some places and not in others. Searching for our individual artists not merely in the bastions of the Western canon but in the neglected byways of oral traditions and rejected heresies, paying homage to the Tolstois among the Zulus, Prousts of the Papuans (to respond to Saul Bellow's notorious challenge),[75] and artists of the graffito and the B-film, argues not for a narrow range of cultural excellence but, on the contrary, for a wider construction of inspiration than may be found in any culture. It may well be true that there are no Tolstois among the Zulus, but it is also proper to ask how many Tolstois there are among the Russians; for such highly original individuals are rare both in groups that have writing and in those that do not. It is also worth noting that different cultures are good at different things and admire different talents; what strikes us as original is often not what that culture values but what ours values, and what may be, in its own culture, better named not original but deviant. The trick is to learn to understand (perhaps even to love) both what *that* culture regards as original and what that culture may scorn but we may admire.

The question of Tolstoys among the Zulus is a question about who decides which works and authors are "good," and on what basis. My emphasis upon the individual *at all levels of society*, from high culture to popular culture, is designed to address this question as well as the deconstructionist objection to universalism and to the sort of humanism I am advocating: the objection that humanism falsely universalizes an ideological fiction based on the interests of the privileged. This position also argues ultimately for that particular flash of difference that is best illuminated by the context of sameness. And where the emphasis on the characteristics of a whole class or culture fails to take into account not only parallels in other cultures but originality in any culture, the emphasis on one individual (in comparison with other, less inspired individual tellers) can at least pinpoint the moment of inspiration, if not account for it. The arguments that I have made for *pointillism* and will make for *bricolage* are designed to counter naïve claims about novelty and to stress the creative dimension of thinking.

The individual spark of originality should be sought in other cultures as well as in our own. In his discussion of the analogical imagination, David Tracy sounds a note of warning: analogical concepts must never lose what he calls "the tensive power of the negative. If that power is lost, analogical concepts become mere categories of easy likenesses slipping quietly from their status as similarities-in-difference to mere likenesses, falling finally into the sterility of a relaxed univocality and a facilely affirmative harmony."[76] In my own rather similar-and-different context, mythological rather than theological, the role of "the tensive power of the negative" is played by what some might call "the tensive power of historical specificity" and I would call "the tensive power of the individual." To lose awareness of this power is to fall into the "facilely affirmative harmony" of reductionist schools of comparative mythology. Yet to lose awareness of the "similarity-in-difference" is also fatal to our enterprise. We must strike a balance between centripetal and centrifugal forces in a myth.

Geoffrey Hartman has argued that a text (such as the Bible, his immediate concern) or a myth (our concern) may be "a glorious patchwork," the combined work of many individual hands, and the fact "that the seams show through, as in modern collages, can be an artistic, though not a theological, virtue."[77] Since myths are as much the province of artists as of theologians, I would join Hartman in his defense of their seamy side. But even theologians, as Tracy has demonstrated, may be not only pluralistic but artistic; I agree with him wholeheartedly that "Where art is marginalized, religion is privatized."[78] It is generally assumed that the focus on individual artists is a form of privatization, that only culturally particularized studies are truly public. But I do not see why careful comparison of individual texts should not be public, precisely in the sense of illuminating qualities that are shared by a large number of individuals. I would hope that a good comparatist could strive simultaneously to demarginalize art (to use artistic examples in comparative studies) and to deprivatize religion (to show how these individual examples are relevant to a very broad human continuum).

The comparatist is part scientist, part artist, but this is too seldom acknowledged. As Laurie Patton has put it, "Microscopes are used by both artists and scientists, and their legacy is both poetic and rational. Historians of religions, with all of their methodologies, are not so lucky. The idea that one can be exact, scientifically interesting, and poetic at the same time has been lost as the history of religions veers between aping the human sciences and aping the literary world, and doing a good job at neither."[79] But we can see the glass as half full, rather than half empty, and argue that the comparatist has, appropriately, a double claim on the microscope (and telescope): as artist and as scholar.

The idea that the study of mythology is a scientific enterprise has haunted and perverted this discipline from Max Müller (*Lectures on the Science of Language*) to Jung (*Essays on a Science of Mythology*) and Lévi-Strauss (*Introduction to a Science of Mythology*—though Lévi-Strauss later claimed that his American publisher gave his work this title without his knowledge).[80] But if we acknowledge our debt to art rather than to science, we do not have to submit to criteria like falsifiability. We could also use our status as artists to grant, as J. Z. Smith argues, that what the comparatist creates is not "out here" but in the comparatist's mind. Yet this would be to give away too much, for, as I have argued about the implied spider, it is not *only* in the individual scholar's mind; it is also out there, in other peoples' minds. Indeed, we trust the artist, not as we trust the scientist—because of our ability to falsify or duplicate her experiments or even to apply her formulas—

but rather because we have faith in her ability, like that of a scientist, to see connections (however subjective) among phenomena that really are out there. Jessye Norman argued that art does "'from the inside out," as she put it, precisely what, I am arguing, comparative mythology does from the bottom up: "Art brings us together as a family because it is an individual expression of a universal sentiment."[81]

Art is not "just" art. After all, a novelist does not create *ab ovo, de nihilo*, any more than the spider (or mythmaker) can; the poet uses available words, with all their associations. And on the other hand, science is not "just" science; as Thomas Kuhn[82] and others have shown, there is a great deal of subjectivity and cultural construction in many branches of science. So art and science form, each within itself and together, another continuum, with degrees of dependence on a combination of the data out there and the inspiration in here. And on this continuum, the comparatist stands halfway between the "pure" artist and the "empirical" scientist.

For the phenomena that the comparatist deals with are "out there" to a greater degree than are the materials of most artists, such as those who paint on entirely blank canvas. The comparatist, like the surrealist, selects pieces of *objets trouvés*; the comparatist is not a painter but a collagist, indeed a bricolagist (or a *bricoleur*), just like the mythmakers themselves. Annie Dillard wrote a wonderful book of "found poems," each constructed entirely out of someone else's words—edited and rearranged so that they speak with Annie Dillard's unmistakable voice.[83] This is a particularly vivid instance of the work of a mythmaking *bricoleur*. It is also a less obvious yet equally valid paradigm for the work of both the artist and the scientist, and for the work of the comparatist.

Chapter 4

Micromyths, Macromyths, and Multivocality

The Myth with No Point of View

Chapter 1 discussed the inherent ability of myths to compare the views of the microscope and the telescope. Chapters 2 and 3 suggested that myths from different cultures are both comparative and comparable. This chapter will discuss the micromyth and the macromyth as scholarly constructions that make comparison possible.

Myths are retold over and over again for several reasons: because the community becomes attached to the signifiers, and they become authoritative and historically evocative; because myths are at hand, available, like the scraps of the *bricoleur*, and using them is easier than creating from scratch; and because they are intrinsically charismatic. But perhaps the greatest of all of myth's survival tactics is its ability to stand on its head. The very word *myth* is one of a small but interesting group of words that mean, usually for reasons of historical conflation, both one thing and its opposite (like *cleave*—meaning both "adhere [to]" and "split [apart]"). There is an old bon mot, sometimes ascribed to Sir Hamilton A. R. Gibb of Oxford and Harvard, that every Arabic word has its primary meaning, then its opposite meaning, then something to do with a camel, and lastly something obscene.[1] Similarly, it was said at Harvard, when I was there in the '6os, that every Sanskrit word means itself, its opposite, a name of God, and a position in sexual intercourse. As we saw in the introduction, the word *myth* has two very strong, very opposite meanings, depending on one's point of view: "truth" and "lie." Even the proto-demythologizer himself, Plato, spoke with a forked tongue when he spoke about myths.

But it is really myth itself that hunts with the hounds of truth and runs with the hare (or fox) of antitruth. For often, through the years, the truth becomes regarded as a lie, or the lie as a truth. Salman Rushdie has argued that "all stories are haunted by the ghosts of the stories they might have been,"[2] and that "*For every story there is an anti-story*. . . . every story . . . has a *shadow self*, and if you pour this anti-story into the story, the two cancel each other out, and bingo! End of story."[3] Roberto Calasso sees this double edge as an intrinsic quality of myths:

> Myths are made up of actions that include their opposites within themselves. The hero kills the monster, but even as he does so we perceive that the opposite is also true: the monster kills the hero. The hero carries off the princess, yet even as he does we perceive that the opposite is also true: the hero deserts the princess. How can we be sure? The variants tell us. They keep the mythical blood in circulation. Let's imagine that all the variants of a certain myth have been lost, erased by some invisible hand. Would the myth still be the same? Here one arrives at the hairline distinction between myth and every other kind of narrative. Even without its variants, the myth includes its opposite.[4]

Indeed, we might single this out as one of the defining characteristics of a myth, in contrast with other sorts of narratives (such as novels): a myth is a much-retold narrative that is transparent to a variety of constructions of meaning, a neutral structure that allows paradoxical meanings to be held in a charged tension. This transparency—the quality of a lens—allows a myth, more than other forms of narrative, to be shared by a group (who, as individuals, have various points of view) and to survive through time (through different generations with different points of view).[5]

The transparency of myth has at least three significant effects: (1) any single telling may incorporate various voices; (2) any myth may generate different retellings, different variants, each with its own voice; and (3) any single telling is subject to various reinterpretations, both within the tradition and from scholars outside the tradition. In this chapter, I consider each of these three related aspects of myth, beginning with the transparency that makes them all possible and going on to the political implications of this multivalence and multivocality of myths.

Transparency comes from the experience behind the myth, which is transparent or neutral at least in the sense that it is capable of being interpreted from any number of different points of view. Although we cannot have access to an untold experience, we may hypothesize an untold story, a nonexistent story told with no point of view at all. This hypothetical story is a scholarly construct that functions like, but does not equal, the hypothetical experience that lies behind the myths. E. M. Forster made a distinction between a story and a plot: " 'The king died and then the queen died,' is a story. 'The king died and then the queen died of grief,' is a plot."[6] He went on:

> Consider the death of the queen. If it is in a story we say "and then?" If it is in a plot we ask "why?" That is the fundamental difference between these two aspects of the novel. A plot cannot be told to a gaping audience of cave men or to a tyrannical sultan or to their modern descendant the movie-public. They can only be kept awake by "and then—and then—" They can only supply curiosity. But a plot demands intelligence and memory also.[7]

I think "cave men" (by which Forster, who lived and wrote in India, surely is referring to contemporary non-Western listeners) and "the movie-public" (in which I include myself) are quite capable of listening to a plot. Indeed, the distinction I wish to make between story and plot assumes that very few people ever listen to a story at all, that the great majority of texts are plots, not stories—that they keep asking, "Why?" and offering different answers. A myth is a story; but each retelling, each text is a plot. If there could be an experience without a telling, it would be possible to say, "This happened" (the story) without saying why it happened, or what was the point of it happening (the plot). But we can never have access to such an experience.

Although, as we have just noted, the word *myth* is often used nowadays to designate an idea (particularly a wrong idea), the one thing a myth most certainly is *not* is an idea. It is a narrative that makes possible any number of ideas but does not commit itself to any single one. A myth is like a gun for hire, a mercenary soldier: it can be made to fight for anyone. Thus, for example, William R. Bowden remarks of a particular mythic theme, the bed trick (the story of Tamar and Judah, Helena and Bertram), "The ethics of the bed trick is determined by the intentions and the nature of the perpetrator; the trick is neither good nor bad in itself. . . . The bed trick is a morally neutral device used by the dramatists in an essentially moral context."[8] A myth's attitude to dogma is like that of the great Sam Goldwyn who, when asked why he didn't make movies with messages, replied, "When I want to send a message, I send for Western Union." Goldwyn was speaking against overt messages; myths (not, as we shall see, texts that tell myths) are indifferent, rather than antipathetic, to any specific messages, overt or covert.

But can there be a myth with no point of view at all? Yes and no. The hypothesis of an unmarked, neutral experience involving a woman, a man, a garden, a tree, a fruit, a serpent, and knowledge allows us to understand how the dominant reading of the Hebrew Bible could tell that story as it does (a subtle serpent, forbidden fruit, evil woman, disobedient and destructive knowledge), while other tellings of that myth cast it differently (a benevolent Goddess in her form of life-giving serpent and tree, giving the blessing of the fruit of useful knowledge that makes human life possible). This alternative reading of Genesis implies not a Fall but a progression from the Garden of Eden (a place of ignorance and constriction) to the wider world, a place of open possibility, of freedom and knowledge (not to mention the pleasures of sex),[9] the gift of the seductive woman or the subtle serpent. This reading, which argues that eternal seduction is the price of liberty, is often said (usually by feminists) to have existed in the ancient Near East alongside the biblical text,[10] but there is no textual evidence for this. The positive reading of the serpent (though not of the woman) was, however, accepted in the Ophite version of Genesis, in which God is evil and the serpent is good;[11] yet since *ophis*, serpent, is a feminine noun in Greek, it may have had feminine overtones too.[12] The positive reading of the serpent was further developed by Romantics such as Shelley, who saw a direct parallel between Satan's gift of the fruit and Prometheus's gift of fire—a gift which, like the fruit in Eden, provoked the wrath of the jealous gods and the creation of the first, disastrously seductive woman, Pandora.[13] Shelley remarked, in his introduction to *Prometheus Unbound*, that "The only imaginary being resembling in any degree Prometheus, is Satan," and he argued that he could just as well have written about Satan in Eden, but chose not to do so because of the negative assumptions about Satan that a (presumably Christian) reader would bring to the text.[14] Mark Twain had his own take on Genesis 3: "Adam was but human—this explains it all. He did not want the apple for the apple's sake; he only wanted it because it was forbidden. The mistake was in not forbidding the serpent; then he would have eaten the serpent."[15]

A hilarious proto-Freudian spoof of the myth of Eden was composed by Royall Tyler in 1793:

> Innocent of nuptial blisses,
> Unknown to him the balm of life,
> With unmeaning, wild caresses,
> Adam teaz'd his virgin wife.

As her arm Eve held him hard in,
And toy'd him with her roving hand,
In the middle of Love's Garden,
She saw the Tree of Knowledge stand.

....

Her soft hand then half embrac'd it,
Her heaving breasts to his inclin'd,
She op'd her coral lips to taste it,
But first she peel'd its russet rind.

....

But when its nectar'd juice she tasted,
Dissolving Eve could only sigh;
"I feel—I feel, my life is wasted,
This hour I eat, and now I die."

But when she saw the tree so lofty,
Sapless and shrunk in size so small;
Pointing she whisper'd Adam softly:
"See! there is DEATH! and there's the FALL!"[16]

There is actually a basis for this interpretive tradition among the Kabbal-ists, some of whom saw the tree in Eden as a phallus[17] (but did not, I think, spell out the implications of the Fall as a detumescence).

The texts that I have just cited are only a few of the thousands of vari-ants, in words and images, that have been rung on the theme of the Gar-den of Eden, one of the most reworked and varied themes in the history of Western civilization. The fact that these very different constructions of the myth of Genesis are not only possible but attested makes it possible for a scholar to let the polarized interpretations cancel one another out, leaving an ideal, Platonic form of the myth in which the tree, woman, serpent, and fruit are morally neutral.

But can a morally uninflected myth have meanings? I think so. The "neutral" elements of myths have inherent meanings, to which other, suc-cessive layers of meanings are attracted. We might formulate the "neutral" or uninflected hypothetical myth of Eden thus: "A woman and a serpent in a tree gave a man a fruit to eat, created by a deity, which brought him knowledge." This already tells us a great deal. It tells us that women rather than men are responsible for change (though we can disagree as to wheth-er this particular change was good or bad), that women rather than men supply the original food (mother's milk; can't you just hear Adam com-plaining, "What, fig casserole again? Can't we have some new fruit"), that food has something to do with sex, that both food and sex have something to do with knowledge, and so forth. But the most basic meaning shared by all variants of this or any cross-culturally attested myth is that the experience reflected in the myth is important, so important that several different cultures have selected it (or, if you prefer, constructed it), rather than one of the million other experiences that human beings have, as the basis of their myth.

Many Voices

This quality of myth, its ability to contain in latent form several different attitudes to the events that it depicts, allows each different telling to draw out, as it were, the attitude that it finds compatible. But each telling may have within itself, simultaneously, several points of view, several voices. Thus when we have seen the variants of the myth of the man, the woman, and the serpent, etc., we can take another, harder look at the inflected version that we know (in this case, the Book of Genesis). And then we can notice the text's ambivalence about the tree (there are, after all, *two* trees) and indeed about the woman and the fruit, even in the story as it is told in the Hebrew Bible, a text often alleged to have a single point of view ("patriarchal"). Setting aside the possibilities raised by multiple authorship, any perceptive author is simultaneously aware of the points of view of all the characters in the story. Homer tells the *Iliad* from the vantage point of a dead while male; but he allows Thersites to show us the underside of the Trojan war. Shakespeare both condemns and defends Othello; the voice of Feste in *Twelfth Night*, or of the Fool in *King Lear*, is a built-in voice of subversion.

Myth is like opera in its ability to represent several different people saying different things at the same time; in an opera, you can hear them all at once as separate voices, instead of the incomprehensible babble that results in real life if several people speak at once. The multivocality that characterizes myth reaches its apotheosis in the quartet from *Rigoletto*, the sextet from *Lucia di Lammamoor*, and the final trio from *Rosenkavalier*, when each character speaks from his or her heart, each voice contributing to a single tapestry of song. In Richard Strauss's *Capriccio*, people "talk" during the performance of a string quartet (they actually sing their "talking"), as they do during the Italian tenor's aria in Strauss's *Rosenkavalier* and during the mythic performance in his *Ariadne*. (When I attended a dress rehearsal of *Capriccio* in Chicago at the Lyric Opera in 1994, the people sitting near me in the audience were talking during the scene where people talk during the music, which infuriated me until I realized how very appropriate it was). People do not often literally talk at the same time in myths, but their various ideas, their symbols, their agendas are running at the same time, as Lévi-Strauss has pointed out: one cannot understand myth as a continuous sequence, but only like a musical score, reading all the lines simultaneously.[18] It should not be surprising to learn that Lévi-Strauss uses Wagner as his primary example of the confluence of opera and myth, since Wagner, the most mythical of all opera composers, invented leitmotifs, themes that function precisely like what Lévi-Strauss calls "mythemes," the atomic units of a myth, each with its own significance; when they are combined, their various symbolic values are simultaneously expressed.

Visual icons, like musical images, are even more ambiguous, more transparent, than narratives. Visual images are mythic, in my terms, when they are the keys to a narrative, like freeze frames in films, evoking the whole story. The surrealist paintings of De Chirico or Magritte or Escher function like myths in suggesting narratives and a place that is in two worlds at once, our world and another that plays by different rules. The art of *bricolage*, of *objets trouvés* is intrinsically mythic, as are all the images, from Lascaux to present-day Christian icons, that refer to a story that everyone in that particular culture knows. But they do not always tell us—or indeed the people within the culture—what to think about that story.

Bakhtin has taught us to recognize competing voices in the novel and different interpretive communities within the same text; we can, with profit, use Bakhtinian concepts of multivocality not only to bring women's voices into texts written by men but also to bring the voices of texts composed in one culture into texts composed in other cultures. And Gary Saul Morson, with Michael André Bernstein, has further developed the concept of what he calls sideshadowing:[19] "In contrast to foreshadowing, which projects onto the present a shadow from the future, sideshadowing projects—from the 'side'—the shadow of an alternative present. It allows us to see what might have been and therefore changes our view of what is."[20] Bakhtin and Morson are talking about novels, but I would argue that myths, which participate so much more directly than novels in a multiauthored community, better support Morson's belief in the salutary effects of sideshadowing:

> Sideshadows conjure the ghostly presence of might-have-beens or might-bes. . . . When sideshadowing is used, it seems that distinct temporalities are continually competing for each moment of actuality. Like a king challenged by a pretender with an equal claim to rule, the actual loses some temporal legitimacy. It can no longer be regarded as inevitable, as so firmly ensconced that it does not even

make sense to consider alternatives. Or to adapt one of Bakhtin's favorite metaphors, a present moment subjected to sideshadowing ceases to be Ptolemaic, the unchallenged center of things. It moves instead into a Copernican universe: as there are many planets, so there are many potential presents for each one actualized.[21]

Myths are even more Copernican than novels. Or perhaps we might say that if dogma moves in a Ptolemaic universe and novels move in a Copernican universe, myths move in an Einsteinian universe, a place of true relativity.

One particular trick of myths contributes greatly to their multivocality: the literary convention of nested tellings of stories within stories, which collapses all the tellers from the outermost layer to the central, most immediate one so that often we do not know which voice is speaking; they all speak simultaneously. In the *Mahabharata*, for instance, when the bard tells us what a sage told a king about what another king told yet another king, the translation has to indicate this by saying, " " ' " 'Your majesty. . . .' " ' " "[22] But which king is the majesty being addressed? And whose voice is addressing him? So too, outside the text, the multiauthored, communal character of myths makes them function like palimpsests, building up layer after layer of tellings and interpretations over the centuries, which lend each one its rich patina of ambiguity.

Mieke Bal has argued for this sort of multidimensionality in the interpretation of myths in the Hebrew Bible, including not only the myth of Eden (whose multidimensionality I have just argued for) but also myths about sexual tricksters like Tamar:

Focusing on the different subject-positions involved in narrative has allowed me to differentiate between the status of various expressions. That is how it was possible to notice both the idea of lethal love and its problematic background, its struggle against other views of love, its insecurity. If David kills Uriah for love, we don't need to assume that the overall ideology of the text agrees. And this for the simple reason that there is no overall ideology of the text.

The type of narratological analysis advocated in this study provides insight into what the text presents as problematic. Love is not lethal, but there is a problem for some people who think it is: such is the statement I have read in the stories, if statements there were at all. What went wrong in the history of the reception of these stories is precisely the repression of the problem, hence, of the heterogeneous ideology of the text, which had to be turned into a monolithic one. Textual subjectivity had to be replaced with *the* subject of the text. . . .

The point is that there is none, at least not a single one; the point of literary analysis is that there is no truth, and that this contention can be reasonably argued.[23]

Where Mieke Bal asserts that there is no truth, I would argue rather that there are a number of different truths—or, I would say, perspectives—all expressed in the same story.

In addition to the plurality of tellers and listeners, there are several other factors that extend the many voices, the multivocality, of a myth. And there are several different ways in which to outline the levels of meaning within a myth. One way is to focus on the different voices, asking whether they are male or female, traditional or subversive; or on different agendas, asking whether the text seems to care more about sex, religion, or politics. Some stories seem blatantly Freudian, while some seem to legitimate and establish a religious and/or political dynasty. A. K. Ramanujan preferred to focus on three basic conflicts in myths: high versus low (class, brains, or money); male versus female, and old versus young. On another plane, some stories seem to offer us nothing more or less than an amusing, frivolous tale about the past, while others present a serious, heavy prediction: things end up happening as they must happen. The interaction of oral and written traditions lends greater variety to many retellings; vernacular and noncanonical traditions often retain the structures of the stories told in the canonical texts, but give them different meanings. These are all concerns that apply to all texts to some degree and in different proportions, like the phenomena on the various continuums that we have constructed.

Indeed, a single telling may have so many points of view that ultimately the voices seem to cancel one another out, and there may seem to be no (single, or even dominant) point of view. But each telling, each text, does favor one point of view over all others; if we cannot decide which one, we must simply admit that we do not have enough data, or enough discernment, to find what is in fact there. The political stance of any telling of the myth is not chaos, not Brownian motion: each time anyone tells the myth, there is an inflection in one direction or the other (or both: the serpent might be good and evil, and both the woman and the man might be evil, or neither, or one or the other). The story is not infinitely pliable; it always clusters around a given set of meanings, which it can invert. The storyteller usually takes one basic, initial viewpoint; there are heroes and villains, and the narrator/reader shares the point of view of one character. This is true both in the bare-bones versions of myth and in highly elaborated versions where the storyteller artfully teases out various meanings in a single description or a single speech.

But, although the experience itself has no ideology, no spin, every telling puts a spin on it—indeed, puts several different spins on it. It is not the task of myths to moralize explicitly, but every telling implicitly invites the teller, listener, commentator to moralize. Different variants of myths are driven by different agendas, and so, inevitably, any particular variant does send a message; every teller sends for Western Union. Even by choosing to tell one myth rather than another, the teller is choosing to make one point rather than another. And indeed, if we assume, as surely we must, that the myth in its earliest telling was made by a human with opinions about it, there was always a point of view. But we must also admit that the second telling might have expressed a very different point of view.

Micromyths and Macromyths

The multivocality of myths is a quality that we encounter in actual texts. But a myth—still in the sense of a story embodied in a group of texts—can be analyzed through two kinds of nonoccurring metamyths, which I would call a micromyth and a macromyth. The micromyth is the neutral structure that I have been describing, the nonexistent story with no point of view: "A woman and a serpent in a tree gave a man a fruit. . . ." It is an imaginary text, a scholarly construct that contains the basic elements from which all possible variants could be created, a theoretical construct that will enable us to look at all the variants at once and ask questions of all of them simultaneously. It minimizes, though it cannot entirely exclude, the expression of any point of view. The micromyth is not merely a scaffolding on which each culture erects its own myths; it is more like a trampoline that allows each culture to fly far away to its own specific cultural meanings, leaping to make wildly different variants instead of remaining stuck to a limiting, constraining structure (a description often used for archetypes). After all, even the same skeleton can support very different bodies: Abraham Lincoln and Marilyn Monroe had, basically, the same skeleton (give or take a rib or two).

The micromyth is not a colorless grid, but rather a rainbow or a beam of pure light that seems colorless until it is refracted through the prism of a particular cultural telling. It's like one of those haystacks that Claude Monet kept painting over and over again, not primarily for their own sake (though haystacks are not without meaning—breast shapes, harvest time, autumn, the country) but in order to paint the light at different times of day and year, that same pure beam that, like the spider, no one can see or paint directly. The micromyth is the "third thing," the scholar's own defining interest, which serves now not just as the pivot of two things being compared but as the hub of a wheel to which an infinite number of spokes may be connected.[24] It is therefore highly subjective, like the choice of level of focus that we considered in chapter 1; the story will be quite different depending upon where one chooses to make the cut.

For instance, I have included a deity in my micromyth of the story of Eden; God certainly plays a central part in that story in the Genesis version, and including God in the micromyth enables me to take up theological issues in other variants that also include God. And using the neutral term *deity* allows me to include stories about Goddesses as well as Gods, if I can find them. Some folklorists make a sharp distinction between myth and folktale, on the basis of religious content and other factors, and some do not; here again, I would prefer to see a continuum of narratives more or less mythic, more or less folkloric. But even to do this, one would have to associate *folk* with tales that deal primarily with human problems, often in a profane context and usually with primarily human protagonists and a minimal intervention of the supernatural, while *myth* would deal primarily with cosmic problems, in a sacred context and with supernatural actors.[25] A folklorist who did make this sharp distinction might prefer to exclude God and theology from the micromyth entirely and tell it thus: "A woman and a serpent in a tree gave a man a fruit that brought him knowledge." For my purposes, it is useful to keep the deity in the micromyth.

The subjectivity of this choice does not make the micromyth any more arbitrary than the "third thing," for the scholar chooses not just what interests her personally (if she did, no one would buy the book), but what is important in her time, to her students and colleagues. The micromyth must be situated at the intersection between our questions and those asked by other cultures, in the area that remains when we have jettisoned both contemporary questions peculiar to our own culture and ancient questions that have no analogues in our day. Although the micromyth is subjective and cannot be experienced directly, something that functions very like it can actually be found in texts from cultures other than the Western academic world. In India, for instance, texts often cite a single cryptic verse from an older text, the Veda, and then expand it into a full narrative.[26] And condensed tellings of myths are inserted into the epic, the *Mahabharata*, as a bridge from one narrative to another: the bard says, "What's happening to you now is like what happened to King so-and-so, who did thus-and-so," or "This is the place where King so-and-so did thus-and-so," whereupon someone in the audience asks, "Who was that king and why did he do that? Tell us in expanded detail [*vistarena*]," and the narrator goes back and tells the whole story, filling in the gaps left by the micromyth that he used as bait to snag the curiosity of the audience—including, of course, the audience outside the text.

As a heuristic device the micromyth provides us with a springboard by which to vault over several otherwise insuperable hurdles in the comparative enterprise. It enables us to compare as variants of "the same" basic narrative different versions that embellish that narrative with different points of view. It is useful as an armature that defines a group of texts. The micromyth only superficially resembles what Joseph Campbell called the monomyth;[27] it is more particularly constructed on combinations of specific concrete details.

If we define the micromyth as a sentence, with a subject noun and a verb, often also with an object noun ("A woman and a serpent in a tree gave a man a fruit")—we exclude the adjectives and adverbs that betray the presence of the editorializing and moralizing author. But we must exercise caution in abstracting these small units from our myths, as Clifford Geertz warns when we use Java and Morocco as "optics" for each other: we do not find "a collection of abstractable, easily stateable themes (sex, status, boldness, modesty . . .) differently tied into local bundles, the same notes set into different melodies."[28] Themes as abstract as these (status, modesty), and as heavily value-laden, will necessarily shift their weight in transit like baggage in an airplane. We must be far more modest in selecting our units. But the metaphor implicit in Geertz's comparative model—that Java and Morocco serve as "optics," i.e. lenses, for each other—implies that we can, with care, look at one culture through another.

The building blocks I have in mind pivot upon verbs, like the building blocks that Vladimir Propp isolated and called "moves."[29] For a noun, such as a serpent, may symbolize so many polarized things—wisdom and evil, rebirth (sloughing) and death (poison), masculinity (the phallus) and femininity (the coiled power), water (the element of many serpents) and fire (the flame of its tongue)—indeed, it may seem to symbolize almost anything, though closer inspection reveals that it symbolizes certain large groups of somethings. When we add a verb, such as "gives" or "bites," the meanings of the resulting micromyth are more circumscribed than the meanings of the noun alone, because the meaning of the micromyth is constructed in the area in which the two terms, the noun and the verb, intersect, each activating a particular subarea within the larger potential area of meaning of the other term: another Venn diagram (or spider's web).

David E. Bynum has articulated another good reason to focus on what he calls motifs (and I call micromyths) rather than on nouns (what he calls symbols):

> A symbol is by nature a perfectly adequate purveyor of meaning in its own right whenever it passes between persons who are initiated into its symbolism. But a narrative motif by itself means nothing and *can-*

not even be identified apart from the other motifs surrounding it in the story-patterns to which it belongs. Moreover, when one is not privy to the symbolism of an image used symbolically, it means little or nothing, and no amount of effort will suffice to extract its symbolism from it alone, because symbolism is meaning *associated* with an image and not resident in the image itself. But in their proper patterns, narrative motifs bear certain meanings inherent in narrative regardless of whether anyone apprehends that meaning or puts it to any extra-narrative use whatsoever. In order to use a symbol effectively, one must (as in enactments of ritual) be taught in detail what it symbolizes, but to convey the generic ideas in narrative motifs one learns to tell stories.[30]

If a serpent is a symbol, one has to know what it symbolizes in the particular culture that tells a story about it. But the more verbal theme of incest or mutilation in a story has a generic meaning that one learns from any variant, a meaning that is then often further complicated by taking on a particular cultural meaning as well.

The micromyth makes it possible for us to find meanings shared by all the cultures that share the myth, meanings over and behind the individual cultural inflections. It allows us to isolate within a group of myths a core that no teller of those myths from any culture would find foreign, but that still retains some intrinsic meaning that is not limited to any single text. It allows us to outline the borders of the sphere of influence of any particular myth. It is also useful as a source of some basic cross-cultural meanings that may not be explicit, or even conscious, in individual tellings but are there, latent, and give the punch to the manifest meaning that may at first appear to be the only meaning of any culturally specific retelling. Just how interesting those cross-cultural meanings are is determined by the balance between, on the one hand, a structure simple enough to accommodate a significant number of variants and, on the other hand, a corpus of detail complex enough to constitute a distinct, unique myth. It comes down, again, to the subjective question of where to make the cut. For you can state any myth in a series of forms that can be arranged on a continuum: you can say, "A man and a woman had children," and it applies to a million stories and hardly tells us anything we do not already know. Or you can include all the details of the Genesis story of Adam and Eve, which is not quite like any other myth. Depending on where you draw the line of details, you can argue that the stories are more similar or more different. I choose to make the cut for the micromyth where they are relatively similar, and to begin by investigating what it is that they share. This is a minimalist approach.

The micromyth, however, systematically eliminates all the detail that gives the myth its color and complexity, if not its meaning. It threatens to reduce the group of myths to a truly common denominator (which Raymond Jameson sees as a virtue, when he argues that folklore themes present "the lowest common denominator of human nature, the nuclei of human aspirations and human terror").[31] Superficial comparatists (among whom I include Campbell) stop at the micromyth, at the stripped-down plot where several versions intersect. They quit before the hard work begins; if you just point out how *The Tibetan Book of the Dead* is like Dante's *Inferno,* you can see some interesting things, but you don't see what you see when you go on to learn Italian and Tibetan. Abandoning the mythic analysis when you have just isolated the micromyth is like abandoning psychoanalysis at the point when the personality has been dismantled, before it has been rebuilt. To put it differently: comparison involves a "second naïveté" like the one implicit in our emphasis on the individual: the initial comparison is superficial, but the human meaning deepens as the comparison leads us into the individual culture and then goes below the cultures to still deeper levels of human meaning.

For in order to note the particular spin that each individual telling (not merely each individual culture) puts on the basic tale, including details that no other telling has, we must use the basic units we have formulated, the micromyths, to construct a macromyth. Of course, we could never get all the details from all the variants, and if we did the resulting study would make Frazer's *The Golden Bough* look like a sound bite. (*The Golden Bough* is actually the closest thing to an extant macromyth that I know, though it is not constructed the way I would do it; Frazer makes the cut for the implicit micromyth of the killed and resurrected king/priest at a point so stripped down that it includes far too many texts). But we might hope for analyses that would be inclusive not only in their range of details but in the range of genres from which they mine those details. We can get *enough* details to make a persuasive case, if not an argument,[32] through the numerological rather than logical method that I characterized as working from the bottom up. Or we might make what Lawrence Sullivan, referring to the workings of myths themselves, calls an "argument of images."[33]

David E. Bynum suggests that the "purpose in comparing variants of fable and extracting generic motifs from them is precisely to lighten the otherwise heavy work of deciphering variants, which, if taken one by one and without reference to each other, constitutes a truly insurmountable labor of decipherment."[34] I would qualify this statement by emphasizing that the micromyth does indeed enable us to decipher the individual variants *with* "reference to each other," but that this is still a great, though not insurmountable, "labor of decipherment." I agree with Jameson when he suggests that the task of the comparatist is "to examine the variations of a symbol and to determine the reasons for these variations."[35]

The macromyth is a composite of the details of many variants and insights; it arranges texts, and micromyths, in their possible systematic relationships. It suggests, though it cannot entirely encompass, the expression of all points of view in order to build up a multinational multimyth, a collage in which a storyteller from any culture could find many things that she had never—yet—dreamed of, but that might expand her own particular insight into the shared myth. This is a maximalist approach. The macromyth makes possible the cross-cultural rather than the universalist enterprise.

The micromyth ("A woman and a serpent in a tree . . .") is below the text (the text being, in this case, Genesis 3), smaller than the text; the macromyth is above the text, sometimes larger than the text (the macromyth being, in this case, an extended version of the brief survey I have offered of some variants of the micromyth: the Ophites, Royall Tyler, Shelley, Mark Twain, etc.). The nonexistent, uninflected micromyth that the scholar constructs out of the actually occurring, inflected myth confronted in any analysis of a text is like a condensed soup cube: the scholar confronts the soup (a particular variant of the myth) and boils it down to the soup cube, the basic stock (the micromyth), only to cook it up again into all sorts of soups (various detailed myths confronted in actual individual texts) and finally into the great narrative bouillabaisse that is the macromyth (the comparison of many variants).[36] Thus in the example I have been using, the scholar confronts the text (the book of Genesis) and extracts from it the micromyth ("A woman and a serpent in a tree . . ."); she uses that to relate the texts of Shelley, Twain, and so forth to the Hebrew Bible; and finally she creates the macromyth that incorporates the Bible, Shelley, and all the others. The macromyth is then the object of interpretation of the meaning of the myth on the comparative level, an interpretation of the many different cultural and individual variants of the myth of the origins of sexuality, food, and knowledge.

Let me offer another example, the story of Cinderella. We might begin with two texts, one from Mongolia about a girl who loses a fur slipper, another, from Paris, about a girl who loses a glass slipper. (In chapter 6 I will consider the argument that the Mongolian version was the source of the French version). From these two texts we would extract a micromyth about a girl who loses a slipper (jettisoning from our basic unit the various substances of the slipper) or, even more basic, about a girl who loses some object of clothing (such as a ring). The macromyth would include all variants (a girl loses a fur slipper, a glass slipper, a ring, and so forth).

Scholars' readings are also part of the macromyth: what Freud said about Oedipus, what A. K. Ramanujan said about Cinderella.[37] From there we could go on to ask questions of the macromyth that we could not ask of any of the individual versions: How is glass different from fur? How can both of them be related to the story of a lost girl? What do they mean together? Why do these stories regard a woman's foot as the key to her identity? Why do some variants regard a ring, or the ability to cook a particular dish, as the equivalent of the shoe in other variants? What do a ring and a shoe mean, together, for the cultural formulation of a woman's sexual identity? And so forth.

Some elements that are held in common by all versions of that story carry a shared meaning: stepmothers can be cruel; the meek shall inherit the earth; and so forth. Ramanujan reminds us that "Cinderella tales tend to be similar not only in 'deep' structures, but even in particular surface details. . . . The identifying object is a slipper in the European tale, food in the Kannada, a ring in the classical Sanskrit. Like items of vocabulary in a language, cultural content is clearest in such details—though, as we have seen, even abstract structures must be interpreted for cultural and contextual meanings."[38] But only when we have the macromyth can we notice that when the slipper is made of glass, which does not, like fur, stretch, the test of foot size has far greater effect. Only from the macromyth do we realize that glass is not merely glass but not-fur, that the French version doesn't bark, as it were, at the furriness of Cinderella (whose fur feet may indicate, for instance, that she is an oversexual woman, a suggestion that is supported by an Indian story of a fur-footed demoness—another comparative insight).[39] Marina Warner notes how the glass and fur illuminate each other:

> The glass slipper works to dematerialize the troubling aspects of [Cinderella's] nature, her natural fleshiness, her hairy vitality, and so to give a sign of her new, socialized value. The slipper becomes the glass in which a princess sees her worth brightly mirrored. As the beast is to the blonde, so the webbed foot or ass's hoof of the storyteller is to Cinderella's glass slipper.[40]

Or, one might say, hair is to glass as nature is to culture. A modern, politically correct retelling remarks that, at the ball, "She tried to escape, but her impractical glass slippers made it nearly impossible. Fortunately for her, none of the other womyn were shod any better."[41] So now glass equals male chauvinism. The possibilities are great—but not infinite. The method of comparison from the bottom up would start with only the barest clue from the structure (that some object identifies the Cinderella figure) and go on to ask what the variants of that object (foot, food, ring, fur, glass) have to tell us, together, about the range of ways in which a person may be identified.

The Myth with Points of View

There are many myths, like the story of the serpent in the garden, that have been used even within a single culture to argue for diametrically opposed morals, political theories, or social codes. Some are independent variants of a single theme, which can stand on their own and express their own point of view without reacting against anything else, though they may take on greater depth if the audience knows other, opposing variants. This is true of, for instance, the many tellings of Cinderella in many different cultures.[42] It is also true of the many tellings of the *Ramayana* in India, which are aware of one another through what has been called "intertextuality"[43] but which do not necessarily, at least explicitly, respond to one another or to some "original" *Ramayana*.

One of the reasons why myths generate so many variants is that they wrestle with insoluble paradoxes, as Claude Lévi-Strauss noted long ago,[44] and they inevitably fail to pin the paradox to the mat. The failure to fit a round peg into a square hole generates potentially infinite ways of *not* fitting a round peg into a square hole—hence our multiple variants. An anecdote is told about Thomas Edison who, after some nine thousand unsuccessful attempts to devise a new type of storage battery, was asked, "Isn't it a shame that with the tremendous amount of work you have done you haven't been able to get any results?" Edison replied, "Results! Why, man, I have gotten a lot of results! I know several thousand things that won't work."[45] Myths, too, know thousands of things that won't work.

But sometimes this ongoing system of trial and error leaves logical holes in a myth large enough, as the Irish saying goes, to drive a coach and horses through. For most traditions, the hole becomes part of the story; you tell it that way, note the pothole, and walk around it. The community ignores the hole until someone falls in; this is what Mieke Bal calls "the repression of the problem." But as the years go on and sensibilities change, suddenly someone notices the hole; some smartass kid shouts out that the emperor has no clothes, and then a new suit has to be woven for him, a new episode inserted in the myth to cover its logical nakedness, suddenly exposed after so many years of polite, tacit agreement to ignore it. Then a new telling emerges to confront—or to paper over again—the newly exposed hole.

This process is captured in a terse parable by Franz Kafka:

Leopards break into the temple and drink to the dregs what is in the sacrificial pitchers; this is repeated over and over again; finally it can be calculated in advance, and it becomes a part of the ceremony.[46]

The commentary that calls attention explicitly to what everyone has ignored also becomes a part of the ceremony, a part of the text.

Another, delightful instance of this process is provided by Evelyn Waugh's portrait of Mr Tendril, the vicar in an English village, a man who totally disregards context: "His sermons had been composed in his more active days for delivery at the garrison chapel [in India]; he had done nothing to adapt them to the changed conditions of his ministry and they mostly concluded with some reference to homes and dear ones far away."[47] His Christmas sermon was his masterpiece:

> "How difficult it is for us," he began, blandly surveying his congregation, who coughed into their mufflers and chafed their chilblains under their woolen gloves, "to realize that this is indeed Christmas. Instead of the glowing log fire and windows tight shuttered against the drifting snow, we have only the harsh glare of an alien sun; instead of the happy circle of loved faces, of home and family, we have the uncomprehending stares of the subjugated, though no doubt grateful, heathen. Instead of the placid ox and ass of Bethlehem," said the vicar, slightly losing the thread of his comparisons, "we have for companions the ravening tiger and the exotic camel, the furtive jackal and the ponderous elephant. . . ." And so on, through the pages of faded manuscript.[48]

The "subjugated, though no doubt grateful, heathen" are conflated with "the furtive jackal" and contrasted, by Fluellenish comparison, with "the placid ox and ass of Bethlehem"; the heathen are not only like animals, but like unholy animals. Yet the racism of the sermon loses its force in the new context of the English village, where both heathens and jackals are unknown. Moreover, the sermon gradually undergoes a sea change without altering a syllable of the text; after a while it loses its original subtext of "How we colonials do long for England" and even its next subtext of "What an idiot this vicar is" to evolve into a new tradition:

> The words had temporarily touched the heart of many an obdurate trooper, and hearing them again, as he had heard them year after year since Mr Tendril had come to the parish, Tony and most of Tony's guests felt that it was an integral part of their Christmas festivities; one with which they would find it very hard to dispense.

"The ravening tiger and exotic camel" had long been bywords in the family, of frequent recurrence in all their games.[49]

The ritual has become transformed to accommodate the vicar's now frozen, wildly inappropriate sermon; in this new context, through the process that we have considered at some length, that sermon has taken on a totally different, and entirely appropriate, subtext. The mistake (the parson's assumption that all the English villagers were soldiers in India) becomes part of the Christmas ritual (enjoying the parson's predictable, inane sermon).

To take another sort of example: early parts of the Sanskrit epic, the *Ramayana*, tell us that the demon Ravana never forced Sita to his bed, though he captured her because he was infatuated with her and held her captive for many years. Later parts of the *Ramayana*, puzzled by the demon's uncharacteristic self-restraint, added another story to explain it in retrospect: he once raped a woman, and she cursed him to die if he ever forced another woman.[50] Another version adds that that woman was reborn as Sita.[51] In this way the epic plugs its holes, incorporating variants into itself and expanding upon the laconic plot just as Shakespeare, in my reading, expands upon the story of Tamar and Judah. Like sand in an oyster, the insoluble problem is an irritant that keeps generating literary pearls; like a string suspended in a supersaturated solution (which is to say, a culture), it keeps generating literary crystals.

The different ways in which the "same" story can be interpreted within a single culture (or a closely related group of cultures) may be seen in a myth that is as important to the Indo-European world as the myth of Eden is to the world of Judaism and Christianity: the story of Yama and his sister Yami. In the telling composed in Sanskrit in Northwest India in about 1,000 B.C.E., Yami, the sister, urges her brother Yama to commit incest with her, and he refuses. In the Iranian version, composed in the related Indo-Iranian language called Avestan at a slightly later period in Iran, Yama (now called Yima) accedes to his sister's wishes, and thus the human race is created. The shared experience recorded in both stories is the attempted incestuous seduction by the sister; in one branch of the Indo-Iranian tree it succeeds; in the other, it fails. It is the same myth and not the same myth.

But there is another way in which myths generate variants: by inspiring not two parallel versions of the same story but explicit parodies, which assume that the audience knows the version being imitated and use that assumption to challenge its point of view. (The two versions of the Indo-Iranian incest myth may actually fall into this category, though it is difficult to know from the historical evidence.) We have already seen this process at work in the myth of Genesis, with satires (or at least subversive responses) by people like Shelley, Royall Tyler, and Mark Twain.

Fairy tales too can be told in order to make diametrically opposed points. Here is a charming contemporary inversion of the story of the Frog Prince:

> Two guys "with the experience that comes with age," [are] playing tennis. At one point, the ball rolls into some bushes, and when one of the players goes to retrieve it he is confronted by a frog who claims to be a beautiful princess who has been turned into a frog by a mischievous wizard. If the player will kiss her, the frog assures him, she'll revert to her princess state and marry him, and they'll both live happily ever after. The player pockets the frog and returns to the game. After a bit, the frog, inside the player's pocket, croaks, "Sir, did you forget about me? I'm this beautiful princess, turned into a frog, if you kiss me . . ." and so forth, to which she receives the reply, "Dear lady frog, I will be completely honest with you. I have reached the age at which I would rather have a talking frog than a new wife."[52]

Red Riding Hood also used to be told, in Europe, in ways very different from the ways it is told to American children, in which (usually: there are variants here too) the wolf eats the grandmother and is about to eat Red Riding Hood (or—variant—has just eaten Red Riding Hood) when the Huntsman comes and shoots him. In some of the older tellings, Red (Riding Hood) eats her grandmother and climbs into bed with the wolf.[53] We are telling it still differently now; a 1989 "Far Side" cartoon by Gary Larson depicts the wolf on a psychiatrist's couch, saying, "You know, it was supposed to be just a story about a little kid and a wolf, but off and on I've been dressing up as the grandmother ever since." And it is being told in different ways now in Japan; in one variant, the wolf eats Red Riding Hood and falls asleep, and the hunter takes Red Riding Hood out of the wolf's belly and substitutes stones (a motif that may have been borrowed from the Greek story of the stone substituted for Zeus in the belly of his father, Chronos,[54] or just from the more closely related Grimm story of the stone in the belly of the wolf who swallowed the seven kids). In another Japanese version, "The wolf apologizes to Little Red Riding Hood and promises to be good from now on."[55]

Another example of such a 180-degree turnabout may be seen in three variants of another Jewish story. In one, from the Babylonian Talmud (compiled after the fourth century C.E.), the heroine, like Tamar and Helena, has to masquerade as another woman in order to get her husband into bed:

The wife of Hiya Bar Ashi said, "It has been some years now that he
has abstained from [sexual relations with] me." One day, when he
was studying in his garden, she adorned herself and paraded in front
of him. He said to her: "Who are you?" She said: "I am a prostitute
named Harutha [Freedom] returning from my day's work." He de-
manded her [sexual services]. She said to him, "Then bring me the
pommegranate that is on the topmost branch." He jumped and
brought it to her. When he came home his wife was stoking the
oven. He climbed up and sat in it. She said to him: "What's this all
about?" He said to her: "Here's what happened." She said to him:
"That was me." He said: "Nevertheless, my intention was to do something forbidden."[56]

The pommegranate, the apple of Granada, seems to function, like the ring
of Tamar and Helena or the slipper of Cinderella, as proof that it was the
man's wife with whom he indulged his evil inclination. But in this Rab-
binic text the apple of Granada may also carry overtones of that other apple
with which a woman persuaded her husband, in Eden, to accede to *her*
evil intention.

A related text tells another story about a rabbi named Hiyya:

Judith, the wife of Rabbi Hiyya, had suffered great pains in childbirth. She changed her clothing and appeared before Rabbi Hiyya.
She asked, "Is a woman commanded to be fruitful and multiply?" He
told her, "No." She departed and drank a sterilizing potion. When
finally her action became known, he said to her: "I wish you had
borne me one more set of twins [or: issue of the womb]."[57]

The phrase "she changed her clothing" may have indicated no more than
the change out of childbearing clothes, impure clothes, but it might also
suggest a disguise, a reading that is supported by the husband's ignorance
of "her action" (disguise, or abortion?). In retelling this story, the feminist
Dena Davis expands upon this possibility:

She went out of the back door of their house, changed her clothing,
and appeared at the front door in disguise. "Rabbi," she asked him,
"is a woman commanded to propagate the race?" "No," he replied.
Out the front door she went, around the house, removed her disguise, and drank a sterilizing potion. . . .[58]

In this interpretation, the wife uses her disguise to obtain from her husband a favor that is the very opposite of that sought by the first wife: not sex
or a child but knowledge about whether or not women are required to have

children. Where the rabbi in the first story did not want to have sex with his wife, the wife in this story does not want to bear more of the rabbi's children. Where in the first text she tricked him into doing something, here she tricks him into letting her not do something, as it were.

There is a rough symmetry, a causal link, if not an identity, between having sex and having children, that might allow us to argue that the second text is in many ways an inversion of the first. The modern feminist interpretation reads a more developed agenda into the wife's trick, now seen as an attempt to thwart the ancient patriarchal demand for as many male heirs as possible. The obstacle to the wife's wish is now said to be the husband's famous piety, interpreted as the reason for his resistance to birth control; the wife now appears disguised "as one of the many women in the town who would ask Rabbi Hiyya for advice." This reading assumes that "Judith knew that, according to the Talmud, the obligation 'to be fruitful and multiply' devolved upon men but not upon women." It assumes that "She also knew that unusual pain in childbirth was one of the many reasons for which Jewish law allowed a woman to use a contraceptive or a sterilizing agent." (In fact, the wife in the second text does not know these things, but finds them out in the course of the story.) These assumptions make the third text, the feminist reading, a more extreme inversion of the first. What all three have in common is the assumption that to have a child, to find out if she must have a child, or not to have a child, the wife has to pretend to be someone else. But the three texts say very different things about the uses of this trick.

The chameleon quality of myth works in opposition to the more monolithic and dogmatic aspects of religion; where myth encourages a wide range of beliefs, dogma would narrow that range. Martin Buber made this point very well indeed:

> All positive religion rests on an enormous simplification of the manifold and wildly engulfing forces that invade us: it is the subduing of the fullness of existence. All myth, in contrast, is the expression of the fullness of existence, its image, its sign; it drinks incessantly from the gushing fountains of life. Hence religion fights myth where it cannot absorb and incorporate it. . . . It is strange and wonderful to observe how in this battle religion ever again wins the apparent victory, myth ever again wins the real one.[59]

What Buber says about religion, I would limit to dogma. With that corrective, I think Buber's statement a marvelous testimony to myth's ability to keep open the doors of the imagination within the most constricting dogmatic frameworks. It has been said that a language is a dialect with an army;[60] I would say that a dogma is a myth with an army.

Inverted Political Versions

To speak of an army is to speak of politics. Roland Barthes sees myth as essentially nonpolitical; but whereas I would see myth as *pre*political, he see it as *post*political, as a text from which politics has apparently been extracted:

> What the world supplies to myth is an historical reality, defined, even if this goes back quite a while, by the way in which men have produced or used it; and what myth gives in return is a *natural* image of this reality. . . . A conjuring trick has taken place; it has turned reality inside out, it has emptied it of history and has filled it with nature. . . . *Myth is depoliticized speech.*[61]

Barthes is speaking here of right-wing myths that pretend to be depoliticized, neutralized, but his remarks apply, I think, only to the neutral, non-existent micromyth. I would add to his statement: each telling keeps the image of nature but also puts the history back into the myth.

Different tellings of the same myth may make explicit different political agendas embedded in it. Ancient myths have always been recycled for various, opposed political purposes. Alan Dundes has assembled many versions of "The Blood Libel Legend" accusing the Jews of torturing and eating Christian children,[62] but Carlo Ginzburg has demonstrated that a very similar cluster of accusations was leveled against other people besides the Jews—Christians (eating Roman children), lepers, gypsies, witches.[63] This compelling image of hate could be directed at almost any marginal figure: in the dark of bigotry, all the people you hate look alike.

We can see the protean political nature of myths at work in a few examples that I have taken from contemporary culture. They are mythic not in any explicit religious content but in the looser secular terms that Barthes has defined for such contemporary mythic practices as wrestling,[64] and in my own terms of a story transparent to polarized retellings. These are myths that swing both ways, politically speaking, and have generated separate, polarized variants. A rather touching reversal of this sort took place in a single, pregnant phrase in Moscow in 1991, the moment of glasnost. Moscow subways have no safety devices to protect people who get caught in the doors; instead, Muscovites are subjected to a droning voice that repeats, over and over ad nauseam, "Warning, the doors are closing." In 1991, people started wearing T-shirts depicting subway doors made of prison bars and inscribed with the motto: "Warning, the doors are opening."

Two very different versions of the same switch-hitting story by Alexandre Dumas were filmed a decade apart. In 1929, Douglas Fairbanks made *The Iron Mask*,[65] playing the part of d'Artagnan, who protected the good king Louis XIV when the evil Rochefort (Ulrich Haupt) tried to put the king's (evil) twin brother on the throne of France. The film was remade in 1939 as *The Man in the Iron Mask*,[66] with Warren William as d'Artagnan, but now with a twist: this time, d'Artagnan was the protector not of the king, now regarded as evil (Louis Hayward), but of the twin, now regarded as virtuous. A later set of variants of this set of variants is *The Prisoner of Zenda*, which in its book form (1896) and in the Ronald Colman movie (1937) reverts to the second type of *The Man in the Iron Mask*, with the evil king and the good twin; it is all about the honor of the upper classes, which forms a bond between the true king of Ruritania and the Englishman (a member of the Coldstream Guards) who doubles for him (and teaches him his job: the king is a drunk, the Englishman a prince among men).[67] But the Peter Sellers satire (1979) blows the class bonding out of the water: the English double is a cockney, and the point of the film is the contrast between the men's classes (and, as in the earlier version, their morals).[68]

Another example of a political myth that bats for both teams is the Irish antiwar folksong, "Johnny, I Hardly Knew You," which speaks of the returning soldier's disfiguring mutilations. ("Oh my darling dear, you looked so queer, Johnny, I hardly knew you.") This song was then, amazingly, transformed into the pro-war American Civil War song, "When Johnny Comes Marching Home" ("And we'll all be gay when Johnny comes marching home!"). The story is the same: the soldier returns home from war and is greeted by his mother. But the plot is entirely different: in one he returns in tragedy, in the other, in triumph.

On a lighter level, there is the story of the boy in the Civil War who is saved when a bullet strikes the deck of cards he had stashed in his breast pocket, while his comrade, carrying a Bible, is killed.[69] This is already a reversal of the assumed myth: the Bible saves you, the gambling deck kills you; A. E. Housman once expressed the blasphemous hope that a copy of *The Shropshire Lad* taken into battle would stop a bullet aimed at a soldier's heart. But it is reversed in yet another way in Woody Allen's story about the man who always carries in his breast pocket a bullet (a gift from his mother), which saves his life when a berserk Evangelist hurls from a hotel window a Gideon Bible that hits him in the chest: "That Bible would have gone through my heart, if it wasn't for the bullet."[70]

Another good example of a political myth turned on its head in explicitly inverted separate tellings is the American myth of the cowboys and Injuns. The basic narrative remains stable: the cowboys move West, the Injuns attack, the cowboys circle the wagons, the Injuns kill some of the cowboys, the cavalry arrives at the eleventh hour, and they and the cowboys massacre all the Injuns. When I was growing up in the '40s and '50s we saw films with these plots, and we cheered for the good cowboys and booed the evil Injuns. Now we see the same films (*Dances with Wolves*[71] is a good example), but we cheer for the good Injuns and boo the evil cowboys. "The same" myth, but now a different idea has been attached to it. "The same" narrative (based on the undeniable outlines of actual history, which I would include in what I am calling experience): the white man did move West, and many white men and women and Native Americans died in the resulting clash of cultures), and even "the same" characters, but a very different meaning. We might have assumed that the Injuns also told more or less "the same" story except that they always rooted for the Injuns, but until recently no one but anthropologists, perhaps, certainly no one in Hollywood, cared about those variants of the myth. The change of point of view was well demonstrated in a recent television program telling the story from the Native American point of view, entitled, "How the West Was Lost." Yet another development on this theme came in the film *Into the West*,[72] which conflates the myth of the cowboys riding into the American West with the Irish myth of the land in the west where no one ever grows old; two little boys, who are Travellers (Tinkers, Gypsies), ride into the west of Ireland on their magic white horse that comes from the west of Ireland and is named Tir Na Nog (Land of the West); they sing cowboy songs and watch cowboy films, and are persecuted by the police. At the end, the little one asks his brother, "Are the Travellers Cowboys or Indians?" To which, of course, no answer is given.

A striking example of a myth that has grafted very different political meanings onto the basic narrative, from ancient times to the present, is the Old Norse myth of the Valkyries, which already had a richly multivalent set of meanings in the medieval texts of the German *Nibelungenlied* and the Norse *Volsungasaga*: the daughters of Wotan, riding on the horses of the storm, gather up fallen warriors and bring them to a glorious afterlife in Valhala. Wagner added new, Aryan triumphalist layers to the meaning of the Valkyries in his cycle of operas known as *The Ring of the Nibelung*, and the Nazis in turn reinterpreted both the ancient myth and the Wagnerian variant for their own anti-Semitic purposes. The Wagnerian variant took on the status of a true mythic retelling; people still find, and I think will for many generations continue to find, beauty and meaning in it. The Nazi variant lasted far too long, but ultimately it did not succeed as a myth;

it is no longer generally regarded as a valid retelling of the ancient tale. More recently, Francis Ford Coppola used the Wagnerian music of the Valkyries to refer simultaneously to Wagner, the Nazis, and the American forces in Vietnam (not to mention Joseph Conrad in the novel *Heart of Darkness*) in his film *Apocalypse Now*:[73]

> When the US Airborne Cavalry in Coppola's film started out on those famous operations christened "search and destroy" by General Westmoreland, seeking out towns suspected of being Viet Cong, they did so only with light music, with Muzak. Wagner's "Ride of the Valkyries," the pretty, old light show of 1876, droned in all the earphones of all the war helicopters. A feedback between music-drama and war technology transformed the Valkyries, Wotan's deadly daughters, into on-board MG-guards, their storm-horses into helicopters, and Bayreuth into Hollywood.[74]

When Coppola played the Valkyries' music as the helicopters attacked, he was simultaneously implying that the helicopters were like Valkyries (flying and choosing the dead) and like Nazis (waging an evil war), but only the first meaning was literally there in the music; to get the second meaning, you had to know that the Nazis had used the myth in their own way, as did Coppola in his. Clearly it behooves us to distinguish among the very different uses to which the basic theme has been put, but at the same time we must acknowledge that our understanding of Coppola's film is greatly enhanced by an understanding of both the *Nibelungenlied* and modern German history—two tellings, one on each side of the historic moment of Wagner.

Inverted Political Readings of Contemporary Mythic Texts

It may happen that, as in the story of Rabbi Hiya's wife or the myth of Eden, one telling of a myth states the traditional view and another text subverts it. How does one telling replace another?[75] A variety of factors may make this happen. Sometimes the times change and make possible a new telling; myth reflects the changes in actual life and may in turn inspire changes in actual life.[76] Sometimes someone with power makes a new telling stick; sometimes the new telling is just so good that people want it instead of the old one. But inverted tellings need not replace one another; since a single multivocal myth may express diametrically opposed viewpoints, a single telling may express the traditional view cheek by jowl with a view that subverts it. And even an apparently monolithic telling may be interpreted differently by different people in the tradition (and by different scholars), and say diametrically opposed things to different readers/listeners. In many tellings, different political opinions are simultaneously expressed and are probably differently perceived by individuals in the audience.

Salman Rushdie has focused on this process in Greek myths. He has argued that the myths of Arachne, Niobe, and Prometheus seem to say that we must not challenge the gods (or, by implication, those in power), for if we do they will destroy us. But the myths actually demonstrate the opposite, that the gods (or those in power) are so vengeful and petty that they deserve to be challenged, and that those who challenge them live forever in human memory—in the myth.[77]

This double edge in interpretations of a single myth (or, in the case I am about to cite, a ritual) may be seen in interpretations of Guy Fawkes's Day, on which, every year, the British light bonfires and burn a "guy" in effigy, explicitly to commemorate Guy Fawkes's unsuccessful attempt to blow up king, Lords, and Commons in Westminster Palace on November 5, 1605. This is a festival about a political event; even Frazer demurred when his followers insisted that the bonfire was "associated intensely, if vaguely, with a tradition of sacred fires, coming down from prehistory."[78] But one reason for the enduring popularity of Guy Fawkes's Day is that it is celebrated with equal enthusiasm by people who think that they are symbolically blowing up Parliament to commemorate Guy Fawkes's admirable revolutionary zeal and by people who think that they are blowing up Guy Fawkes, commemorating the failure of that dastardly upstart. As Ronald Hutton explains, "The anniversary flourished because of the flexibility of its message: to some it was still an opportunity to berate Catholics, to others one to eulogize monarchy and condemn rebellion," while, on the other hand, "Some tories disliked it because it eulogized a revolution."[79] People were, after all, doing what Guy Fawkes had done: burning things up, but also, paradoxically (or as I would say, mythically), pretending to burn *him*. The theme continued to be malleable: in the 1980s, some people burned effigies of Margaret Thatcher as the Guy.[80]

A similar process of divergent interpretations was applied to the film *Invasion of the Body Snatchers*,[81] in which the invading aliens may be read either as communists (possessing people who thereafter hand over their minds to Mars, a.k.a. Moscow) or as McCarthyites, red-baiters. During the same period, the McCarthy era, Arthur Miller wrote *The Crucible*, which was generally perceived to be simultaneously about the witches (or alleged witches) hunted in Salem and about the communists (or alleged communists) hunted by McCarthy. But when *The Crucible* was revived in 1996, Miller said in interviews that it was now simultaneously about fundamentalism and/or political correctness.

On the other side of the cold war, when Yuri Grigorovich at the Bolshoi ballet staged his version of the ballet *Spartacus* in 1968, "Although impeccably Soviet on the surface, the allegory worked both ways: was it the brave Thracians or the fascistic Roman legions who represented the Soviet state? Grigorovich was playing dangerous games, and it wasn't long before the state called his bluff and insisted that he make an overt ideological statement in his work."[82] So too in Prague in 1992, at a performance of Wagner's *Rienzi* that was self-consciously contemporary, the audience wondered uneasily whom to identify with the corrupt regime—Hitler or Havel?

People have used myth for very different political ends, not only reactionary (which we always knew) but revolutionary (which mythologists have generally failed to note). Barthes wrongly damned myths for being inevitably reactionary,[83] and Mircea Eliade often equally wrongly blessed them for the same quality when he asserted that myths always look to the past, that they are always about origins (though he also noted that they can look toward the future).[84] I prefer the formulation of the theologian Teilhard de Chardin, that the myth of Eden, the myth of the Golden Age, is a myth about the future.[85]

Hilda Kuper tells of the subversive use of what I, though not she, would call a myth in Swaziland in the 1930s, when a British official told the Swazi king that his people must give up some of their hunting land for the British to build a landing strip on it:

> The councillors thought of a way to prevent the transaction. The proposed ground was the site of an old royal village, marked by the shady tree under which the council of King Mbandzeni [the last independent Swazi king, r. 1872–89] had met in debate. To prepare the ground the tree would have to be removed. On their advice the King said that the ground could be used if the tree were not touched. There have since been negotiations to buy land from a European.[86]

As Bruce Lincoln points out about the story of the council under the tree (which he calls a myth in a much narrower and more idiosyncratic sense than I do), "It would make no difference were it a total fabrication, although in strictly practical terms it is considerably more difficult to win authoritative status for a story that previously lacked credibility. . . . Insofar as these claims were accepted—by the Swazi and by the British—those who advanced them had succeeded in creating, at least temporarily, a new myth."[87] In other words, even if the tree was not a sacred tree, or wasn't in that field, the councilors could have modified the tribe's myth, moving the sacred tree into a place where it could through the implicit process of comparison invoke the powers of *The Golden Bough* or the tree in Eden. Indeed, their story invoked a whole micromyth connecting the Swazi tree with other mythical trees in the minds of the British to make them do what the Swazi wanted them to do. In a similar way, what Jean Comaroff has called the "subversive bricoleur" combines colonial and African (Tshidi) traditions for new purposes.[88] And this is an old trick: in the *Mahabharata*, when the heroes want to make sure no one will disturb the tree where they have hidden their weapons, they hang a corpse in the tree and spread the word that it is the corpse of their 180-year-old-granny, and that it is their family custom (*kula-dharma*) to treat a dead body like that—a grotesque misrepresentation of the funeral rites represented elsewhere in that same text.[89]

Myths do not merely reflect the eternal, reactionary archetype or even the present hegemonic *Zeitgeist*; they can subvert the dominant paradigm. Revolutionary myths express what David Tracy has called not the status quo but the fluxus quo.[90] George Sorel wrote that the myth of the general strike gives the workers hope, even though the strike may never happen.[91] Granted, myths, like most preserved texts, tell the story of the winners and belong to the winners, and winners have, alas, usually been on the right (though not *in* the right). As Marina Warner demonstrates, traditional storytellers, "negotiating the audience's inclination, may well entrench bigotry."[92] But myths may also oppose prevailing prejudice. Storytellers may, like judo wrestlers, use the very weight of archetypes to throw them, and with them to throw the prejudices that have colored them for centuries. Call it deconstruction, call it subversion, or just call it creative storytelling.

Chapter 5

Mother Goose and the Voices of Women

Old Wives' Tales

Let us now consider, among the many competing voices in multivocal myths, the voices of women, regarding them, from the standpoint of cultural morphologies, as a social group whose shared interests span cultures.

I remarked in the introduction that it never occurred to me that anyone would have to argue for the comparative method, which seemed so obviously useful—until I discovered that many people objected to it. I feel even stronger about this chapter, in which the argument that there are women's voices in men's texts seems to me not only blatantly obvious but already well argued by a number of scholars before me. Yet many people either do not believe it or believe that to assert it is reactionary, and some of them have set widely followed agendas for the academy's study of women.

Feminist scholarship, from the second wave to the present, has used men's writings to learn *about* women: Shakespeare and Chaucer are read for insights into the lives of women, even their attitudes and behavior, as are manuals of proper deportment, satires on women's uses of cosmetics, even early pornography.[1] But feminists realized that these texts often presented their "data" from a misogynist point of view; it was assumed that the texts could not speak from a woman's point of view, or advance her interests. And while most women's studies programs today quite reasonably add works by women to an expanding canon, arguing that Zora Neale Hurston and Toni

Morrison are greater writers than some of the lesser (dead white) males on many petrified (patrified?) lists, many young students in women's studies programs still assume (a) that (only) women should study (only) women and (b) that this can be done (only) by studying (only) those texts known to have been written by women. Against these still-prevalent assumptions, I must therefore defend the prosaic argument that both men and women are capable of both recording and hearing both men's and women's voices, and I must defend it by calling upon allies who have thought longer and harder about it than I have.[2] This chapter is, therefore, the least original link in the chain of my argument, but it is an essential link.

We know that men wrote the texts of ancient Israel and India, and most of the texts of ancient Greece and medieval Europe; indeed, most of our ancient texts (Greek, Hebrew, Sanskrit) and even dominant modern tellings of traditional stories (Perrault, the Grimms, Disney) have been transmitted by men in one way or another. We know that women have been silenced, that extant written texts may have suppressed or distorted women's voices in earlier texts. Feminists have drawn our attention to the difference that gender makes in discourse, some arguing that this difference is social, others that women themselves are essentially different, still others that women are strategically different.[3] But most of them agree that women's writing is essentially different from men's, and that this is the voice we have lost and now have to retrieve from history.

I believe this to be true, but I think this truth has obscured another that I want to defend here: that these voices were not entirely silenced, that we can retrieve them from existing patriarchal texts. Texts composed by men often differ in interesting and significant ways from those composed by women, but not entirely, and some more than others. I argue that it is time to stop asking whose voice is the author of the text. We can ask whether the text expresses women's concerns and interests, points of view; but we must also acknowledge that a man can express such concerns and interests too, and a woman might not. It is precisely because feminists are successfully excavating silenced women's voices that we now have the luxury of going back to men's texts without either damning them for their lack of such voices or ignoring the traces of such voices in them. As in other matters that I have touched upon, I want to erase the either/or, to find women's voices in both women's texts and men's texts (or anonymous texts).

There was a time not so long ago (beginning with Simone de Beauvoir's attack on Freud in *The Second Sex*, in 1949, and continuing through Mary Daly's definition of "therapist" as "the/rapist") when some people stopped reading Freud, newly aware of his sexism, of how much he left out of his portrait of the human psyche when he ignored the female psyche as subject. But now that feminists have begun to illuminate what Freud left out, we can read him again; they complete him for us. Indeed, psychoanalytic feminist scholarship, beginning with Juliet Mitchell's *Psychoanalysis and Feminism* in 1974, has become the cutting edge in Freudian scholarship; the feminists have, ironically, retrieved Freud from the dustheap to which other factions would consign him. This argument depends upon a spirit of true pluralism in the academy. But it is also an argument that builds on feminism's contribution to our understanding of multivocality.

I want to use "men's" texts—the Bible, Homer, Shakespeare, Sanskrit literature—not merely critically, to demonstrate that their dominant (but not only) agenda may be sexist; nor (or not merely) to undercut their influence and privileged status by demonstrating their errors, biases, and limitations. I want to find meanings in them that transcend their gender errors, and in some cases to find gendered meanings in them that transcend their gender errors. In reading Freud's study of Dora, for example, I would search for his insights into the interpretation of texts, many of which are valid despite his serious lapse (a Freudian slip?) in totally disregarding Dora as a subject,[4] a blind spot in a vision otherwise in large part still useful to us. As I argued for colonial scholarship, I don't want to throw out the Freudian baby with the sexist bathwater.

One of the contributions that deconstruction has made to our project is in its attempts to dismantle (male) subjectivity. In the writings of Freud and most continental philosophers, no female subject is possible; but now that we have tried to imagine what a female subject could be like, we see that there is no male subject, either. And I would rush in, where deconstructionists deign to tread, to argue that there is no American subject, or Jewish subject, or black subject. The labels force us to go out of the project through the same door by which we came in. The solution should be to imagine a human subject, which is what I propose to do. And this is more likely to be accomplished not with philosophical texts, which really do have male authors who exclude the female, but with mythological and folk texts that may or may not assume a male subject (a flexibility enhanced by the assumed anonymity of mythological texts).

Although we might expect to hear women's voices more clearly within texts composed and transmitted by women, first we have to identify those texts. Now that we have modern texts composed by women and have begun to recover more texts composed by women in the recent past, can we use them to tease out patterns of difference between male-authored and female-authored texts, and then look for the female patterns in texts from the past to establish female authorship even in anonymous works? It is not quite so simple. Such a project is saddled not only with the general problems of time travel and boundary-jumping that we encounter in using Shakespeare to flesh out the Hebrew Bible but also with problems specific to gender: the problem of men's voices in women's texts as well as the less obvious problem of women's voices in men's texts.

We begin with a paradox: women are regarded as the traditional purveyors of myths and folktales, but most of those tales are "patriarchal," which I take to mean two things: first, men have controlled most of the written records of such stories and second, most of these records depict women in a most unfavorable light. How then can we hear women's voices in them?

Let us consider the first part of the paradox, the assertion that women tell the stories. Plato refers to myth as the property of mothers and nurses,[5] and this has remained the dominant view: "old wives tales" are "old" in the double sense of the antiquity of the story (the old tale) and the age of the traditional storytellers (the old wives), the women in charge of the care and feeding of myths. Marina Warner, in her study of the character of Mother Goose, the web-footed old woman regarded in Europe as the author of fairy tales, has demonstrated that the old wives' tale about old wives is largely true, that women often *were* the tellers of the tales.[6]

But in fact, we usually do not know the gender of the teller of an ancient tale. And even if we turn from ancient tales (where we must work from internal arguments) to contemporary ones (where we can actually collect tales told by women, where at least we know the person at the end of the storytelling chain), and if we try to consider the differences between male and female authors, we still find ourselves on shifting ground. Texts, as we have seen, have many voices and serve many interests.

Folklorists have attempted to identify constellations of subject matter characteristic of "women's stories." H. M. and N. K. Chadwick argued that the stories about David in the Hebrew Bible were written by or for women, on account of the great amount of women's activities in them.[7] Clearly such a criterion is far too general; men too are interested in women. Other scholars have tried to narrow the area of subject matter to such domains as women's domestic or marital activities. Thus A. K. Ramanujan defined women's stories through their concerns, such as an emphasis on the adventure that begins *after* marriage, in contrast with men's tellings that emphasize the events leading *up to* marriage[8] — for the male teller apparently assumes that they all live happily ever after, while the female teller knows that the trouble is just beginning. Barbara Leavy agrees that "Tales of a search for the lost wife (Type 400) are held to be favored by men, tales concerning a search for a lost husband (Type 425) favored by women, in both cases the searcher's gender correlated with that of the most likely teller of the tale."[9] "Beauty and the Beast" and "Cinderella" are women's stories because they reflect both women's predicaments and women's points of view; Bengt Holbek observed that men and women often tell the same tales in characteristically different ways, but the difference often lies in the subjects that are expanded or deleted, not in the moral or political stance.[10]

Ramanujan has argued that in men's stories the snake is usually the enemy and is killed, while in women's stories snakes are father figures, friendly phalluses, usually maternal uncles, who help the women.[11] But snakes are very slippery characters, morally ambiguous (and not always killed) even in putatively male-authored texts like Genesis. Midas Dekkers argued for a gendered asymmetry in the authorship and subject matter of stories about bestiality:

> Compared with reality, in which it is virtually always men who actually copulate with animals, in art the roles are completely reversed. Since most artists over the centuries have been men, the reason for this role-reversal is obvious: because it corresponds with male fantasies. . . . The fact that the man identifies with the animal is best illustrated by all those myths and stories in which a man actually turns into an animal. . . . As always a man identifies with the active party: the animal. He is the stallion, the dog, the bull, the lusty monster with its outsized organ. . . . His fantasy is destroyed by the woman as beast. This is why *King Kong* was a box-office success and *Queen Kong* was not.[12]

Dekkers is certainly wrong about the prevalence of male beasts, as any folklorist could have told him—think of all the Swan Maidens and Mermaids and Mélusines and Undines and Japanese Fox Women. And it needs no feminist come from the grave to point out the chain of biased assumptions in his argument. When the women have stopped shouting (What about women artists? What about active women? And finally, How do you know what women dream about, Mr. Dekkers?), the men will surely protest, "Speak for yourself, Midas." But Dekkers is right about one thing: the stories about female animals are different from those about male animals. This is hardly surprising, since both female animals and female humans behave in ways different from males, a fact available to both male and female authors. Considerations such as these cast doubt on the project of identifying women's texts by their choice of subject matter, which turns out not to be a reliable criterion after all.

For instance, one question that we might expect texts composed by and/or for women to ask is, Why should having a baby hurt so much? Indeed, we might add this to our list of the questions that myths pose in many cultures. This question is not, however, asked by classical religious texts with the frequency of others (Why are we here? etc.), perhaps because the putative (male) authors of those texts did not usually have firsthand experience of giving birth. One medieval, male-authored French text argues that the pains of childbirth are greatly overrated: "I marvel no more at it than at a hen or a goose that lays an egg as big as a fist through an opening where a little finger could not have passed."[13]

As for India, Ramanujan included childbirth as one of the topics that defined women's tales,[14] and V. Narayana Rao has remarked, "Men are not very interested in the details of pain women undergo in childbirth. . . . Only in the women's song versions of the *Ramayana* do we find a description of Kausalya in labor, graphically depicting the pain associated with it."[15] So too, a vivid description of birth pangs in various parts of the body is recorded in an Indian palm-lead manuscript that, Sarah Caldwell remarks, includes "immediate and intimate details that strike me as very likely to have been composed by a woman (although I have no independent evidence to confirm this intuition)."[16] And indeed it is graphic: "My ankles are paining . . . my nails are paining . . . the joints are paining . . . there is pain all over the body. . . . There was pain in the vagina, the whole body was paining."[17] Yet Caldwell wisely prefers to refer to this as a "female-centered" rather than a "women's" text that shows a strong concern for the female point of view but is not necessarily by a female author.

Since pain is one of the great human universals, why should women's pain, more particularly the pain with which women bear male as well as female children, be given relatively short shrift? Questions about suffering in childbirth are not unanswerable in quite the same way as the other questions about origins are. We know, for instance, that the conditions necessary to make the womb secure enough for nine months also make it difficult to let go easily. That giving birth should be hard work is fairly obvious. But why agony? And why, in the ancient world and the third world today, so often fatal to both mother and child?

In fact these questions are asked, by texts presumably composed by men, in several different cultures. Within the Jewish tradition, we have already noted in passing that the Book of Job asks, "Do you tell the antelope to calve or ease her when she is in labor?" And we have seen the story of Judith, the wife of Rabbi Hiyya, who had suffered such pain in childbirth that she wanted no more children. So too, Genesis (3.16), which we considered in chapter 4, tells us that God said to Eve, "I will greatly multiply your pain in childbearing; in pain you shall bring forth children, yet your desire shall be for your husband." And Sanskrit texts tell us that the embryo suffers agonies in the womb,[18] while Latin texts say that Hera (later called Juno), jealous of women that Zeus had impregnated, magnified the childbirth pains of one of them, Alcmena, by having the goddess of childbirth sit at the door with knees crossed and fingers interlocked to prevent the child's delivery, listening to the woman's moans.[19] Stories of this sort suggest that not only hard work (labor, travail) like that of men, but also serious pain was regarded by texts that we have every reason to believe were male-authored not only as an inevitable component of giving birth, but also as a puzzle that had to be addressed.

No experience is immediately accessible; as soon as we try to tell it to someone else, it is mediated by words. And this is particularly true of pain, which, as Elaine Scarry has argued, baffles language. For a woman to tell anyone else about her childbirth pains, she has to translate the experience into words; and a man has the same access to those words as she or another woman has, though they may not mean the same thing to him; he can take the words and write about childbirth pain. In the same way, and perhaps through the same method—listening to women talk—D. H. Lawrence, in *Lady Chatterly's Lover*, could write convincingly about what a woman experiences in orgasm.

Women's Points of View

If we cannot infallibly identify a woman's interests in subject matter, what about in standpoint? This too is problematic. Ramanujan argues that there is a noticeable difference in the points of view of women's tales and men's tales: "[Women's] stories present an alternative way of looking at things. Genders are genres. The world of women is not the world of men"; stories collected from women express "an alternative set of values and attitudes, theories of action other than the official ones."[20] And indeed, sometimes women's stories do raise different issues, or subvert the dominant (male) paradigms. As V. Narayana Rao has pointed out, "A . . . strategy of subverting authority while outwardly respecting it is found in the *Ramayana* songs sung by non-Brahmin women."[21]

But again, matters are not quite so simple. There is, for instance, the ironic fact that it is precisely the asymmetry of power in real life that produces some of the apparent convergences of points of view in stories. Thus Margaret Mills suggests that "Men's and women's tales share a preference for women acting in male roles rather than for men acting in female roles," but this may be explained by the fact that "women covet male 'options' and that men have more options."[22] Because in the real world it is easier to be a man than to be a woman, both male and female storytellers portray women, more than men, as gender benders; inequality in real life leads to an apparent equality in the depiction of that inequality in stories.

Ann Grodzins Gold has illuminated a different complexity in Rajasthani folktales told by a man:

> The construction of femaleness that is generated may be a vigorous and positive one, even though it emerges from an apparently misogynous text. . . . Episodes of [sexual] violence, such as Gopi Chand's abuse of Moti De, are described with a kind of relish that might be seen as playing to sadistic [male] sexual fantasies. However—and this may be what initially captivated me about the tale—the women in it not only have genuine power, they also have character. They speak their minds and act accordingly. . . . As a whole the Rajasthani Gopi Chand transmits a world view in which gender is construed flexibly, the attributes of the different sexes are at times interchangeable, and misogyny coexists with a view of women as definitively the better half.[23]

Gold's analysis separates the question, "Are the women depicted in this text nice?" from "Can they exercise power?" It also separates both of these questions from the more reductionist question, "Is there a woman's voice in this text?" and separates the slant of the explicit text from the slant of the implicit subtext. This is a most welcome corrective to the current tendency to identify as "women's texts" those that display women as powerful or women as good.

For powerful women are often depicted only in order to be destroyed or showed to be evil, and what "goodness" is is also up for grabs; if women defeat the system, this can be construed perhaps by other women as clever and resourceful, but by men as dishonest and corrupting. Sometimes the affirmation of powerful women is undercut by a moralizing ending (the destruction of the evil powerful woman), and sometimes that ending is just tacked on (like the alternative film endings that we encountered in chapter 1) and the force of the story resides in the tale up until the end. But sometimes when a powerful woman is destroyed at the end, the end is the whole point for which the rest of the text sets us up.

For example, Aeschylus presents us, at the start of his ancient Greek trilogy, with a powerful woman, Clytaemnestra, of whom the very first thing we learn is that she has "the mind of a man";[24] but at the end he shows us that she, and any woman like her, has no recourse against matricide and no vote in Athens.[25] The logic of what I would call the Clytaemnestra Syndrome seems to be that the more intrinsically powerful, and hence dangerous, women are perceived to be, the greater the perceived need to keep them far away from the actual use of any political power in the world. So too, where goddesses are powerful and hence dangerous, human women are perceived to be powerful and dangerous, and the same measures must be taken to control them. The fates of the devotees of Athena, Inanna, Mary, and Kali should discourage Goddess-feminists from pursuing this track any farther. If the history of the worship of goddesses teaches us anything at all about the empowerment of women, it is that spiritual power may very well flow from heaven to earth, but political power flows from earth to heaven.[26] The fact that most of the ancient goddess texts were composed by men should give us pause; but I wish to argue that even if such texts were composed by women (as they often are nowadays), they should still give us pause.

Often the stories told by women do not seem to express a woman's point of view at all. Narayana Rao admits that "Women in these [Ramayana] songs never openly defy propriety: they behave properly, even giving themselves advice that the male masters of the household would accept and appreciate."[27] Moreover, the subversive/revolutionary voice and the woman's voice don't always coincide. As Barbara Leavy remarks, "A female narrator in no way guarantees a feminist point of view, whereas a male narrator may for many reasons prove insightful concerning woman's lot; the apportioning of tale types to male and female narrators consequently raises as many questions as it answers."[28]

Marina Warner, who argues for the female authorship of many fairy tales, has asked the right questions: "If and when women are narrating, why are the female characters so cruel? . . . Why have women continued to speak at all within this body of story which defames them so profoundly?"[29] It does not appear clearly in the female teller's interest to insist on the wickedness of all women, an idea which might taint her by association. What sort of woman would tell that sort of story about that sort of woman? The traditional proto-feminist answer to this question has been, "Not a woman at all, a man, that's who, stupid." But once we have established that women did indeed tell many of these tales, we must ask why they would depict women so unfairly.

One answer is that all women are not the same; and when we take account of *difference*—difference of class, beauty, brains, family life, or, most significant, of age—we can see that some women were opposed to other women in just as many ways as they were opposed to some (or all) men. Nurses may tell children stories about bad mothers in order to make the children love them (the nurses) more than their mothers, or may just use female bogeymen to frighten children into obedience. Or, if the teller is a grandmother or a mother-in-law, the tale may express her fear and resentment of her granddaughters or daughters-in-law; so she makes the mother in the story vanish, "replaces her with a monster, and then produces herself within the pages of the story, as if by enchantment, often in many different guises as a wonder-worker on their behalf, the good old fairy, the fairy godmother."[30]

And of course there must have been different points of view not only in different tellers, but also in different audiences. Some scholars have tried to avoid the problems of authorship by defining "women's stories" not as stories told *by* women but as stories told *for* or *to* women. It is easier, though not always easy, to determine the audience of a text: who listened to it or read it? But again the value of such knowledge is defused by the realization that where some people choose to read or hear, others are forced; where some like what they hear, others do not; and even when they like it, it may not advance their interests—and interests may be a more interesting, or important, focus than voice. Sorting out the voices in myths that can be placed in context demonstrates how very complex context is, for two different listeners even in the same group may think the myth means two different things.

Jeanine Basinger, in *How Hollywood Spoke to Women*, offers a definition of women's films—films made for and about rather than by women— that could stand in for women's myths and folktales:

> A woman's film is one that places at the center of its universe a female who is trying to deal with the emotional, social and psychological problems that are specifically connected to the fact that she is a woman. . . . She is forced to make some kind of choice between options that are mutually exclusive, and these options will be visualized as two contradictory paths, one of which will empower and/or liberate her in some way, however minor, and one of which will provide her with love. These problems are made concrete by various plot developments, and since they are often contradictory, they are represented in the story as a form of choice the woman must make between options that are mutually exclusive.[31]

It might be possible to hazard an educated guess as to the gender of the intended audience, though not the author, of a text by looking for markers such as those suggested by Basinger. But since men must make very similar choices, it would be no better than a guess. For just as male authors are, as we noted above, interested in women, so too male audiences are interested in the reasons why women choose (or do not choose) them.

These are often ambivalent agendas in which even the wicked stepmother, the villain of the piece in so many stories, may have a voice:

> Certainly women strove against women because they wished to promote their own childrens' interests over those of another woman's

offspring; the economic dependence of wives and mothers on the male breadwinner exacerbated—and still does—the divisions that may first spring from preferences for a child of one's flesh. But another set of conditions set women against women, and the misogyny of fairy tales reflects them from a woman's point of view: rivalry for the prince's love.[32]

The conflicting points of view of women occur *outside* the text, in the world, before they are projected *within* the stories as a source of apparent misogyny. The "female hatred and cruelty" in these stories engage women both outside and inside the frame, as subjects and objects, audiences and authors, fictional characters and storytellers, and as both participants and targets, victimizers and victims. Misogyny is both a subject and an object of many of these texts.

Sometimes, as in many variants of "Beauty and the Beast" and "Cinderella," the villain is the father, who tries to force his daughter to marry a man she does not want—or even to marry him, her father; such a story would have a clear enough meaning to an audience of women "who fully expected to be given away by their fathers to men who might well strike them as monsters."[33] In many other tales, however, the villains are women who "struggle against their often younger rivals to retain the security that their husbands or their fathers afford them."[34] And on a deeper level, we see that the husbands or fathers—the sources of the desired security—are the ultimate tyrants standing behind the apparent female tyrants. Ramanujan too suggests that in women's stories, the enemies are often human women; in men's stories, the enemies may be supernatural women (witches) or men. It is interesting to note that women are often the enemies of women in their own stories, as well as the enemies of men in men's stories: heads they lose, tails they lose. Such contextual studies demonstrate how little we can conclude about a story's meaning even when we do know who told the story, and this consoles us when we do not have access to our tellers and cannot determine if the teller is male or female. Even if we knew, we would not know.

Men's Voices in Women's Texts

We must also bear in mind the likelihood that even women authors will share the dominant mythology of their culture; they learn and assimilate the images that men have of them, and express those images in their own storytelling. Men's voices work on women on the subconscious level, through what some feminists call false consciousness. This is why, as many folklorists have noted and as we have just seen, women's tellings often do *not* subvert the patriarchal point of view at all, but merely offer ways either to satisfy or to evade it.

We must distinguish this invisible projection of men's ideas into the minds of real women from the conscious form of ventriloquism in which men write texts in which fictional women appear to speak. This sort of ventriloquism is not usually designed to deceive an audience; it is just a pose, a convention, that bears the same relationship to false consciousness as a flamboyant drag queen bears to a person masquerading as someone of the other sex and/or gender to fool someone in a marriage (and, subsequently, a lawsuit).[35] In male ventriloquism of this sort you can see the puppet; and the voice says, like the voice of the wizard in *The Wizard of Oz*, "Pay no attention to the man [*sic*, not the woman] behind the curtain." (We all knew that Lassie was played, in the film, by a male dog.) Ruth Padel has nicely termed this the "man-made" text's way of "fabricating a woman's voice, making her sing (like a torturer, you might say) of her pain for men's pleasure."[36] This syndrome, epitomized in Flaubert's famous assertion, "I am Emma Bovary," also characterizes Scheherazade, perhaps the most famous woman storyteller of all time, who uses her stories to subvert the sexual violence of the man who has the power of life and death over her. But Scheherazade's voice was written by a man, and Flaubert was not Emma (though for that matter, he was not Emma's lover, Rodolphe Boulanger, either).

When a man pretends to speak as a woman, it is not usually to her benefit; the dominant class gets the last word, as usual, and can present the woman's story in a twisted light. And sometimes this ventriloquism is not so obvious, as in the case of Mother Goose, who may not have been a woman at all but only a male fantasy "of nursery, of nurture, of female magic, of woman at the hearth."[37] Warner points out a particularly Machiavellian reason why male authors of the tales might make women the speakers *within* the tales (like Scheherazade): "Attributing to women testimony about women's wrongs and wrongdoings gives them added value: men might be expected to find women flighty, rapacious, self-seeking, cruel and lustful, but if women say such things about themselves, then the matter is settled. What some women say against others can be usefully turned against them."[38] In addition, and on the other hand, the attribution of texts to female authors on the *outer* frame, as tellers (like Mother Goose), might invalidate their testimony against women: "If fairy tales are mere old wives' tales because they are told by women, is then what they say necessarily false, a mere trifle, including what they say about women? Or does the lowness of the genre, assumed on account of the lowness of its authors, permit a greater degree of truth-telling, as the jester's cap protects the fool from the consequences of his frank speech?"[39]

In India, some men wrote texts that they presented as texts composed by women. John Stratton Hawley has argued that men may have written much of the poetry attributed to the greatest of India's women poets, Mira Bai:

> It is possible that some of the poems of "Mira" were composed by men . . . since both sexes sing both sets of poems. . . . On the basis of the poetry itself, there seems good reason to believe that many of the poets who used Mira's name—in addition to Mira herself, if there ever was such a person, were women, as were a great many in their audience.[40]

There is an entire genre of Tamil poems known as *pillaittamil*, composed by male poets speaking with the voices of women addressing young children (who are in many cases incarnations of God). Paula Richman suggests that we think of this as "cross-speaking," on a parallel with "cross-dressing." Yet here too there is an asymmetry:

> It is males . . . who enjoy the rhetorical mobility that they attain by taking on a maternal voice. No parallel prestigious literary genre exists in Tamil that enables female poets to take on the voice of a father. One might also see the genre as affirming the dichotomization of male and female activities because when the male poet takes on a "female" voice, he reiterates the ascription of domestic duties to women.[41]

And Richman goes on to remind us of the constraining implications of this appropriation of the female voice:

> As one saying goes, in the presence of Krishna (a male deity), all of humanity is female. . . . By this line of reasoning, taking on a maternal voice in a *pillaitamil* would be a way of expressing devotion to a male deity.

Another example of this sort of ventriloquism may be seen in a Telugu text in which love poems composed by men speaking as women for the love of (a male) god are then recast as poems sung by courtesans about their customers,[42] a text that may thus be viewed as poems by men pretending to speak for women (both courtesans and female devotees). Yet actual men and women might have shared the authorship of these poems to some degree, though we will never know who or when or how much. Perhaps we might do best to differentiate between proximate and ultimate narrators, acknowledging their complex presence in any text.

Women's Voices in Men's Texts

But just as there are men's voices in women's heads (and hence women's texts), so too women's voices are often closeted within patriarchal texts. How tightly shut is that closet door? Even when the final recension is controlled by a man, women's voices may speak through it. Just as the dominated often reproduce the opinions of the dominators, so it is also true, though less so and less well known, that the dominators mirror the opinions of the dominated. The dominated do get their foot in the (closet) door; the dominant culture is often strongly, if unofficially, influenced by those whom it subordinates. (This point, the agency of the oppressed, was acknowledged by Edward Said himself in the modified version of his theory of Orientalism expressed in *Culture and Imperialism*).[43] Texts controlled by men do not necessarily represent a man's point of view. Men cannot always erase entirely the female voices that they appropriate or imitate. To put it differently, we might say that even when a man finds it useful to appropriate the speech of women and to set it in a context that serves his purposes, he must preserve that speech with some fidelity if it is to be credible. This move, however, has its dangers, for the audience may choose to hear and honor the speech that he has appropriated while ignoring or mocking its recontextualization.[44]

What do these stories by male authors tell us about the feelings of women? More than you might think. Texts by male authors reveal the assumptions that men have held about women, but they also, sometimes, reveal the ways women have devised to deal with these assumptions. Men may express images of themselves that they have learned from women. Several male scholars have hypothesized about women's voices in male-controlled texts; Thomas Laqueur remarks about medieval European medical texts: "The Hippocratic corpus and book 10 of Aristotle's *History of Animals*, for example, may well represent the voices of women, and other works give accounts much like these."[45] And A. T. Hatto says of the Swan Maiden tales, "At the human level the story has to do with the pitiable lot of a girl from another tribe and territory who has been trapped into an unsuitable union through the guile and strength of a man. So much does it tell the woman's side of the story . . . that one suspects its first tellers may have been women."[46] Indeed, Hatto remarks that the tale reflects two sorts of women's points of view: the sympathetic view of the swan maiden told "from within," that is, from the swan woman's standpoint; and the "scathing" view of her "from without," that is, from the standpoint of the women in the culture to whom her husband brings her, women who hate her as "the foreign woman."

Jungian ideas of androgyny lead Jungian folklorists to hear female voices in male authors, for from a Jungian standpoint it is difficult to distinguish between "a genuine female point of view and that of a man expressing some aspect of his personality traditionally deemed feminine: the mere existence of a female character does not prove either."[47] French feminists such as Hélène Cixous, Luce Irigiray, and Julia Kristeva, Lacanian rather than Jungian, have also taken account of the possibility that men can write feminist tracts (and have inspired the genre of writing by men as well as women called *écriture féminine*); they have even read Freud for feminist ends (psychoanalyzing his own slips and omissions). Certainly some men can reproduce women as subjects, with voices. Here again, what we want is not a dichotomy (women can only write about—or understand—women) but a continuum: some men come closer to others in recognizing women's subjectivity. The statement "She was a gorgeous blonde, just asking for it, so I fucked her good and then beat her up," operates, after all, on a rather different level of discourse from the statement "What does he know of love for children—of my love for Seriozha, whom I gave up for him? And this desire to hurt me! No, he must be in love with another woman: it can't be anything else." The first statement I have reconstructed from the memory of furtive adolescent readings of Mickey Spillane; the second (which deals directly with the question of men's inability to know what women think and feel) is by Tolstoi,[48] who was neither a woman nor good to women (as his published correspondence with his wife makes horrifyingly clear) but who understood some women very well indeed and was, in this very real sense, Anna Karenina, just as Shakespeare was, in the same sense, Helena in *All's Well*, and Flaubert was Emma. Tolstoi's assumption in this passage that a woman is likely to be thinking of a man is typical, and part of the problem that feminism is now addressing; but still, his women don't *always* think about men.

Mieke Bal has argued that there may be a woman's point of view woven into the putatively paternalistic Hebrew Bible,[49] and Harold Bloom has argued both that a woman *could* have written the "J" parts of the Hebrew Bible and that men have written many texts that speak with women's voices.[50] Adrien J. Bledstein, her tongue even farther in her cheek than Harold Bloom's was in his, has argued that J, whose style is marked by "characterizations, themes, irony and a healing sense of humor," is Tamar, the daughter of David, who could have written during the latter part of David's and the early years of Solomon's reign.[51] This suggestion is more imaginative than convincing, but it does make us think about other possibilities that we may have overlooked. Even less convincing is the argument made by S. D. Goitein, who was convinced that he could tell the gender of the author in the Bible even when he heard women's poetry spoken by men and men's by women;[52] "female narrative structure" was characterized, he maintained, by repetition, particularly double and triple repetition.[53]

Often this game degenerates into little more than sexist stereotypes. Donald Keene expresses his astonishment that so many masterpieces of Japanese literature were written by women and goes on to characterize what is feminine about their poetry: the abandoned woman imagines that she will fade away like the dew and yields despondently to her fate, in contrast with a poem written by a man disappointed in love, who "has no desire to fade away like the dew" but would prefer to become "an object insensitive to the pangs of love. This difference between masculine and feminine expression is obvious, and parallels may of course be found in many other literatures."[54] Keene sees this passivity not as a Japanese stereotype (or, as I see it, a Western stereotype about Japanese literature) but as a cross-cultural characteristic of women's poetry. He goes on to describe another poem and comments: "There can hardly be a more intensely feminine piece of writing. It is concerned almost exclusively with the personal feelings of the author. . . . She writes with a candor no man could approximate."[55] I cannot judge the validity of this approach to Japanese literature, though I smell a bias, but it is nonsense when applied cross-culturally.

It certainly does not apply to India. Since women were excluded from the Sanskritic tradition preserved in the myths recorded in the Vedas and the Puranas, we might hazard the guess that women's contribution was stronger in the realm of the vernacular, oral folklore, but it would be difficult to substantiate such a claim—especially since there is no clear demarcation between the so-called "great" and "little" variants of any story. For although the classical Indian myths were almost always written and recorded by men, there is good evidence within the tradition itself that women— the old wives—were the source of some, if not indeed most, of the storytelling; theirs might well have been an oral contribution to the tales ultimately written down by men.

Even an aggressively male author is a man who has a mother, a wife, and probably a mistress, and therefore he has women's voices in his head. In South India, as Ramanujan admits, men hear women's stories:

> Sometimes the tales that are told by women are also told by men, but a single inquiry makes it clear that, invariably, the men had heard them first from a woman in a domestic setting, usually in childhood. Young boys and girls are told such tales by older women who feed

them in the evening, in the kitchen—which is exclusively the realm of women. Boys, as they grow older (often no older than six or seven), may drop out of these tale-telling sessions, while girls continue until adolescence. Thus, these nonprofessional tellers of tales tend to be predominantly women.[56]

Yet there are also many Indian settings in which older men, no longer boys tied to their mothers, learn stories from men when women are not present at all, just as women learn stories from women;[57] under such circumstances there is likely to be a significant difference between tellings by men and by women. Similarly, Ruth Padel has noted that in England, where by 1870 women were responsible for most middle-class popular songs, male Edwardian classical scholars would have heard, as children, "their mothers sing drawing-room songs composed by women."[58] Yet those boys grew up to go to their clubs, where women were not allowed and where, as in American men's locker rooms, women were not present to challenge what men said about them to other men.

Androgynous Language

I argued in chapter 4 that a text may represent more than one point of view or intellectual culture. To the extent that the two genders are two cultures, they too may coexist in a text in this way. In some societies, women and men literally speak different languages (just as in our own culture John Gray has argued, mythologically, that American men speak languages from Mars, women languages from Venus).[59] When Kevin Costner wanted to learn an Indian dialect for his film *Dances with Wolves*, he didn't realize that there were different grammatical forms for men and women; he learned the language from a woman, and hence, apparently unknowingly, throughout the film referred to himself as "she" and "her."

The stories of Beauty and the Beast and the Swan Maiden, which imagine that women are married to men of different species, may well reflect the actual experience of women married to men from distant tribes, who literally did not speak their language. At a crucial period in Japan, all the court poets were trying to write in Chinese. Women, however, were not expected to learn Chinese, which was "considered to be unladylike. The women of the court in fact sometimes learned Chinese, but it was considered to be in bad taste if they revealed this." The poetry composed in Japanese by women during this period, and by men addressing themselves to women, is what preserved the tradition of writing in Japanese.[60]

In the *Rig Veda* and the *Mahabharata*, women are represented as speaking in Sanskrit; but by the time of the Sanskrit dramas, in about the fifth century of the common era, women were only allowed to speak Prakrit, a dialect. In the *Ocean of Rivers of Story*, a medieval Sanskrit text, a woman commits adultery with the king of the gods, her husband comes home early and surprises them, and her lover takes the form of a cat. When her husband asks, "Who is here?" she replies, "It's just the tomcat," in Prakrit. But she uses her linguistic restriction as a weapon, producing an ambiguity that saves her. For *majjao* ("the tomcat") may be a dialect version of either of two Sanskrit words: *mad-jaro*, meaning "my lover," or *marjaro*, meaning "the cat" (from the verb *mrij*, to wash, because the cat constantly washes itself). Since the woman both lied and did not lie (it was her lover, but in the form of a cat), she is given a modified curse, which is, appropriately, another pun: her husband says, "Since you behave like a rolling stone [literally, since you have an evil nature (*shiila*)], you will become a stone (*shilaa*)."[61]

Ramanujan may have had this sort of thing in mind when he remarked that women's stories "remind one of the double plots of Shakespearean or Sanskrit plays, with a diglossia articulating different worlds of the solemn and the comic, verse and prose, the cosmic and the familial"[62]—or the microscope and the telescope. In some societies, folklore genres themselves are divided between the genders so that, for instance, men may tell their stories in verse, women in prose—or the reverse. There are entirely distinct genres of Arabic women's stories, as Lila Abu-lugod[63] and Sabra Webber[64] have demonstrated. It has been argued that in some cultures, even when men and women speak the same words, the words have different meanings; speaking the same language "in itself is not sufficient evidence that both sexes stand in the same relationship to that language."[65] In Lacanian feminist theory, language is phallocentric and women are relegated to the margins of the symbolic order simply by speaking the man's language.[66] So are the lower classes: Edmund Leach's famous article on the difference between English words for animals and for the foods made from them (calf/veal, pig/pork, sheep/mutton) omits to mention that the animals have Anglo-Saxon names given by their lower-class herders, the foods French names given by their Norman chefs and upper-class diners.[67] Jews, like women, often spoke two languages in Europe: Yiddish at home, German or Russian or Polish in public. Indeed, the voices of the lower castes were lost in India, along with the voices of women. So too, our only access to the suppressed voices of Native Americans may be through the filter of the writings of white anthropologists, or to pre-Christian Celtic religions through the writings of the Christians who converted them, or to the Aztecs through the writings of the Spanish who destroyed them. This is not the kind of access we would have chosen, but it is often all we have, and better than total silence.

But sometimes language is the one thing that men and women share. Ramanujan has also argued that many Hindu men have both a mother tongue (the everyday language, such as Tamil, spoken by women downstairs, in the back, in the kitchen) and a father tongue (once Sanskrit, more recently English, the literary *lingua franca* spoken—or at least discussed—by men in the front rooms).[68] Many South Asian women have a different sort of linguistic androgyny: they speak the languages of their father's house (their native village) and their husband's house. To this degree, South Asians are often linguistically androgynous. Yet as I have argued elsewhere,[69] androgynes are seldom "egalitarian" creatures; rather, one or the other sex almost always predominates (guess which one). Moreover, even if texts are androgynous they most often wear trousers rather than skirts; they are more often clothed in the ideology of men than that of women.[70]

Stephanie Jamison has argued that language was a unifying bond between men and women in ancient India. She notes that the texts of ancient India preserve only "the tediously proverbial tip of the iceberg, and what we are after—women's discourses—are way below the waterline." Moreover:

> The composers of our texts of limited content participated in many different discourses in their lives, only one of which they preserved. And the stuff of discourses—words and syntactic constructions—travel through many levels of discourse and do not shed all their associations when going from one to another. In other words, linguistic levels are not watertight. We can use language as a periscope to peer below the waterline, if we can tap into the associational nexus that the elements of language are part of. Language, more than most cultural institutions, is the property of all speakers, both female and male, who will have similar, though not identical, sets of associational complexes.[71]

Thus men's conversations with women may have constituted a discourse which, though consciously excluded from the Sanskrit texts, subconsciously ("below the waterline") seeped in. At this point, Jamison veers off to make her point—that we can learn about women by reading men's texts carefully—without explicitly arguing my point—that we can find women's voices in men's texts. The image that she uses, the periscope, is a lens metaphor that often signals a leap between two levels in a myth, here the artificially separated levels of two genders within a single language.

Women's voices in men's texts in ancient India are often submerged under Jamison's waterline of the subconscious. The Tantras, ancient and medieval texts about sexual rituals, were certainly composed with a male subject in mind; it is hard to imagine how a woman would respond to passages instructing her to place her penis in the vagina of a woman and thus to raise the semen from her testicles up through her spine to her head.[72] But Miranda Shaw hears women's voices in at least certain Tantras:

> The unstated premise seems to be that if women are present in a text, it must a priori be as objects of male subjectivity. . . . I argue that since these texts were not created by men in isolation from women, they do not express exclusively male views. These views grew out of communal exploration and practice and proceed from the insights of *both women and men*. Indeed, many of the insights contained in Tantric writings can only find their source in practices done by women and men together. . . . I contend that the extensive descriptions of the interactions and shared practices of women and men are in themselves sufficient evidence that the *yogini-tantras* are the products of circles consisting of both women and men. . . .
>
> Reading texts as repositories of the insights of both men and women, rather than approaching them as texts written solely by and for men, opens new avenues of interpretation. Passages on women can be examined for potential evidence of how women viewed and experienced their own lives. This hermeneutical approach raises the possibility that women helped to create and at times dictated the categories within which men viewed them, the terms on which men approached them, and the conditions under which they would accept male companionship.[73]

I am less confident that texts that objectify women in shared rituals necessarily transmit women's categories, but I think they can often reveal particular women's insights.

Salvaging Women's Voices

Here are some examples of what I would call women's voices in men's texts. Feminists have analyzed a number of Western misogynist works, among them a particular genre that denounces marriage — from the man's standpoint. Yet these texts often reproduce the voices of women, if only to disagree with them. Judith Kegan Gardiner argues that the anonymous late medieval French prose satire *Les Quinze Joies de Mariage* "gives an unusually full and vivid rendering of women's complaints about marriage, often in the form of naturalistic direct dialogue. . . . We can read past the narrator's dourly misogynistic comments on his material and instead listen to the direct dialogue he reports."[74] For example, the narrator of the text "is upset by a double standard in marriage and considers it a great pain and trial to the faithful party. He differs from many recent writers by assuming that it is the woman who will be unfaithful."[75] In this instance, the (feminist) reader has to turn the text on its head to make the point useful to women, who can respond more directly to the woman's complaint that bearing children has made her old and ugly before her time.[76] Throughout, although the author presents the woman's point of view as wrong, he does present it, and "portrays women as oppressed by their reproductive biology, by their subjection to ill health, by social custom, by the double standard of sexuality, and by the indissolubility of medieval marriage."[77]

A parallel to this text is provided by one section of the Sanskrit text of the *Kamasutra*, which was composed in India in the early centuries of the common era, historically must have been written by a man, and reflects primarily male concerns. Like the French text on the joys of marriage, the *Kamasutra* often quotes women in direct speech, but unlike the French text, it is surprisingly sympathetic to women, particularly to what they suffer from inadequate husbands.[78] The discussion of why women commit adultery doesn't take the traditional patriarchal party line that one finds in most Sanskrit texts (such as an earlier text on Hindu religious and social law, *The Laws of Manu*: "Good looks do not matter to [women], nor do they care about youth; 'A man!' they say, and enjoy sex with him, whether he is good-looking or ugly").[79] The *Kamasutra* begins with a far more egalitarian, if equally cynical, formulation: "A woman desires whatever attractive man she sees, and so does a man desire every attractive woman. But for various considerations, the matter goes no farther."[80] The text is still an example of men who assume that women don't think about anything but men; and it is still written in the service of the hero, the would-be adulterer, who reasons, if all women are keen to give it away, why shouldn't one of them give it to him? But the author reproduces women's voices sympathetically when he imagines various women's reasons not to commit adultery:

> "He is propositioning me in an insulting way" or "He has no tie to me; he is attached to someone else" or "His face cannot keep a secret" or "His affection and regard are all for his friends" or "He is too passionate and forceful" or "He has always treated me just as a friend"; "Though I have given him hints with my face and gestures, he does not understand" or "I would not want anything unpleasant to happen to him because of me" or "If I am discovered, I will be thrown out by my own people" or . . .[81]

Unlike the French text, the *Kamasutra* does not disagree with the woman at all; the would-be seducer takes the woman's misgivings seriously, even if only to disarm her. The text goes on to outline a list of women likely to commit adultery, ostensibly so that the male reader of the text can learn to manipulate and exploit such women, but perhaps inadvertently as a most empathetic exposition of the reasons inadequate husbands drive away their wives:

> The following are women who can be gotten without any trouble, who can be had by means of mere perseverance: a woman who stands at the door; who looks out from her porch onto the main street; who hangs about the house of the young man who is her neighbor; who is always staring (at you); a woman sent as a messenger, who looks sideways at you; one whose husband has taken a co-wife for no good reason; who hates her husband, or is hated by him; who has no one to look after her; who has no children; who is always in the house of her relatives; whose children have died; who is fond of society; who is addicted to pleasure; the wife of an actor; a young woman whose husband has died; a poor woman fond of enjoying herself; the wife of the oldest of several brothers; a woman who is very proud; a woman whose husband is inadequate; a woman who is proud of her skills; a woman who is distressed by her husband's foolishness or by his lack of distinction or by his greediness; a woman who was chosen as a bride when she was still a young girl, but somehow was not obtained by that man, and now has been married to someone else; a woman who longs for a man whose intelligence, nature, and wisdom are compatible to her and not contrary to her own personality; a woman who is by nature given to taking sides; a woman who has been dishonoured (by her husband) when she has done nothing wrong; one who is put down by women whose beauty and so forth are the same as hers; whose husband travels a lot; the wife of a man who is jealous, foul-smelling, too clean, impotent, a slow-poke, unmanly, a hunchback, a dwarf, deformed, a jeweler, vulgar, bad-smelling, sick, or old.[82]

It needs no Indologist come from the grave to gloss this passage, though it might help to know that Manu says that sex with the wife of an actor is not a sin[83] and that jewelers in the ancient world used chemicals that might have rendered them impotent. It is also interesting to note that in ancient India, the belief that a woman might hate her husband was hardly unique to the *Kamasutra*. "Hated by her husband" or "hating her husband" (the compound can be tantalizingly ambiguous in Sanskrit) is an established taxonomic category in ancient Indian texts; a woman in the *Rig Veda* is "hated by/hating her husband,"[84] and other Vedic texts contrast the "favorite" wife with the "avoided" wife.[85] Even Manu, who states that "A virtuous wife should constantly serve her husband like a god, even if he behaves badly, freely indulges his lust, and is devoid of any good qualities,"[86] grants that "A husband should wait for one year for a wife who hates him. . . . If she hates him because he is insane, fallen, impotent, without seed, or suffering from a disease caused by his evil, she should not be deserted or deprived of her inheritance."[87] Most of the *Kamasutra*'s reasons make perfectly good sense to a contemporary Western reader (even reasons for the jeweler's wife to commit adultery: seeing the rich gifts that other men gave to their women but that never came to her). And, by and large, these reasons express a woman's point of view.

Nor is it necessarily the case that one sort of man composed this text and another composed the misogynistic *Laws of Manu*. They may well have been composed by the same man, or at least the same sort of man, who in his moments of piety excoriated women whom he regarded as evil and in his moments of relaxation sought them out (and perhaps redefined them). Thus when such a man wrote a legal text he would imagine the point of view of the husband (which he could do well, since he was almost certainly someone's husband); but when he composed the *Kamasutra* he put on (or, perhaps, took off) the hat (or pants) of the lover, which may well have also been his own hat; and, having talked to his wife (and his mistress), he was able to express the woman's point of view. There was no special caste of adulterous scribes who were the custodians of a genre that lobbied for adultery. With one hand (presumably the right), our educated Brahmin wrote the dharma texts; with the other (presumably the left), he wrote stories in praise of adultery. In any case, in writing the *Kamasutra*, he—whoever he was—incorporated the voices of women. It is interesting to note that in both cases—the French and the ancient Hindu—we find meanings that have value for us only by transcending, if not totally disregarding, the original context and, in fact, the fairly patent intentions of the author. Were we to remain within the strict bounds of the historical context, we could not notice that there are, in fact, women's voices speaking against their moment in history, indeed against their author.

A recent Western satire brings out yet other voices in a retelling of the *Kamasutra* that claims to satisfy the contemporary need for "a *Kama Sutra* that is in line with a postpatriarchal, postcolonial, postgender, and perhaps even postcoital world."[88] Here are some high points:

If the man feels that the Bull Elephant embrace is inappropriate—
if it, for example, represents a macho stereotype that he is trying

to transcend—he should express this perspective and explain why the Howler Monkey embrace would make him feel more comfortable. . . . When the lovers decide to join in any of the Animal Embraces mentioned above, and in others such as The Vulture Has Second Thoughts, The Mule Escapes Exploitation, and The Antelopes Form a Support Group, they first enter into deep meditation, facing one another, breathing deeply, and . . . then call into question the very idea of using animal names to describe human sexual activities. Rejecting this subtle mode of domination of the natural world, they separate, enter once again into profound meditation, and fall asleep. . . . As the moment of union approaches, however, their awareness grows that . . . vows that suggest that Shiva and Shakti are "primordial" or "universal" may be deeply offensive to members of other faith communities. In a spirit of profound respect for religious pluralism, they draw apart, and the man's lingam withers.[89]

Feminism, ecology, and religious pluralism, all noble causes, can be tacked onto the sexist, ecologically innocent, and narrowly Hindu text; but here the voices are not only false but, for once, unassimilable, and the lingam withers.

More seriously, the multivocality of Indian stories makes it impossible to be sure that we are hearing a male or female voice at any time: a sympathetic man may mirror a woman's point of view. And if we grant that these stories are not entirely male creations, we may view some of these myths from the standpoint of the man and others from the standpoint of the woman, even if we cannot prove that a man expressed the former and a woman the latter. The gender of the person who tells the story is not necessarily the gender of the dominant voice in the story.

Ann Grodzins Gold compares the gendered tellings of her Rajasthani sources with the ancient Sanskrit texts translated by other scholars, including Sudhir Kakar and myself. She writes:

> I have noted that their major sources are largely male-authored (in the case of texts) or from the male viewpoint (in case of ethnography). By thus contrasting their sources (male) with mine (female), I have not posed a "his" and a "hers" theory of separate worlds and worldviews. Rather, both visions coexist and are available to both sexes. Men can and do partake at times of the kinds of female-generated visions explored here, even as women often articulate perfectly and subscribe behaviorally to the prevalent set of values I have heuristically described as having male orientations and origins.[90]

This balanced viewpoint is very useful in considering the voices expressed in texts whose authors are not available for us to interview.

The classical twelfth-century Japanese novel *The Changelings* is about a brother and sister, each of whom changes genders several times: the biological male, whom the narrator refers to by his apparent gender, as the "sister," impregnates the imperial princess, while the biological female, the "brother," is impregnated as the result of a rape. This results in surprising sentences on the order of, "He was ashamed to tell anyone that he was pregnant," and "She realized that the imperial princess was bearing her child." This text, of the type known as *monogatari,* is of unknown authorship: it might be by a man or by a woman. The English translator speculates that it might have been "written by a woman who had actually experienced something like the sexual complications of the heroine of the tale. This would account for the blend of masculine and feminine elements in the work, and however bizarre or unrealistic this theory may seem, it cannot be totally ruled out, for *monogatari* very often contain autobiographical elements."[91] So too, *Orlando,* a novel about an androgyne, was written by the bisexual Virginia Woolf. In these cases, the author of the text would be an androgyne, at least in the sense of having bisexual experience.

The confusion of male and female voices in a reworked text is well demonstrated by a famous case from the classics. Sappho, a woman poet in ancient Greece, once wrote a poem about a man looking at a woman whom she (Sappho) too desired:

> He seems as fortunate as the gods to me, the man who sits opposite you and listens nearby to your sweet voice and lovely laughter. Truly that sets my heart trembling in my breast. For when I look at you for a moment, then it is no longer possible for me to speak; my tongue has snapped, at once a subtle fire has stolen beneath my flesh, I see nothing with my eyes, my ears hum, sweat pours from me, a trembling seizes me all over, I am greener than grass, and it seems to me that I am little short of dying. . . .[92]

Thus we have a woman (Sappho) looking at a man looking at a woman. Then Catullus, a male poet in ancient Rome, translated that poem, almost word for word, both from Greek to Latin and from a female gaze to a male gaze:

> He seems to me to be equal to a god, he, if it may be, seems to surpass the very gods, who sitting opposite you again and again gazes at you and hears you sweetly laughing. Such a thing takes away all my senses, alas! for whenever I see you, Lesbia, at once no sound of

voice remains within my mouth, but my tongue falters, a subtle flame steals down through my limbs, my ears ring with inward humming, my eyes are shrouded in twofold night. . . .[93]

Now we have, apparently, a man (Catullus) looking at a man looking at a woman. But if we look behind the text into the context, we realize that we have a man (Catullus) looking at a woman (Sappho—who was from the island of Lesbos, and hence resonates quite specifically with the name of Catullus's Lesbia, his faithless mistress in several other poems as well—a name inspired by Sappho?) looking at a man looking at a woman. And our knowledge of Catullus's poem colors our reading of Sappho's, helping us to see that in Sappho too the gaze is fragmented: though the poem begins with Sappho's gaze, midway it shifts (with "greener than grass" and "it seems") to the gaze of someone else, forcing "a contradictory double perspective."[94] As in Borges's story of Pierre Menard, the same words take on entirely different meanings. It is too simple, though not entirely untrue, to say that Catullus stole Sappho's poem, or even Sappho's voice.

A similar interaction may be seen in the joint composition of a poem on an appropriately androgynous subject by William Butler Yeats and his close friend Lady Dorothy Wellesley. Dorothy Wellesley first wrote an unrhymed ballad (published in 1937 in the Cuala Broadsides) based upon an incident in the *Historia mei Temporis* of the Abbé Michel de Bourdeille, about a bed-trick involving a man and a woman, and her maid, who, when they die, are buried together; three rosebushes grow out of the graves, their roots tangled together. Yeats then wrote his own, rhymed version of the poem, "The Three Bushes," which he still considered *her* poem; in a letter to her, he said, "Here you have a masterpiece. (I have just put in the rhymes, made it a ballad)."[95] In addition to the rhyme, he put in a refrain that echoes the old sexist proverb about cats in the dark:

And maybe we are all the same
Where no candles are,
And maybe we are all the same
That strip the body bare.[96]

Yeats then published, as his own, this much-revised version of Dorothy Wellesley's ballad.[97] Their two poems had fused, like the rosebushes, into one androgynous text. In a very real sense, Yeats had stolen (or at least transformed) Wellesley's voice, as Catullus had stolen/transformed Sappho's. We need to know this for the sake of Sappho and Dorothy Wellesley. But as far as Catullus and Yeats are concerned, we have two richly androgynous texts.

Even where it is possible to determine the gender of the actual author of a text such as a modern novel or a contemporary myth or folktale, the ideas in that text may have been received from people of different genders. Women may not share the male fantasies that drive many of our texts, but women also fantasize, often in the presence of men. And once the story is told, we may see in it simultaneously a woman's point of view and a man's, no matter who told it. The author of a myth is a tradition, not just one human male; and traditions have women in them too. Feminist discourse at its best generally rejects dichotomy of all sorts, including male voice versus female voice, in favor of the sort of continuum that we have found useful in other aspects of mythological analysis. And in a culture in which men and women speak to one another (which is to say, in most cultures), we might do best to regard the authors of most texts as androgynes.

Chapter 6

Textual Pluralism and Academic Pluralism

The Archetype

In chapter 3 I tried to defend comparison against charges that it lacks rigor, advances unfalsifiable universalist hypotheses, and is politically unhealthy. This last accusation sometimes takes the form of the contention that transcultural themes perpetuate stereotypes of gender, some of which we have just considered in chapter 5. Marina Warner has argued that "The theory of archetypes, which is essentially ahistorical, helps to confirm gender inevitability and to imprison male and female in stock definitions."[1] She regards the archetype as the enemy not only of social change but also of social justice: "When history falls away from a subject, we are left with Otherness, and all its power to compact enmity, recharge it and recirculate it. An archetype is a hollow thing, but a dangerous one, a figure or image which through usage has been uncoupled from the circumstances which brought it into being, and goes on spreading false consciousness."[2]

Warner attacks the psychoanalyst Bruno Bettelheim's analysis of the split between the good and evil mother in the Cinderella corpus[3] for effacing from memory "the historical reasons for women's cruelty within the home" and ratifying "the expectation of strife as healthy and the resulting hatred as therapeutic."[4] In short, she says, "this archetypal approach leeches history out of fairy tale." Thus fairy-tale conventions become sticks with which to beat young women, clichés "used by moralists to enforce discipline (and appearance) on growing girls."[5] Warner scolds Bettelheim for making the evil stepmother "seem natural, even intrinsic to the mother-child relationship,"[6] and thereby in a sense justifying that evil. But since the acts of cruelty by women in the stories represent "not an ineluctable or Oedipal condition" but social stratagems, "mothers or stepmothers today need not be inculpated *en masse*."[7] "As individual women's voices have become absorbed into the corporate body of male-dominated decision-makers," the misogynist depictions of wicked stepmothers, bad fairies, ogresses, spoiled princesses, and ugly sisters have "come to look dangerously like the way things are."[8]

But it is by no means the case that what we regard as archetypal, universal, or even natural ("the ways things are") is immutable or desirable; it is merely *given*. And we can change that; indeed it is easier to change if we acknowledge that it *is* given. "I have seen the enemy, and he is us" is surely true of archetypes. Moreover, I have argued that the great cross-cultural themes of myth are not given or natural, that they are merely widespread responses to shared experiences that are, in a sense, given and natural. If the great mythic themes are social and artistic rather than biological (or psychological), they are not built into the brain and can certainly be changed. But to the extent that they are expressed in linguistic patterns that may well be built into the mind, deeply embedded and strongly compelling, they can only be changed within the rules of the game—which often means inverting given patterns or breaking dichotomies down into continuums, rather than creating new patterns with entirely different structures. Mythmakers know this, which is why all of them—including our own contemporary spin doctors—are *bricoleurs* rather than patented inventors.

Mircea Eliade took pains to distinguish his "exemplary models" or "paradigms" from Jung's archetypes:

> In using the term "archetype," I neglected to specify that I was not referring to the archetypes described by Professor C. G. Jung. This was a regrettable error. For to use, in an entirely different meaning, a term that plays a role of primary importance in Jung's psychology could lead to confusion. I need scarcely say that, for Professor Jung, the archetypes are structures of the collective unconscious. But in my book I nowhere touch upon the problems of depth psychology nor do I use the concept of the collective unconscious. As I have said, I use the term "archetype," just as Eugenio d'Ors does, as a synonym for "exemplary model" or "paradigm."[9]

Yet, as Carlo Ginzburg has pointed out, "Eliade dissociates himself from the Jungian notion of the archetype only in the preface to the English translation of his *Le mythe de l'eternal retour*. . . . Previously, he had used this idea quite lavishly."[10] On the other hand, to use the Jungian term "in an entirely different meaning" is simply to do what myths (and *bricoleurs*) always do: tell the same story but reverse, or at least modify, its meaning. I think it is safer to avoid the word "archetype" altogether, given all the baggage it has acquired in its journey from Plato via Jung to us. But we still need to account for the shared materials of myths.

Diffusion and Survival

Jonathan Z. Smith rightly notes that most comparatists assume that "the only possibilities for utilizing comparisons are to make assertions regarding dependence," and that "in such an enterprise, it would appear, dissimilarity is assumed to be the norm; similarities are to be explained as either the result of the 'psychic unity' of humankind, or the result of 'borrowing.' "[11] The "psychic unity" argument is about survival, while the "borrowing" argument is about diffusion. The solution to this quandary seems to me to be to explain similarity by both/and: a degree of human (if not psychic) unity (as I argued in chapter 3) and a degree of borrowing or "dependence" (as I am about to argue now), plus a restructuring in each new situation.

Within the area of "borrowing," we might begin with the most specific register on which the myth operates, and we may account for the similarities between stories on this level by historical contact, diffusion. An appropriate metaphor, I think, for the network of diffused narratives with no common origin is not the family tree that folklorists used to favor, but rather a banyan tree, which must have an original root but sends down so many subsequent roots from its branches (other variants) that one can no longer tell which was the original. The pattern of banyan roots is rather like a Venn diagram of family resemblances, or the web of an invisible spider.

Sometimes "the same" story—that is, not merely the broad outline but certain otherwise arbitrary details, such as proper names and distinct cultural artifacts—appears in two different cultures. In such instances, there has almost always been some possibility of contact between the two cultures, even in the case of the most remote islands, given the omnipresence of Indo-European invaders, ancient merchants, and Buddhist and Christian proselytizers, and an ancient land link between Asia and North America across the Bering Strait. There are no Galapagos Islands for myths. Therefore when we find "the same" myth in two different cultures, it is more likely that one culture borrowed the story from the other than that the story was independently created, in parallel, by both cultures. If "the same" story is told by a Greek and a Roman, we may hazard a guess that the Roman heard it (or read it) from a Greek.

Nineteenth-century folklorists tended to chase all variants back to India, postulating the mediating element of Islamic culture as the carrier; some scholars think that Shakespeare's *All's Well That Ends Well* is based upon the ancient Indian story of Muladeva's wife recorded in a medieval Sanskrit text, *The Ocean of the Rivers of Story*. N. M. Penzer, the editor of the translation of that text, remarks in a footnote: "This story is known in Europe and may perhaps be the original source of Shakespeare's *All's Well That Ends Well*. At any rate there is a slight resemblance in the leading idea of the two stories."[12] W. W. Lawrence mocked this sort of enterprise: "Oriental analogues are frequently of considerable significance, even though we realize that all our chickens are not to be hatched out of eggs from India."[13] Yet the riddle of the chicken and the egg is precisely what we need to express the unanswerable question of which came from which. All that we really know, after all, when we find a story recorded in ancient India and in medieval Europe, is that the Indian version was recorded (but by no means necessarily composed or imagined) long before the European version. R. Howard Bloch has rightly and wittily satirizied the "diffusionist" school with their "long caravan of tales stretching from the banks of the Ganges to the Seine."[14] Indeed, before we jump to the conclusion that the plot of *All's Well* came from India to England, like tea or the words *punch* and *pajama* and *verandah* and *bungalow*, it is well to recall that Shakespeare may also have been inspired by the Semitic story of Tamar and Judah. Tracing the genealogy of a story is a mug's game.

For an example of the genealogical method, let us return to the story of Cinderella. Folklorists have long asserted that this story developed (through a disease of language that would have delighted Max Müller) from a story from China or Mongolia (remember those small feet as the standard of female beauty) in which the slipper was originally made of fur or ermine, which was *vair* in the French translation and which Perrault (who first recorded the story in French) misheard, presumably from some other Francophone teller, as the homophone *verre*—glass. This argument has persisted because, as Alan Dundes notes, "It crept into such authoritative sources as the *Encyclopedia Britannica*. . . . Could the *Encyclopedia Britannica* be wrong?"[15] In fact, the *Britannica* places the disease of language at a different point, not in the translation from Chinese to French or French to French, but "in the English version, a translation of Perrault's *Cendrillon*."[16]

Dundes challenges this argument by noting that the slipper is glass in cultures where there is no such homophone; that "fur" is also a reference to the pubic hair[17] (and may survive in an atavistic form in the fur that the heroine often wears as a disguise—donkeyskin, catskin, etc.); and, most definitive, that Perrault did not use the word *verre*.[18] Whatever its history, however, the glass has its own meaning. As Warner points out: "The logic of the symbolism, whether [Perrault] chose it or happened upon it, is perfect."[19] And so, even if a linguistic mistake was not the original reason for the shift from fur to glass, the glass slipper has now become an essential part of the European myth about Cinderella, and a story about a girl in a glass slipper is a new story, with new meanings: the fragility of the woman, the imposition of culture (glass) on nature (the furry foot), and so forth. A glass slipper would make a woman tottering, small—just like the foot-binding in the putative Chinese original. Dundes concedes that "It is clear that the 'glass' slipper which occurs in several versions of the tale of Cinderella (AT 510A) is an appropriate symbol for virginity. Glass is fragile and once broken cannot be repaired."[20] It is still the same slipper, and not the same slipper. The Chinese genealogy has not explained the story.

Tale-tracking has political implications. Tellers tend to regard their own culture as the source and other cultures as the borrowers and to deny that they themselves have borrowed from other cultures, for reasons of status and hierarchy: to be upstream, to be the giver rather than the receiver, is to be superior. (Recall the old Soviet claims that Russians invented the telephone, etc.). Outside the culture, British (and German) scholars may well have been inspired to trace stories back to India (and China: the colonies), in part as an outgrowth of the nineteenth-century craze for origins (the source of the Nile, the source of Language [itself an old search, as in Herodotus's experiment with the infant who said "bread" in Phrygian]) but also as a way of feminizing these cultures, as David Henry Hwang reminded us in *M. Butterfly*: "The East is feminine—weak, delicate, poor . . . but good at art, and full of inscrutable wisdom—the feminine mystique."[21] They tell good stories, but they need us to run their country. This was also a way of privileging the past of India over its present, as Sanskrit and the ancient Vedas were valued over vernacular languages and contemporary, "idolatrous," Hinduism: the thinking becomes, they *used* to tell great stories, but they need us *now* to run their country.

But the problem of diffusion is more basic than the mechanical complexities or political agendas of this sort of tale-tracking. For on the one hand, diffusion still fails to account for the particular genius of each telling—the genius (with or without the inspiration of a linguistic slip) of a glass slipper instead of a fur slipper. And on the other hand, the lineage of a story does not explain its endurance. When two different cultures tell a very similar story, it is because that story expresses a sentiment that is native to both. The Indian stories that are merely Indian, whose meaning is entirely contingent upon their role in Indian society, do not, like certain wines, "travel well"; they do not survive the journey to appear in Shakespeare's plays. And this suggests that even when we know the historical diffusion of a story (and in general we do not), we must take into consideration its more general appeal, its cross-cultural meanings, the culturally nonspecific register on which the myth can be played. Like Typhoid Mary, myths transmit memories from one culture to another through images and themes whose meanings those who receive them may not be aware of.

Claude Lévi-Strauss met the problem of cross-cultural parallels head on in his attempts to account for certain striking similarities in what he called "split representation" in the art of Asia and America (a subject that, like the two related cultures that explore it, involves two halves of a single substance):

> Do we rest, then, on the horns of a dilemma which condemns us either to deny history or to remain blind to similarities so often confirmed? . . . These studies have been jeopardized even more by intellectual pharisees who prefer to deny obvious relationships because science does not yet provide an adequate method for their interpretation. . . .
>
> How shall we explain the recurrence of a far from natural method of representation among cultures so widely separated in time and space? The simplest hypothesis is that of historical contact or independent development from a common civilization. But even if this hypothesis is refuted by facts, or if, as seems more likely, it should lack adequate evidence, attempts at interpretation are not necessarily doomed to failure. I shall go further: Even if the most ambitious reconstructions of the diffusionist school were to be confirmed, we should still be faced with an essential problem which has nothing to do with history. Why should a cultural trait that has been borrowed or diffused through a long historical period remain intact? Stability is no less mysterious than change. . . . External connections can explain transmission, but only internal connections can account for persistence.[22]

Once again we cannot sidestep the problem of cross-cultural meaning. The fact of historical diffusion does not get us off the hook of the problems inherent in the hypothesis of independent origination (reinventing the mythic wheel each time from "the same" experience). On the contrary, we need that hypothesis to explain why, in historical diffusion, some elements are retained while others are not. Lévi-Strauss further advanced this point in *The Story of Lynx*, arguing not only that borrowing is never haphazard but also that what is borrowed is not just fitted into a preexist-ing structure: the borrowing takes place because of the similarity in struc-ture between myths in the culture that "lends" them and myths in the cul-ture that "borrows" them. And what explains this similarity of structure? He is unwilling to say, but his other writings imply the "internal connec-tions" of a shared mental structure, that is, a "common origin" not of the myths themselves (as Jung has argued) but of the mental structures that create the myths.

Carlo Ginzburg strikes a useful compromise position, which Ioan Culianu formulated as a stance "against the two dominant cultures of our epoch: a historicism without structure and a structuralism without histo-ry."[23] Ginzburg argues that the same schema of images (in this particular case, the blood libel) was used by different peoples, even if those images took on different meanings: cultural convergences may be explained by diffusion or by "derivation from structural characteristics of the human mind."[24] Ginzburg rejects the idea of a genealogical tree as "a model which is Romantic even before it is positivist,"[25] and he seems at first to reject the idea of "derivation from structural characteristics of the human mind" (or "psychic unity of mankind") when he rejects the Jungian expla-nation of universal, archetypal structures preserved in the human mind (citing with approbation Walter Benjamin: "he considered Jung's psy-chology 'the devil's work through and through, which should be attacked with white magic' ").[26]

Instead, Ginzburg opts for a particular sort of diffusion, not from a com-mon source, and he supports this by calling upon Wittgenstein's theory of "family likenesses" in ideas, the Venn diagram model: a basic set of images attract "other elements, whose presence is fluctuating, contingent: they are sometimes absent, sometimes present in an attenuated form. Their superimposition and intersection impart to the figures constitutive of the series . . . a family likeness."[27] These basic images, like the mythemes in Lévi-Strauss's image of the *bricoleur,* can be used in various combinations to make the myth.

But by throwing Jung to the sharks, Ginzburg is forced to find some other way of explaining why, when one culture borrows from another, cer-tain elements are kept and others are not. Lévi-Strauss, pinch hitting for Jung (as he does surprisingly often), bails Ginzburg out of this quandary. For although in opting for historical diffusion Ginzburg implicitly rejects Lévi-Strauss's hypothesis of (universal) "structural characteristics of the human mind" to explain why the same phenomena *recur,* he does use Lévi-Strauss's *Structural Anthropology* to explain why they are *retained,* cit-ing the passage about "split representations" and concluding:

To understand the reasons for this twofold characteristic—persistence in time, dispersion in space—it seems necessary to follow a different route, one that has been indicated earlier ["derivation from structural characteristics of the human mind"]. But there is no reason to suppose that these perspectives are mutually exclusive. We shall therefore seek to integrate in the analysis the external historical data and the internal structural characteristics of the transmitted phenomena.[28]

Thus he argues that historical diffusion and Lévi-Strauss's hypothesis of universal "structural characteristics of the human mind" can be integrated. In this way Ginzburg is able to explain both what happened (history) and why it kept happening (structure), to run with the universalist fox and to hunt with the contextualized hounds (or, as the case may be, hedgehogs).

Any theory of family resemblances, such as Ginzburg's, is susceptible to the pitfalls that J. Z. Smith has pointed out.[29] Smith's critique favors the comparative method that argues for homology, assuming diffusion from common ancestors, over the comparative method that argues from analogy, assuming independent origination and no common origin, and depends on superficial convergence.[30] But I would try to avoid so sharp a dichotomy between the two approaches. Leaning on David Tracy's idea of the analogical imagination, I suggest that a comparatist needs both an analogical and a homological imagination. It is also interesting, and perhaps relevant, to note that the word "affinity," which originally means a relationship by marriage—that is to say, an analogical relationship, in contrast with consanguinity, a homological relationship—comes to mean a spiritual attraction or a structural resemblance from a common source—a homological rather than an analogical relationship. This linguistic confusion reminds us that family resemblance is not by blood alone.

And analogy, in Tracy's reading, by no means preludes a consideration for history:

> I am not in fact leaving history when I interpret a tradition. Rather I am entering that history with a deep consciousness of it. I am willing to accept the risk that the subject matter of this particular text articulates a question worth asking and a response worth considering. When the text is a classic, I am also recognizing that its "excess of meaning" both demands constant interpretation and bears a certain kind of timeliness—namely the timeliness of a classic expression radically rooted in its own historical time and calling to my own historicity. That is, the classical text is not in some timeless moment which needs mere repetition. Rather its kind of timelessness as permanent timeliness is the only one proper to any expression of the

finite, temporal, historical beings we are. The classic text's real disclosure is its claim to attention on the ground that an event of understanding proper to finite human beings has here found expression. The classic text's fate is that only its constant reinterpretation by later finite, historical, temporal beings who will risk asking it questions and listening, critically and tactfully, to its responses can actualize the event of understanding beyond its present fixation in a text.[31]

The "event of understanding" in a classic myth speaks to other "events of understanding" in other times, and is joined to them by the always foiled attempt to go behind the understanding to the shared human experience that both inspires and eludes the myth.

The Foul Rag and Bones Shop of the Heart

Many of the accusations made against archetypes in the analysis of myths are also made against structure, which is generally regarded as the polar opposite of history: where history is contextualized, structure is decontextualized; where historic is diachronic, structure is synchronic. Let us jump in at the deep end and consider the work of the founder of structural mythology, Claude Lévi-Strauss.

What does structuralism tell us about myths and how to analyze them? These are closely related questions, for the method mirrors the making. Structuralism gives us a pretty good idea of how myths are made. If you take an early story (more precisely, a story that was recorded early, since no one knows when it was first told) and compare it with later tellings, it is as if the first story was dropped and broken into pieces, then put together again differently—not wrongly, just differently. The broken pieces are the atomic units of a myth, what Lévi-Strauss called "mythemes" in response to the "phonemes" of his colleague, the linguist Roman Jakobson. The set of mythemes that the structuralist isolates from any corpus of myths is roughly (but only roughly) equivalent to what I call the micromyth.

In the ecology of narratives, recycling is a very old process indeed. Myths, like all things in constant use, such as Truth in the Midrash, get broken and fixed again, lost and found, and the one who finds and fixes them, the handyman who recycles them, is what Lévi-Strauss calls a *bricoleur*—a term that he made famous even in English-speaking circles—and what the British used to call a "rag-and-bones man."[32] The rags and bones of the stories, the recycled pieces, the mythemes, are made in what William Butler Yeats (in "The Circus Animals") called "the foul rag and bones shop of the heart."

Long before Lévi-Strauss, Emerson mocked the intellectual *bricoleur*: "I am tired of scraps. I do not wish to be a literary or intellectual chiffonnier.

Away with this Jew's rag-bag of ends and tufts of brocade, velvet, and cloth-of-gold; let me spin some yards or miles of helpful twine, a clew to lead to one kingly truth, a cord to bind wholesome and belonging facts."[33] But Geoffrey Hartman defends the *bricoleur* against Emerson's intellectual attack (tactfully also sidestepping its anti-Semitic overtones, which would still find a target in our contemporary rag-and-bones man, Lévi-Strauss): "Emerson's image of the Jew's rag-bag . . . does not have to be an insult, or an indication of abject poverty."[34]

Each telling of a myth draws upon a network of these rags and bones, a kind of Erector set of prefabricated pieces, an identikit with which to construct all the faces of the Other that Levinas alerted us to. (A colleague of mine once told his undergraduate class that the *Odyssey* was like the Parts Department of Western Literature.)[35] Many motifs flow together to make a new story, like the flotilla that goes to Dunkirk in the film of *Mrs Miniver*:[36] little streams of little boats float silently together, their ranks swelling as they join finally in the broad Thames and the even broader Channel, what Hindus call the Ocean of the Rivers of Story. Each piece has its own previous life history and brings its own barnacles into the story. And there are several good reasons to call the rag-bag of themes "the same" even when it undergoes major transformations in different cultures, or in different periods or sectors of the same culture.

Many mythologists accuse Lévi-Strauss of being coldly scientific, probably because he has insisted that the logical patterns of myths can be expressed in a series of mathematical formulas, particularly what he calls the "canonical formula" ($a:b::c:a^{-1}$). It is this sort of thing that has driven Clifford Geertz, for instance, to write of Lévi-Strauss's work:

> "Aloof, closed, cold, airless, cerebral"—all the epithets that collect around any sort of literary absolutism collect around it. Neither picturing lives nor evoking them, neither interpreting them nor explaining them, but rather arranging and rearranging the materials the lives have somehow left behind into formal systems of correspondences—his books seem to exist behind glass, self-sealing discourses into which jaguars, semen, and rotting meat are admitted to become oppositions, inversions, isomorphism.[37]

This is unfair. Lévi-Strauss has always been interested in the messiest, juiciest aspects of human culture—eating and killing and marrying. Is it just that mythology *is* full of those things, and Lévi-Strauss knows it (i.e., that mythology has a dirty mind)? Or is it that he has selected myths that have dirty minds? Or that he imposes his own dirty mind upon the myths that he selects—myths about, as Geertz admits, jaguars, semen, and rotting meat? Hard to say; but the end result is a cold method that analyzes the hot content of myths.

Where his critics see Lévi-Strauss as reducing myths to logical oppositions, I see him as illuminating human ambivalences. After all, he is the one who taught us that every myth is driven by the obsessive need to solve a paradox *that cannot be solved*, a mess that cannot be cleaned up. And it is his obsession too: paradoxes are to him what whales were to Captain Ahab. Lévi-Strauss is talking not merely about *mental* constructs and patterns, but about *emotional* needs and conflicts. Yet he himself insists that he is only revealing structures. What is he repressing, that he keeps insisting he is just interested in the structures (just the facts, ma'am)?

And what makes him insist that he is doing science, as he does in this remarkable passage?

> I am convinced that the number of these systems is not unlimited and that human beings (at play, in their dreams, or in moments of delusion) never create *absolutely*; all they can do is to choose certain combinations from a repertory of ideas which it should be possible to reconstitute. For this one must make an inventory of all the customs which have been observed by oneself or others, the customs pictured in mythology, the customs invoked by both children and grown-ups in their games. The dreams of individuals, whether healthy or sick, should also be taken into account. With all this one could eventually establish a sort of periodical chart of chemical elements analogous to that devised by Mendelier. In this, all customs, whether real or merely possible, would be grouped by families and all that would remain for us to do would be to recognize those which societies had, in point of fact, adopted.[38]

The mythemes in this project are as pure, and as *given*, as elements, and the sum total of human thought can be analyzed as precisely as the compounds formed from the elements. But even in his claims to science, Lévi-Strauss is not "aloof, closed, cold, airless, cerebral," as Geertz described him; he is passionate, irrational, megalomaniac. The precision and scope of this "Mendelierian" table is insanely ambitious (certainly I would never claim that my micromyths and macromyths could be pinned down like elements and compounds), but it is also even theoretically inane. Listing all the theoretically possible customs and then selecting the ones that actually occur is, I think, a method analogous (!) to the method of catching lions in the old joke: "Catch two lions and let one go."

Structuralism is, like myth itself, a neutral construct that could theoretically be used to ask any of a number of questions, to address any of a number of problems. But structuralists tend to group mythemes in dyads, contributing to the general dichotomization of thought that I am arguing against in this book. In *Structural Anthropology*, as well as in subsequent works, Lévi-Strauss asserted that all mythology is dialectic in its attempt to make cognitive sense out of the chaotic data provided by nature, and that this attempt inevitably traps the human imagination in a web of dualisms: each dualism (such as male/female) produces a tension that seems to be resolved by the use of a mediating term (such as androgyny), but then that new term turns out to be one half of a new dualism (such as androgyny/sexlessness), *ad infinitum*.

Myth, Lévi-Strauss argues, is a form of language, and language predisposes us to attempt to understand ourselves and our world by superimposing dialectics, dichotomies, or dualistic grids upon data that may not be binary at all. And underneath language lies the binary nature of the brain itself. Right and left, good and evil, life and death—these are inevitable dichotomies produced by the brain that has two lobes and controls two eyes, two hands. We are split creatures literally by nature, and we process experience like a simple digital machine. Our common sense is binary; the simplest and most efficient way to process experience seems to be by dividing it in half, and then dividing the halves in half, reformulating every question so that there are only two possible answers, yes and no. As Thomas Laqueur remarks, "If structuralism has taught us anything it is that humans impose their sense of opposition onto a world of continuous shades of difference and similarity."[39]

Yet the stories retain those continous shades. Rather than a neat grid, therefore, we would do better to attempt to construct yet another Venn diagram (or spider's web) of interlocking motifs, in which each variant has some of the themes, but not all, and each arranges them differently and, more important, interprets them differently. Or we might construct yet another continuum such as Edmund Leach proposed in his modification of Lévi-Strauss's starkly polarized oppositions: "We need to consider not merely that things in the world can be classified as sacred and not sacred, but also as more sacred and less sacred. So also in social classifications it is not sufficient to have a discrimination me/it, we/they; we also need a graduated scale close/far, more like me/less like me."[40]

Structuralism is a great way to see what questions are being asked over and over; structuralists are haunted by *déjà vu*. Structuralism isolates the themes in a myth; it says, this *is*. But the myth is not a structure, it is a narrative; the myth adds to the structures speculations about the sequence of events, about causation; it says, this happens *because*. Structuralism does not arrange the pieces chronologically or sequentially or causally; the narrative does, and when it changes the arrangement it changes the point of the story, the point of the new answer to the old questions. In E. M. Forster's terms, the structure gives us the story, not the plot. But the myth does not settle for elementary structures; it modifies them and qualifies them in many different ways, and often even rejects them.

If a reader of Lévi-Strauss is foolish enough to seek the punch line, to cut to the chase, to turn to the end of the mystery to find out who did it, then that reader is likely to be disappointed. The formula that Lévi-Strauss often provides at the end, holding it up proudly for us to see, like a cat that brings its master a half-masticated mouse, is anticlimatic; often that formula bleeds the myth of all of its meanings. But before he gets to that end, Lévi-Strauss reveals to us more complex levels of meaning. He tells the stories and tells about the stories and suggests many rich patterns of interpretation before he boils it all down to a set of logical symbols (such as $a:b::c:a^{-1}$). The trick is to jettison Lévi-Strauss right before the moment when he finally deconstructs himself. It is a point that is hard to gauge, and calls to mind the story of the woman on the bus who, when asked by a stranger about a particular stop, advised him, "Just watch me and get off one stop before I do." We must jump off Lévi-Strauss's bus one stop before he does. In order to remain truly engaged with our texts, we must wallow in the mess for a while before the structuralists clean it up for us. I have argued that we must not stop at the empty micromyth but must fill it with texts; so too we must not hasten too quickly to the macromyth, another theoretical construct; we must linger in the texts.

For once we have jumped off the structuralist bus, we are likely to find that we are not there yet. We have to get on another bus (political, theological, psychological), or several buses. We need a lot of transfers on the mythic journey. At the beginning stage of the analysis, it is enough to identify certain unifying structures. Later, when we begin to search for the meanings of the structures and to locate those meanings in particular historical situations, we must venture into the symbolic territory of Eliade, and beyond it into the land of Freud and Mary Douglas and many others. But if one knows what pocket to look in for those transfers, Lévi-Strauss provides them too.

If we need a form of post-post-colonialism, surely we also need a form of post-post-structuralism. David Tracy has noted the ways the flaws of structuralism can be obviated by other kinds of awareness:

It may well be true that Lévi-Strauss' structuralist methods are some-times entangled with the bleak beauty of a despairing structuralist ideology, that Foucault's genealogical method is often entwined with a bitter polemic against any form of humanism, that Barthes' semi-otic method sometimes seems inseparable from a deliberate, if vital-izing, critical perverseness, that Derrida's deconstructionist methods seem to need the aid of *some* determinate meanings as they spill us and all our classic texts into his vitalizing abyss of indeterminacy. Yet all these ideologies possess, after all, their own truth: a suspicion of the illusions, the alienation, often the death and slackness of all self-congratulatory humanisms. Moreover, the ideologies are not intrin-sic to the methods of structuralist, semiotic or deconstructionist ex-planations. The methods—as methods of explanation—stand on their own either to develop and expand our original understanding or to confront and challenge it at the root.[41]

The trick is to apply the methods without the ideologies, indeed to apply the methods in conjunction with other methods (instead of ideologies).

Lévi-Strauss has characterized the structuralist approach as nothing but "the quest for the invariant, or for the invariant elements among superficial differences."[42] Yet if we take a closer look at his system, the mythemes do allow for difference as well as sameness. We can structure competing voic-es as opposed mythemes (Lévi-Strauss does not, but one could), and if we attempt to structure more than two competing voices, we find ourselves once again on a continuum rather than a dialectical grid, which is just where we need to be. The structural mythemes are there, all right, but they must be formulated in such a way that they can be plotted, not graphed. If a man kills his son in one variant, the theme might be inverted so that the son kills his father[43] in another (an inversion that Freud taught us, and Lévi-Strauss, to recognize long ago). For inversion is an intrinsic quality of myth.

Ivan Strenski insists that in a structural study, "Myths reveal no religious truths and deploy no supernatural power."[44] This too I would debate. The neutral structures are not dependent on religious thought as they are in, say, an Eliadean analysis, but they are open to it at any point. Lévi-Strauss includes the cosmological level in many of his analyses, and we can use other sorts of ideas to flesh it out (as he does not), once we have used the structural method to isolate the structures. Since Lévi-Strauss neither priv-ileges nor excludes religious or political questions in myths, by incorporat-ing such questions into a structural analysis we would be staying on the structuralist bus after Lévi-Strauss gets off.

The mythemes, as we have seen, can be arranged in any order, thereby excluding both cause-and-effect and value judgments. But couldn't there be other mythemes to include some of what the story mythemes by definition exclude? Why couldn't domination and subversion be mythemes? Why couldn't good and evil be mythemes? They might function as factors in a micromyth of Genesis, and in fact Edmund Leach includes good and evil in his structural analysis of Genesis and more/less sacred in his modified structural continuum.[45] And why couldn't causation be a mytheme, and chronology, time, history, as they are in the macromyth of the phantom Helen and the shadow Sita? As we will soon see, Lévi-Strauss does in effect create a causal, historical mytheme in *The Story of Lynx*. Would this not be one way to take structuralism farther than most card-carrying structuralists want to go, into political, theological, ethical territories? After all, a mythologist (unlike a folklorist) is free to ask, Is God a mytheme? For a structuralist, the great existential question would be, Is there a Mytheme?

The Greening of Claude Lévi-Strauss[46]

Lévi-Strauss's structural models have, like archetypes, been faulted for being disconnected from history, change, the flow of time: they are said to exist in a Platonic void that would make them equally relevant at all moments in the life of a culture, any culture. But the structural method does not just provide a kind of stasis; the idea of the mediating category in the Hegelian dialectic makes the theory dynamic, as it made Hegel's theory historical: structuralism sees myths as processes of synthesis and change. Moreover, in *Myth and Meaning* Lévi-Strauss makes explicit the connection with history that he has in fact always intended his structures to have, when he argues for the diachronic aspects of myths (changing through time) as well as their synchronic aspects (transcending the barriers of time). He puts historical flesh on the structural bones by tracing the specific cultural development of a corpus of myths.[47]

Lévi-Strauss has raised political aspects of the problem of the same and the different both inside and outside the text in his comparative study of myths of twinship in North America and Europe, *The Story of Lynx* (another subject that, like the "split representations," involves two halves of a single substance—a structuralist's dream). Noting the similarity between the myths about the twins in AmerIndian thought (as he calls it) on the one hand, and Castor and Pollux (the Gemini, or Dioscuroi) in Western mythology on the other, he argues that there is a perceived (and real) similarity in the structure of the AmerIndian and European myths that extends even to the kind of plants and planets associated in the two continents with the two pairs of twins. Yet there are striking dissimilarities between the ideologies of twins in the two cultures. The European myth (epitomized, for Lévi-Strauss, by Montaigne) expresses what he calls the ideology of identity, which excludes the Other; it emphasizes the similarity of the twins and thus the reduction of the other to an image of the self, the annihilation of its difference. The AmerIndian myth (epitomized in the famous case of Montezuma welcoming Cortes as a god) expresses what Lévi-Strauss calls the ideology of opposition, really a kind of synthesis or coexistence that assumes one must interact with the other; it emphasizes the dissimilarity of the twins, and thus the unstable coexistence of self and other. In this AmerIndian worldview, nothing and nobody can exist without an opposite, with which it coexists in unresolved tension. The mythologies of the twins are therefore not themselves identical twins; there is a profound difference between ideologies that exclude or interact with the Other, that annihilate or coexist with difference.

Here Lévi-Strauss tackles the political implications of mythology more directly than in any of his previous work. The clash between the two cultures and their mythologies had tragic consequences for the AmerIndians. Since they defined themselves in terms of their opposites, there already was a place of coexistence for the Europeans (or any other Others) in AmerIndian thought, even before these Others arrived in America. But the conquering Europeans never occupied this place; since they thought in terms of identity, and thus of exclusion, they destroyed the peoples whom they confronted in the New World.

There is, of course, a problem in lumping together all the AmerIndians—the "high" Aztec and the Inca, the "low" Thompson and Tupinamba—as Lévi-Strauss does; do all AmerIndians look alike in the dark? This is particularly problematic since, as he himself argues, the AmerIndians (all of them, presumably) were so highly sensitive to the Other and hence, presumably, to the differences among their own groups. But one might overcome this problem by applying the paradigm to one group at a time, and indeed, they may have been all alike in the particular ways that concern Lévi-Strauss. In any case, his study adds new mythemes to the *bricoleur*'s bag: Europeans/AmerIndians = identity/opposition = exclusion of the Other/interaction with the Other = similar/dissimilar twins = annihilation of difference/coexistence of self and other = colonizing/colonized.

Seventy Different Interpretations

I have argued that structuralism can be enriched, its shortcomings overcome, by combining it with other methods of interpretation. There is a word for this, the "e"-word in academia: eclecticism. Hilary Mantel offered both a challenge to and a defense of methodological eclecticism in the work of John Demos:

"Biography, psychology, sociology, history," he has written: "four corners of one scholar's compass, four viewpoints overlooking a single field of past experience." . . . Once you have decided on such a multi-disciplinary approach, where do you stop? How wide do you open your arms? . . . If you opt to be eclectic, there is no limit to scholarship, no end to your book. Yet you know you are working closer to some sort of truth.[48]

Here the argument is that the danger of losing methodological control is offset by the confidence that somehow one is approaching "some sort of truth." (Perhaps Indologists are more vulnerable to eclecticism than Western historians because, to use Demos's analogy, there are not four but ten points of the compass in Hinduism—our four, plus the four intermediate directions [Southwest, etc.], plus up and down.)

I think eclecticism is essential to the comparatist's methodology. Within the myth there are so many points of view, and outside the myth there are so many different ways of telling the story; and different scholars will produce different micromyths and bring together different texts in their macromyths. For the culture of the interpreter is no more monolithic than the culture of the teller; there are the competing schools of feminists and deconstructionists, Jungians and Freudians, among us, and different interpretations will be produced by different sorts of interpreters (theological, psychological, structural, and so forth). Moreover, each individual interpreter will approach "the same" story in different ways at different times. It follows, therefore, that any cross-cultural analysis will have to be sufficiently multivalent at least to acknowledge the validity of all of these sets of variants, if not necessarily to employ all of them at once. The many refractions of the narrative require multiple techniques—each maintained by a separate discipline—to isolate their various facets, and it is not necessary for a single scholar to encompass them all. I have argued elsewhere for a toolbox of methodologies, which every scholar/*bricoleur* should have and from which she will select what she regards as the most appropriate tool(s) for any particular analysis.[49] This multidisciplinary approach is a solution, but it is also a problem. Are all methodologies created equal? Does the eclectic scholar have to resign from the club of intellectual discrimination and respectability? I hope not.

Every telling of a story is an interpretation, and it has been well argued that no text ever stood in the way of a good interpretation. As the historian

William McNeill once remarked, "Really important texts are those susceptible of being richly and diversely misunderstood. An author can always aspire to that dignity."[50] Alan Dundes has pointed out "that *interpretations* of fairy tales and their appeal may reflect the same unconscious message as the very tales they purportedly claim to explicate."[51] Roland Barthes has rightly insisted that in proposing one meaning, a subjective choice, one must not suppress other meanings; moreover:

> The meaning of a text can be nothing but the plurality of its [symbolic] systems, its infinite (circular) "transcribability": one system transcribes another, but reciprocally as well: with regard to the text, there is no "primary," "natural," "national," "mother" critical language: from the outset, as it is created, the text is multilingual.[52]

But there are limits to the pluralism of interpretation. There is an old Jewish story about a rabbi who gave a particular interpretation of a text and said, "Isn't that right?" "No," replied his opponent. "But there are seventy different interpretations of Torah," said the rabbi. "Yes," said the opponent, "but that is not one of them."

Even Collingwood admitted that, though you can indeed tell the story of Caesar's assassination in various ways, there are ways in which you *can't* tell it: you can't say that Caesar killed Brutus. It is possible both to misinterpret and to misuse myths. We misinterpret them whenever we ignore context and difference, and we misuse them in the ways to which postcolonial discourse has alerted us. We can therefore eliminate some interpretations, but we should still be left with more than one.

The Multiversity

The richness and nuance of the best sort of comparison is nourished in the context of a university: a community in which a number of scholars work together on different projects in different ways. The very fact that so many people are now doing contextualized work frees the comparatist to do something else, to draw upon their work to ground new comparisons. I wish to carve out a space where, alongside the contextualizers doing their valuable work, those of us who work comparatively can do ours too. David E. Bynum argues that there is "no necessary contradiction between a comparative and an ethnically delimited approach to the criticism of oral narrative traditions. So long as they do not become confused one with the other, each approach may in an open mind greatly enhance the potential of the other."[53] Here, as in so much else, we might paraphrase Freud[54] (with apologies to Kierkegaard and his decisive spider): "Where 'either/or' was, there let 'both/and' be." Or I might quote Cyril Connolly, who once attributed his success as an editor to his belief in "god the Either, god the Or, and god the Holy Both."[55]

And I'm talking not about compromise, but about maintaining each of several conflicting views in a balanced tension, like chemical elements resolved into a suspension rather than a solution (if I may borrow Lévi-Strauss's Mendelierian metaphor); there is no solution, in either a chemical or a logical sense, for the elements of a myth. To change the metaphor, we must aspire to what I once characterized (in a very different context) as the pendulum of extremes:[56]

> By refusing to modify its component elements in order to force them into a synthesis, Indian mythology celebrates the idea that the universe is boundlessly various, that everything occurs simultaneously, that all possibilities may exist without excluding each other. . . . [that] untrammelled variety and contradiction are ethically and metaphysically necessary.[57]

And what is true of the myth is also true of the world.

People can also read other books about the cultures that we draw on for our comparative studies. We don't all have to do the same thing or do it in the same way; we can stand on the shoulders of giants, or as the case may be, pygmies, and they can stand on ours. From each her own. My argument here is for the academy, for multicultural, multidisciplinarian approaches. I would hope that the respect for "difference" (and pluralism, and diversity) that prevails in cultural studies would extend to the methodologies within the discipline of the history of religions, and indeed within the academy at large. I have argued against the present trend of studying only one cultural group—Jews, blacks—or, as discussed in chapter 5, only one gender. Now I challenge the trend of limiting those who study any group to those within the group—women studying women, Jews studying Jews—a trend which, if followed slavishly, would automatically eliminate not only my tiny, precious world of cross-cultural comparison but the more general humanism of which it is a part. This is a trend fueled, in large part, by the high moral ground assumed by disciplines, such as feminism and cultural studies, that argue, or imply, that their subject matter (racism, sexism, the class struggle, genocide) has such devastating human consequences that there is no room for error or playfulness or the possibility of more than one answer.

When did scholarship cease to be a collective enterprise? When did interdisciplinary values cease to apply to comparative studies? When did the "uni" in "university" come to refer to ideology? Perhaps we should rename our institutions multiversities (with overtones of multivocal, multivalent, multicultural) or polyversities, if not diversities (let alone inversities—for structuralists—and perversities—for our academic enemies). Whatever we call it, the academic world should never be a place where there is only one poker game in town. It should be a place where we can say, as in an ice cream parlor or hamburger joint: "Make me one with everything" (a phrase that can also be read as a pantheist prayer).

Walking the Tightrope

In the often stormy ocean of stories, a scholar needs to hang on to some rope stretched across the deck; for a mythologist, this rope is the cross-cultural narrative. But it is also a tightrope that the comparatist must walk between universality and essentialism, cultural distinctiveness and cross-cultural resemblance, a tightrope as narrow, but as strong, as the strand of a spider's web. It is, of course, intellectually dangerous to walk that tightrope, and it can also be physically dangerous, indeed near-fatal, for scholars engaged in fieldwork. And here we encounter yet another distorting dichotomy, between textualists and field-workers, similar to the false dichotomy between comparatists and contextualizers. Textualists (like myself) often feel that they are less implicated in the negative fallout of scholarship because they (we) read texts in libraries while others and go out and talk to people in "the field" (in my case, India); the only danger for textualists is of getting it wrong, which is on an entirely different order from the dangers of hepatitis and bus wrecks that field-workers encounter. But the text, like the Other encountered in the field, can change the scholar's life;[58] and although the textualist cannot change the text quite as directly as the anthropologist can change the people encountered in the field, yet scholars do change the text—not just literally, as in Woody Allen's story about *Madame Bovary*, but by changing the text's reception, its value and meaning for others. If we have learned anything at all from postcolonial discourse, it is that the texts scholars publish have an impact on the people they write about, not entirely unlike the more obvious impact of participant-observer anthropologists. Field-workers and textualists, engaging similar problems in different ways, need one another, and the academy needs both of them, the participant observer and the femme de cabinet (or even the butch de cabinet).

That said, I will conclude this book with two examples of the sort of fieldwork dangers that I have in mind. Clifford Geertz tells a story about the interaction between the comparatist and the cultures that are compared. In 1957, as a young anthropologist in Bali, he had the only Jeep and had to decide where to take a child who had a high fever (perhaps cholera):

> I wanted to take him to the only Western doctor on the island. The villagers wanted to take him to the local "curer." If I take him to the curer, and he dies, I feel bad. If I take him to the doctor, and he dies, they think I killed him. . . . We went to both. I think the curer first, just because he was closer. But if both'd been impossible, I would've taken him to the foreign doctor and taken the heat. There are times when you stop being an anthropologist. The bottom line was the kid got better. The Belgian doctor didn't know what was wrong with him. The curer did some chants. The fever went away. Nobody knows why.[59]

Jonathan Walters, a historian of religions trained in Chicago, told me a similar story, which was resolved for him in a similarly ambivalent way. Some years ago, Walters was living in Sri Lanka, studying the religion and the healing methods of the people in a certain village. He was thoroughly committed to the belief that non-Western healing methods have been unjustly neglected by Western science, that in many instances they are more effective than our own. He became dangerously ill with cholera and treated himself with the native remedies, but to no avail: a high fever and dehydration reduced him to a condition in which he could neither eat nor stand up, and he realized that he would probably die if he didn't get the medicine he needed—Western medicine, antibiotics. But to ask to be taken to the American hospital would be to deny all the work he had done during those years, and to deal a slap in the face of the people who had trusted him to cherish the medicines they had taught him. He couldn't bring himself to do it. As he lay there, breathing what he thought to be his last breaths, the people of the village came, put him on a stretcher, and carried him to the place where they carried out their religious healing ceremonies. The healer began a séance for Walters, using the standard techniques to go into a trance. After a while, the god entered the healer and spoke through him: "Let the white man go to the white man's doctor." They took Walters straight to the hospital and he lived to tell the tale, which he came to refer to as "Love, and My Time of Cholera."[60]

This is indeed a story about love, about the conflict between our love (or sometimes hate) for the Other and our commitment to our own worlds. And Walters's story is both the same as and different from Clifford Geertz's story: the historian of religions was ill himself and someone from the other culture made the ambivalent choice, while the anthropologist had to choose when someone from the other culture was ill. Geertz assumes that Western medicine is better; Walters begins by assuming that the other culture's medicine is better, and comes to think that Western medicine is better *for him*. Both stories therefore end with the triumph of Western medicine, science, and scholarship. But the "other" cultures themselves, in both cases, are less dichotomous; they have always had a both/and solution, using their own medicine and Western medicine together; they have the advantage of not being engaged in writing a book or a dissertation on native methods of healing. The anthropologist/comparatist has to learn from them the nonpolarized approach that the Spanish conquistadors failed to learn from the AmerIndians in Lévi-Strauss's *Story of Lynx*. Medical opinions need not be mutually exclusive, nor should any other ideologies. Comparatists should always be able to call for a second opinion. And despite their differences, to me these two autobiographical vignettes are variants of the same story, the story of cross-cultural comparison.

Notes

Introduction: Myth and Metaphor

1. Leon Festinger, *A Theory of Cognitive Dissonance*.
2. Cendrer's *Anthologie Negre*, cited in Susan Feldmann, ed., *African Myths and Tales*. I am grateful to Jonathan Z. Smith for giving me this delightful vignette; personal communication, May 8, 1997.
3. Wendy Doniger O'Flaherty, *Other Peoples' Myths*, 25–33.
4. David Tracy, *The Analogical Imagination*, 102.
5. David Tracy, paper presented in Jerusalem, March, 1994.
6. Mircea Eliade, *Myth and Reality*, 1, 111–13, 147–57. Xenophanes, before Plato, attempted to rationalize Greek myths.
7. Plato, *Timaeus* 26e; see also *Laws* 10.887.c8–e1; *Timaeus* 19d. For the damnation of the use of myth by the poets, see also *Timaeus* 22d; *Republic* 3.394b–c and 2.380c3; *Philebus* 14a.3–5. For a good discussion of this issue, see Marcel Detienne, *The Creation of Mythology*, 86–87; see also O'Flaherty, *Other Peoples' Myths*, 25–33.
8. Plato, *Laws* 10.887.c8–e1
9. Plato, *Timaeus* 29d, 59d, 68d, etc.
10. Plato, *Symposium*.
11. Plato, *Statesman* and *Timaeus*.
12. Plato, *Phaedo* 110 b–114.
13. Plato, *Republic* 10 (621b–c); cf. a similar myth about the voyage of the dead in the *Phaedo*, 113–14.

14. O'Flaherty, *Other Peoples' Myths*.
15. I am grateful to Dominick LaCapra for reminding me of this at Cornell, November 1996, and to Jonathan Z. Smith for pointing out further implications of it in Chicago, May 1997.
16. Wendy Doniger O'Flaherty, "On translating Sanskrit myths."
17. L. Frank Baum, *The Land of Oz*, 67–73.
18. This ringingly assonant phrase belongs to Ralph Williams, expressed in his remarks at Ann Arbor, February 1997.
19. Wendy Doniger, *The Bed Trick*.

1. *Microscopes and Telescopes*

1. T. S. Eliot, "*Ulysses*, Order, and Myth," 177–78.
2. Joseph Epstein, " `U. S. A.' Today," 72.
3. See chapter 6.
4. Claude Lévi-Strauss, *Structural Anthropology*, 210.
5. Benjamin Goldberg, *The Mirror and Man*.
6. A. K. Ramanujan, "When Mirrors are Windows."
7. Roland Barthes, *Mythologies*, 123. Again, he uses *form* and *meaning* in different senses from mine; my point is simply that he uses the same metaphor to talk about them.
8. Cyril Stanley Smith, "Metallurgical Footnotes to the History of Art," 280–92.
9. Victor Hugo, *Les Misérables*, St. Denis, Book III, "The House in the Rue Plumet," Chapter 3, "Foliis ac Frondibus." I am grateful to Ronald Lane Reese, Professor of Physics and Astronomy at Washington and Lee University, for this quote.
10. James Thurber, "University Days," 222–23.
11. Annie Dillard, "Lenses," in *Teaching a Stone To Talk*, 104.
12. Shakespeare, *Hamlet*, 3.1.
13. *Rig Veda* 10.129.5–6; Wendy Doniger O'Flaherty, *The Rig Veda*, 25–26.
14. *Rig Veda* 10.129.1, 7.
15. *Rig Veda* 10.121.5; O'Flaherty, *The Rig Veda*, 26–28.
16. *Aitareya Brahamana* 3.21.
17. Sayana's commentary on *Rig Veda* 1.121.
18. Stephen Mitchell, *The Book of Job*, xxv.
19. *Never on Sunday* (1959), written and directed by Jules Dassin, starring Melina Mercouri and Jules Dassin. Rossini tacked a happy ending onto his opera based on Shakespeare's *Othello* on one occasion when it was to be performed at the Vatican, and the Vatican insisted on certain changes: when Desdemona says (as she does in the usual Rossini version), "I am innocent," this time Othello replies, "Vero?" ("Really?"), and he believes Desdemona and kicks Iago out. Philip Gossett, who edited the critical edition of this opera, pointed out to me that he reproduced the words of the alternative ending and gave the reader a reference to where the full score could be found, but deliberately did *not* reproduce that score in the critical apparatus

in order to discourage anyone from performing the mutilated variant. Philip Gossett, personal communication, December 7, 1996.

20. Shakespeare, *King Lear*, 4.1.
21. Woody Allen, "The Scrolls," 27.
22. Wendy Doniger O'Flaherty, *The Origins of Evil* and *Dreams, Illusion, and Other Realities*.
23. *Mahabharata* 6.23–40.
24. O'Flaherty, *Other Peoples' Myths*, 157.
25. *Bhagavad Gita* 11.25–29 (*Mahabharata* 6.33.25–29).
26. *Bhagavad Gita* 2.3: klaibyam ma sma gamah, Partha . . . tyaktva' ottishtha, Paramtapa.
27. *Mahabharata* 4.32–42.
28. *Mahabharata* 4.66.20.
29. *Mahabharata* 3.148–49. See also the more serious imitation of the *Gita* in the text that Hindus explicitly regard as the "anu-*Gita*," the "after-the-*Gita*," at *Mahabharata* 14.16–50.
30. Mitchell, *The Book of Job*, xxvi–xxvii.
31. *Bhagavata Purana* 10.8.21–45; O'Flaherty, *Dreams, Illusion*, 109–10; *Hindu Myths*, 218–20.
32. *Mahabharata* 14.16.6–12.
33. O'Flaherty, *Dreams, Illusion*.
34. Saul Bellow, *Henderson the Rain King*, 137.
35. Annie Dillard, personal communication, Key West, Florida, December 27, 1996; to be used in her work in progress.
36. Annie Dillard, *The Living*, 70.
37. I believe it was Eli Lilly who first coined this phrase.
38. Thomas Keneally, *Schindler's List*; *Schindler's List* (1993), written by Steven Zaillian, from the novel by Thomas Keneally; directed by Steven Spielberg; starring Liam Neeson.
39. *The Wizard of Oz* (1939), written by L. Frank Baum, Jr., Leon Lee, and Larry Semon, from the novel by L. Frank Baum; directed by Victor Fleming; starring Judy Garland, Bert Lahr, and Ray Bolger. For the color shift, see O'Flaherty, *Other Peoples' Myths*, 158–59.
40. *Oh What a Lovely War* (1969), written by Len Deighton from the stage show by Joan Littlewood; directed by Richard Attenborough.
41. *All Quiet on the Western Front* (1930), written by Lewis Milestone, Maxwell Anderson et al. from the novel by Erich Maria Remarque; directed by Lewis Milestone.
42. *Gone With the Wind* (1939), written by Sidney Howard from the novel by Margaret Michell; directed by Victor Fleming et al.; starring Clark Gable, Vivien Leigh, Olivia de Havilland, Leslie Howard.
43. *Star Trek*, "The Immunity Syndrome," written by Robert Sabaroff, directed by Joseph Pevney, and first aired on January 19, 1968. I am grateful to Peter Gottschalk for finding this episode for me.
44. Shakespeare, *Hamlet*, 1.1.

45. *Casablanca* (1942), written by Julius J. Epstein, Philip G. Epstein, and Howard Koch, from the play *Everybody Comes to Rick's*, by Murray Burnett and Joan Alison; directed by Michael Curtiz; starring Humphrey Bogart, Ingrid Bergman, Claude Rains, Paul Henreid.
46. Claude Lévi-Strauss, "The Story of Asdiwal," 42.
47. Marcel Proust, *Remembrance of Things Past*, English translation cited here, vol. 2, 1118. He is referring to his first book, *Les Plaisirs et les Jours*, according to the editor of the French edition, vol. 4, 618.
48. Andrew Delbanco, *The Death of Satan*, 231.
49. Dillard, "Lenses," 104.
50. O'Flaherty, *Other Peoples' Myths*.
51. Delbanco, *The Death of Satan*, 191.
52. Ibid., 200.
53. Advertisement broadcast on January 18, 1992, on WFMT in Chicago.
54. George Bernard Shaw, *Saint Joan*, 223; cited in O'Flaherty, *Other Peoples' Myths*, 130.

2. Dark Cats, Barking Dogs, Chariots, and Knives

1. Tracy, *The Analogical Imagination*, 410.
2. "Entries," by James Tate, from *Absences: New Poems*. Cited in Tracy, *The Analogical Imagination*, 446.
3. Francis Bacon, "The Unity of Religions." Bacon went on to contrast religions, citing Psalm 139: "with Thee even darkness is light."
4. Plato, *Sophist*, 254a. ff; Cornford translation. (Cf. 218d, where the Stranger says that the Sophist is "a very troublesome sort of creature to hunt down," i.e. to define.) Plato adds that the philosopher "is difficult to see because his region is so bright, for the eye of the vulgar soul cannot endure to keep its gaze fixed on the divine."
5. Erasmus, *Opera Omnia*, 2:82: "Ego certe antequam Plutarchi locum adiissem, hujusce Graeci adagii sensum à Gallico edoctus eram adagio. *De nuici tous chats son gris.*"
6. John Heywood, *Proverbs*, part 1, chapter 5.
7. W. G. F. Hegel, *Phaenomenologie des Geistes*, 19. "Das Eine Wissen, dass im Absoluten alles gleich ist, der unterschiedenden und erfuellten oder Erfuellung suchenden und fordernden Erkenntnis entgegenzusetzen, —oder sein *Absolutes* fuer die Nacht auszugeben, worin, wie man zu sagen pflegt, alle Kuehe schwarz sind, ist die Naivitaet der Leere an Erkenntnis."
8. John Hollander, "Kinneret," in *Selected Poetry*, 6.
9. John Hollander, Rubai #137 of "The Tesserae," in *Tesserae, and Other Poems*.
10. Unsigned, "The Explosion Point of Ideology in China," in *Situationist International Anthology*, ed. and trans. Ken Knabb, 186 and 194.
11. Michael Lester O'Flaherty, personal communication, May 1, 1995.
12. Ernest Gellner, in the *Times Literary Supplement*, September 23, 1994, 3–5.
13. Dashiell Hammett, *The Dain Curse*, 78.

14. Personal communication from David Shulman, March 1996.
15. Terrence Rafferty, "The Avengers: `Die Hard with a Vengeance' and `A Little Princess,'" 92.
16. Wendy Doniger, "Myths and Methods in the Dark."
17. Mary Ann Doane, *Femmes Fatales*, 209; Sigmund Freud, SE 20, 212.
18. Doane, 209 and 212.
19. Eve Kosofsky Sedgwick, *The Epistemology of the Closet*, 33.
20. Horace H. Wilson, *Essays and Lectures, Chiefly on the Religion of the Hindus*, 257–58. I am grateful to Hugh Urban for this reference.
21. Ralph Waldo Ellison, *Invisible Man*.
22. Delbanco, *The Death of Satan*, 194.
23. Carlo Ginzburg, "Morelli, Freud," 19, citing "Filarete," *Trattato di architettura* (Treatise on Architecture).
24. Marshall Sahlins told me this story about Marty Fried; personal communication, Chicago, November 1996.
25. Ginzburg, "Morelli, Freud," 24.
26. Wendy Doniger, "The Mythology of Masquerading Animals, or, Bestiality."
27. Ginzburg, "Morelli, Freud," 26.
28. Ibid., 27.
29. It was used most recently by Jonathan Z. Smith in "Map Is Not Territory," 300–2; and by myself in *Other Peoples' Myths*, 136.
30. Sir Arthur Conan Doyle, "Silver Blaze," 276.
31. Shakespeare, *Hamlet*, 1.5.
32. Personal communication from David Grene, March 1996.
33. David Tracy, personal communication, August 1995.
34. Tracy, *The Analogical Imagination*, 249–50; and *Dialogue with the Other*, 4–6.
35. I am indebted to conversations with Bruce Lincoln for the ideas in this paragraph.
36. Jonathan Z. Smith, *Drudgery Divine*, 51.
37. "Thirdness is nothing but the character of an object which embodies Betweenness or Mediation in its simplest and most rudimentary form. . . . Thirdness, as I use the term, is only a synonym for Representation." Charles Sanders Peirce, "The Reality of Thirdness," 68.
38. Jonathan Z. Smith, "In Comparison a Magic Dwells."
39. Peirce, "The Reality of Thirdness," 64–76.
40. Doniger, *The Bed Trick*.
41. Claude Lévi-Strauss, *The Story of Lynx*, 186.
42. Claude Lévi-Strauss, *The Raw and the Cooked*, 13.
43. Yuri Lotman, "The Semiosphere," 154.
44. Wendy Doniger, "Speaking in Tongues: Deceptive Stories about Sexual Deception"; "Sex, Lies, and Tall Tales"; and "Myths and Methods in the Dark."
45. Erich Auerbach, *Mimesis*, 11.
46. Robert Alter, *The Art of Biblical Narrative*, 7.

47. *Testament of Judah* 14. See Esther Menn, "Judah and Tamar (Genesis 38)" in *Ancient Jewish Exegesis*.

48. Midrash Rabbah, Bereshit Rabbah 85.8, on Genesis 38.15; also Tan. Wayesheb 9.17, v. Sot. 10b, and b. Meg. 10b. *Targum Neofiti* Genesis 38.

49. Doniger, *The Bed Trick*.

50. I owe this insight to Michael Fishbane; personal communication, February 1994.

51. Gary Saul Morson, *Narrative and Freedom*, 12.

52. Hilary Mantel, review of John Demos, *The Unredeemed Captive, London Review of Books*, October 20, 1994, 20.

53. Zwi Jagendorf, " `In the Morning, Behold It Was Leah': Genesis and the Reversal of Sexual Knowledge," 57.

54. Joel Fineman, "Fratricide and Cuckoldry: Shakespeare's Doubles," 427.

55. Nathalie Zemon Davis, *The Return of Martin Guerre*.

56. Adrien Bledstein has, however, argued (in "Binder, Trickster") that in the closely related myth of Jacob and Esau, Isaac pretends to be fooled by Jacob.

57. As David Tracy suggests in *Plurality and Ambiguity*, 19–20.

58. Marliss C. Desens, *The Bed-Trick in English Renaissance*, 16.

59. Claude Lévi-Strauss, *Tristes Tropiques*, 58, italics mine.

60. Barbara Fass Leavy, *In Search of the Swan Maiden*, 28–29.

61. Bialik and Ravnitzky, *The Book of Legends*, 13; Middrash Rabbah, Genesis, 8.5.

62. The jigsaw puzzle metaphor is well known. This particular version comes from Rabbi Lopez Cardozo, now living in Jerusalem, as retold by Shira Leibowitz Schmidt and Roald Hoffmann, personal communication, October 1996.

63. Personal communication from David Tracy, December 1994.

64. Woody Allen, "The Kugelmass Episode," 72; see O'Flaherty, *Other Peoples' Myths*, 140.

65. Shakespeare, *Hamlet*, 1.2.

66. Wendy Doniger, "Sita and Helen, Ahalya and Alcmena: A Comparative Study" and *Splitting Women*.

67. Laura Bohannan, "Shakespeare in the Bush," 28.

68. Jorge Luis Borges, "Pierre Menard, Author of the *Quixote*," 43.

69. Lévi-Strauss, *The Raw and the Cooked*, 13.

70. Wendy Doniger, "Structuralist Universals," 267–81.

71. Milman Parry, *The Making of Homeric Verse* and Albert Lord, *Serbocroatian Heroic Songs*.

72. Robert P. Goldman, "Transsexualism, Gender, and Anxiety in Traditional India," 394 and 397.

73. Personal communication from Caroline Bynum, May 1992. See also Doniger, *Splitting Women*, which argues that gender outweighs culture in myths that are told about women in different cultures.

74. Milan Kundera, *The Unbearable Lightness of Being*, 192.

75. Brent D. Shaw, review of Caroline Walker Bynum's *The Resurrection of the Body*, 47.

76. Richard Ellman, *along the riverrun: Selected Essays*, 204.

77. David Hume, *A Treatise of Human Nature*, 257 (Book I, Part IV, section VI).

78. Ernest Gellner, *The Psychoanalytic Movement, or, The Cunning of Unreason*, 13.

79. *Milinda Panha*, 40, 71, and 108–6 of the Trenckner edition.

80. Personal communication from A. K. Ramanujan, January 1989.

81. A. K. Ramanujan, *Folktales from India*, introduction, xx.

82. A story told by the anthropologist Gary Clevidence; personal communication from Annie Dillard, Key West, December 1996. Bruce Lincoln tells me that Parson Weems invented the cherry tree story in the 1820s—which of course renders all of this highly anachronistic.

83. Personal communication from Dan Gerber, Key West, December 1996.

84. *Milinda Panha*, 40 and 71 of the Trenckner edition.

85. Lawrence Sullivan, *Icanchu's Drum*, 559, 681–82, 870n361.

3. *Implied Spiders and the Politics of Individualism*

1. Marina Warner, *From the Beast to the Blonde: On Fairy Tales and Their Tellers*, 414.

2. C. S. Lewis, cited by Michael Nelson in "One Mythology Among Many: The Spiritual Odyssey of C. S. Lewis," 628.

3. Sir Ernest Gombrich, *The Sense of Order*, 191–92 (see also the critical discussion of Jung on 246–47); and *Topics of Our Time*, 43–44.

4. J. Z. Smith, *Drudgery Divine*, 47.

5. Shakespeare, *Merchant of Venice*, 3.1.

6. See O'Flaherty, *Other Peoples' Myths*, chapter 4, "If I Were A Horse"; and Doniger, "The Mythology of Masquerading Animals."

7. Plato, *The Statesman*, 269B.

8. O'Flaherty, *Dreams, Illusion*, 203.

9. F. Max Müller, *Lectures on the Science of Language*; see esp. "Metaphor."

10. I tried it too, with only middling success, in *Women, Androgynes, and Other Mythical Beasts*.

11. Joan Aitchison, *The Language Web*, 44.

12. Herodotus, *History*, 2.2.

13. Michael D. Coe, review of Steven Pinker's *The Language Instinct*, 7–8.

14. H. S. Terrace, *Nim*.

15. Elaine Scarry, *The Body in Pain*, 5.

16. Clifford Geertz, *After the Fact*, 51.

17. Thomas Laqueur, *Making Sex*, 16.

18. Ibid., 61.

19. A. K. Ramanujan, "Three Hundred Ramayanas," 46.

20. Claude Lévi-Strauss, "The Structural Study of Myth," 208.

21. Claude Lévi-Strauss, *Myth and Meaning*, 11.

22. Scarry, *The Body in Pain*, 182.

23. Judith Butler, *Bodies That Matter*, 68.

24. For a devastating critique of this "encyclopedic" approach, see Jonathan Z. Smith, "Adde Parvum Parvo Magnus Acervus Erit," 249–53.

25. Geertz, *After the Fact*, 28.

26. Clifford Geertz, "Thick Description," 5.

27. Gananath Obeyesekere, *The Work of Culture*, 285.

28. Ibid., 286.

29. Wolfgang Iser, *The Implied Reader*.

30. Wayne Booth, *The Rhetoric of Fiction*, 70–77.

31. Shakespeare, *The Winter's Tale*, 2.1.

32. O'Flaherty, *Other Peoples' Myths*, 160–61; "The Mythology of Masquerading Animals"; *Splitting Women*.

33. *Zohar, The Book of Enlightenment*, 49–50. I am indebted to Roald Hoffmann for calling my attention to this passage at Cornell, November 1996.

34. *Brihadaranyaka Upanishad* 2.1.20.

35. *Mundaka Upanishad* 1.1.7.

36. *Shvetashvatara Upanishad* 5.10.

37. Walt Whitman, "A Noiseless Patient Spider."

38. Greg Nagy, speaking at a conference at the Chicago Humanities Institute, October 12, 1996.

39. Soren Kierkegaard, *Either/or: A Fragment of Life*, I:19. Friedrich Durrenmatt, *The Assignment*, 70, gives a slightly different translation:

> What should come, what should strange times bring? I do not know, I have no presentiment. When a black widow [spider] plunges down from a fixed point to its consequences, it constantly sees an empty space before it, in which it cannot find a firm foothold, no matter how it kicks about. Thus it is with me: before me perpetually an empty space, what drives me forward is a consequence that lies behind me. This life is backward and puzzling, intolerable.

40. Aitchison, *The Language Web*, 2, 58, 91, 95.

41. Wendy Doniger, "A Very Strange Enchanted Boy."

42. Marjorie Garber, *Vice Versa*, 519n66.

43. Shakespeare, *Henry V*, 4.7.

44. Carlo Ginzburg, *Ecstasies: Deciphering the Witches' Sabbath*.

45. J. Z. Smith, *Map Is Not Territory*; *Imagining Religion*.

46. Bruce Lincoln, *Discourse and the Construction of Society*.

47. Sullivan, *Icanchu's Drum*.

48. Geertz, *After the Fact*, 28.

49. There once were two cats of Kilkenny.
Each thought there was one cat too many.
They started to fight,
To scratch and to bite,
And instead of two cats, there weren't any.

50. Henry Fielding, *Tom Jones*, III:3:109.

51. Emmanuel Levinas, *Totality and Infinity*, 198–99.

52. Annie Dillard, *Encounters with Chinese Writers*, 20 and 71.

53. William James, *The Varieties of Religious Experience* (New York: Modern Library edition, 1929), 10; cited in Jonathan Z. Smith, "Fences and Neighbors," 6.

54. I am indebted to Sarah Caldwell for this cogent summary in her introduction to my lecture at Ann Arbor on February 7, 1997.

55. Wilhelm Dilthey, *Pattern and Meaning in History*, 77.

56. Lewis Carroll, *Through the Looking Glass*, chapter 2.

57. Ralph Williams, remarks at Ann Arbor, February 1997.

58. In fact, nominalism is the basis of both extreme difference and universalism, but that is another story.

59. Sir Ernst Gombrich, *The Essential Gombrich*.

60. Personal communication from Lee Siegel, October 28, 1996, re Lockwood Kipling's *Beast and Man in India*.

61. *The Gods Must Be Crazy* (1980), written and directed by Jamie Uys.

62. See, for instance, David Gordon White, *Myths of the Dog-Man*.

63. Jean Pépin, "Christian Judgements on the Analogies between Christianity and Pagan Mythology," 659b.

64. Ibid., 661b.

65. Robert Ackerman, *J. G. Frazer: His Life and Work*, 95 and 189, citing letters by Frazer.

66. As J. Z. Smith argues in *Drudgery Divine*.

67. O'Flaherty, *Other Peoples' Myths*.

68. I am indebted to David Tracy for the little that I know about postmodernism.

69. Fineman, "Fratricide and Cuckoldry: Shakespeare's Doubles," citing René Girard, "Myth and Identity Crisis in *A Midsummer-Night's Dream*," Colloquium of SUNY Buffalo, Winter 1969.

70. Sedgwick, *The Epistemology of the Closet*, 23.

71. Jacques Derrida, "Violence and Metaphysics."

72. Hilary Mantel, reviewing John Demos, *The Unredeemed Captive*, *London Review of Books*, October 20, 1994, 20.

73. Dillard, *Encounters with Chinese Writers*, 4.

74. Joan W. Scott, "Gender and the Politics of Higher Education," ms., 15.

75. Charles Taylor discusses this statement, often attributed to Saul Bellow, in his *Multiculturalism*, 42: "When Saul Bellow is famously quoted as saying something like, 'When the Zulus produce a Tolstoy we will read him,' this is taken as a quintessential statement of European arrogance, not just because Bellow is allegedly being *de facto* insensitive to the value of Zulu culture, but frequently also because it is seen to reflect a denial in principle of human equality." Taylor added a footnote, which also says what I want to say (42n18): "I have no idea whether this statement was actually made in this form by Saul Bellow, or by anyone else. I report it only because it captures a widespread attitude, which is, of course, why the story had currency in the first place." Bellow later denied having said this, but James Atlas, who first quoted it in his profile of Allan Bloom in *The New York Times*, insisted on it again in his profile of Bellow in *The New Yorker*, "The Shadow in the Garden," 84.

76. Tracy, *The Analogical Imagination*, 410.

77. Geoffrey H. Hartman, "Midrash as Law and Literature," 339.

78. Tracy, *The Analogical Imagination*, 13.

79. Laurie Patton, introductory remarks at this lecture, Emory, January 1997.

80. Claude Lévi-Strauss, personal communication, Paris, October 1980.

81. Jessye Norman, speaking at Radcliffe College, June 6, 1997.

82. Thomas Kuhn, *The Nature of Scientific Revolution*.

83. Annie Dillard, *Mornings Like This*.

4. Micromyths, Macromyths, and Multivocality

1. Personal communication from Joel Kraemer, January 1996.

2. Salman Rushdie, *Shame*, 116.

3. Salman Rushdie, *Haroun and the Sea of Stories*, 160.

4. Roberto Calasso, *The Marriage of Cadmus and Harmony*, 280.

5. O'Flaherty, *Other Peoples' Myths*, chapter 2.

6. E. M. Forster, *Aspects of the Novel*, 130.

7. Ibid., 130–31.

8. William R. Bowden, "The Bed-Trick, 1603–1642," 118.

9. It is not explicit in the text of Genesis that Adam and Eve did not have sex before the Fall; all that is said is that they only became aware of their nakedness then. There is much debate about this—Milton said they did in fact have sex before—but I interpret the text to imply that their sexual awareness came only after the Fall.

10. See Elizabeth G. Davis, *The First Sex*; also Robert Graves, *Adam's Rib* and, more recently, Karen Ziegler, "Creation Myths: Bridge to Human Wholeness," 15: "There is much evidence that suggests that in the ancient Near and Middle East, the serpent was linked to wisdom, prophecy, and esoteric knowledge. . . . In Sumaria [sic], the goddess Nidaba was . . . at times depicted as a serpent."

11. Ireneus 1.31.

12. I am grateful to Elaine Pagels for the suggestion about *ophis*; personal communication, May 14, 1997.

13. Hesiod, *Works and Days*, 54–105, and *Theogony*, 535–616. See Nicole Loraux, "Origins of Mankind in Greek Myths: Born to Die"; Laura Mulvey, "Pandora: Topographies of the Mask and Curiosity"; Froma Zeitlin, "Signifying Difference: The Case of Hesiod's Pandora."

14. Shelley, *Prometheus Unbound*, Preface, 35–36.

15. Mark Twain, *Pudd'nhead Wilson and Other Tales*, epigram for chapter 2.

16. Royall Tyler, "The Origin of Evil," 1793.

17. Moshe Idel, personal communication, January 1995.

18. Lévi-Strauss, "Myth and Music," in *Myth and Meaning*, 44–54.

19. Gary Saul Morson, "Sideshadowing," 117–72 of *Narrative and Freedom*.

20. Gary Saul Morson, *Narrative and Freedom*, 11.

21. Ibid.

22. O'Flaherty, *Dreams, Illusion*, 129.

23. Mieke Bal, *Lethal Love*, 131–32.

24. For another use of this metaphor of the wheel or the roundhouse, to which all variants return, see O'Flaherty, *Other Peoples' Myths*.

25. O'Flaherty, *Tales of Sex and Violence*, 10.

26. The Brahmanas and the *Brihaddevata*. See Laurie L. Patton, *Myth as Argument*.

27. Joseph Campbell, *The Hero with a Thousand Faces*.

28. Geertz, *After the Fact*, 28.

29. Vladimir Propp, *The Morphology of the Folktale*.

30. David E. Bynum, *The Daemon in the Wood*, 80–81.

31. Raymond D. Jameson, *Three Lectures on Chinese Folklore*, 17.

32. For a devastating critique of the argument from the "density of the 'factual' material presented," see J. Z. Smith, "Adde Parvum Parvo Magnus Acervus Erit," 252–53.

33. Sullivan, *Icanchu's Drum*, 20.

34. D. E. Bynum, *The Daemon in the Wood*, 78.

35. Jameson, *Three Lectures on Chinese Folklore*, 17.

36. See J. Z. Smith, "Sacred Persistence," 39–40, for a rather different use of the metaphor of canon as a list of foods that is first limited and then expanded.

37. A. K. Ramanujan, "Hanchi: A Kannada Cinderella."

38. Ibid., 272.

39. *Jaiminiya Brahmana* 2.269–70; O'Flaherty, *Tales of Sex and Violence*, 105–7.

40. Warner, *From the Beast to the Blonde*, 362.

41. James Finn Garner, *Politically Correct Bedtime Stories*, 35.

42. Alan Dundes, *Cinderella: A Casebook*.

43. A. K. Ramanujan, "Two Realms of Kannada Folklore."

44. Lévi-Strauss, "The Story of Asdiwal," 29–30; *Structural Anthropology*, 229; *The Savage Mind*, 22.

45. Frank Lewis Dyer, *Edison*, 2:615–16.

46. Franz Kafka, "Leopards in the Temple." J. Z. Smith uses this parable to make a rather different point in "The Bare Facts of Ritual," 53, citing a different translation of Kafka from "Reflections on Sin, Hope, and the True Way," in Kafka, *The Great Wall of China* (New York, 1970), 165.

47. Evelyn Waugh, *A Handful of Dust*, 29.

48. Ibid., 59.

49. Ibid., 60.

50. *Ramayana* 7.26.8–47, plus the verse excised from the Critical Edition after verse 47. See Doniger, *Splitting Women*.

51. *Ramayana* 7.17.1–31.

52. Adam Michnik, interview, *The New Yorker*, December 9, 1996, 52.

53. Mary Douglas, "Children Consumed and Child Cannibals," 43.

54. Hesiod, *Theogony*.

55. Nicholas D. Kristof, "Big Wolves Aren't So Bad in Japan." *The New York Times*, Wednesday, December 4, 1996.

56. Babylonian Talmud (Tractate Kiddushin 81b). I am indebted to Melila Hellner for this citation and translation.

57. Yebamoth 65b. Trans. Gregory Spinner.

58. Dena S. Davis, "Beyond Rabbi Hiyya's Wife," 11.

59. Martin Buber, *The Legend of the Baal-Shem*, introduction, 11.

60. And was often cited during the Ebonics fracas in 1997.

61. Barthes, *Mythologies*, 142–43.

62. Alan Dundes, ed., *The Blood Libel Legend*.

63. Ginzburg, *Ecstasies*, 74.

64. Roland Barthes, "The World of Wrestling," in *Mythologies*, 15–24; Bruce Lincoln, "Dialectic Manipulations and the Preservation of the Status Quo: 'All-Star Wrestling,' " in *Discourse and the Construction of Society*, 148–59.

65. *The Iron Mask* (1929), written by Elton Thomas (Douglas Fairbanks) from the novel *Ten Years After*, by Alexander Dumas; directed by Allan Dwan.

66. *The Man in the Iron Mask* (1939), written by George Bruce from the novel by Alexander Dumas; directed by James Whale.

67. Sir Anthony Hope, *The Prisoner of Zenda* (1896); *The Prisoner of Zenda*, 1937, written by John Balderston, Wills Root, Donald Ogden Stewart, from the novel by Anthony Hope; directed by John Cromwell; starring Ronald Colman, Douglas Fairbanks Jr., Madeleine Carroll.

68. *The Prisoner of Zenda*, 1979, written by Dick Clement, Ian La Frenals; directed by Richard Quine; starring Peter Sellers, Lionel Jeffries, Elke Sommer.

69. Bell Irvin Wiley, *Johnny Reb: The Common Soldier of the Confederacy*, 40.

70. Woody Allen, live recording of a nightclub act at Mr. Kelly's in Chicago in 1964; copyright Liberty Records, 1968; EMI Records, 1990.

71. *Dances with Wolves* (1990), written by Michael Blake from his novel, directed by Kevin Costner.

72. *Into the West* (Irish, 1992), written by Jim Sheridan and David Keating, from a story by Michael Pearce; directed by Mike Newell, with Gabriel Byrne and Ellen Barkin.

73. *Apocalypse Now* (1979), written by John Milius and Francis Coppola, directed by Francis Ford Coppola.

74. Friedrich Kittler, "World-Breath: On Wagner's Media Technology," 234.

75. This was Kazi Joshua's excellent question, in May 1997.

76. O'Flaherty, *Other Peoples' Myths*, 155–56, 165.

77. Salman Rushdie, commencement speech, Bard College, May 1996.

78. Ronald Hutton, *The Stations of the Sun*, 393.

79. Ibid., 396 and 403.

80. Ibid., 405.

81. *Invasion of the Body Snatchers* (1956), written by Daniel Mainwaring, from the novel by Jack Finney; directed by Don Siegel; starring Kevin McCarthy, Dana Wynter; remade in 1978, written by W. D. Richter; directed by Philip Kaufman; starring Donald Sutherland, Brooke Adams, Leonard Nimoy, Jeff Goldblum, Kevin McCarthy.

82. Luke Jennings, "Nights at the Ballet," 76.

83. Barthes, *Mythologies*.

84. Mircea Eliade, "Eschatology and Cosmogony," in *Myth and Reality*, 54–74, especially 55–56.

85. Pierre Teilhard de Chardin, *Christianity and Evolution*, 40–41; O'Flaherty, *The Origins of Evil*, 35.

86. Hilda Kuper, *The Uniform of Colour*, 103–4; cited by Lincoln, *Discourse and the Construction of Society*, 27.

87. Lincoln, *Discourse and the Construction of Society*, 28.

88. Jean Comaroff, *Body of Power*, 12.

89. *Mahabharata* 4.5.

90. David Tracy, *On Naming the Present*, 16.

91. George Sorel, *Reflections on Violence*.

92. Warner, *From the Beast to the Blonde*, 409.

5. *Mother Goose and the Voices of Women*

1. I am grateful to Judith Kegan Gardiner for reminding me of this; personal communication, Radcliffe College, June 7, 1997.

2. See for instance, Jean Bethke Elshtain, "Feminist Political Rhetoric and Women's Studies."

3. Gayatri Spivak, "Can the subaltern speak?"; Diana Fuss, *Essentially Speaking: Feminism, Nature, and Difference*.

4. *In Dora's Case*, eds. Charles Bernheimer and Claire Kahane.

5. Plato, *Republic* 350 e, 376e–377d, 381 e; *Laws* 10.887.c8–e1.

6. Warner, *From the Beast to the Blonde*.

7. H. M. and N. K. Chadwick, *The Growth of Literature*.

8. A. K. Ramanujan, "Toward a Counter-system: Women's Tales," 53.

9. Barbara Fass Leavy, *In Search of the Swan Maiden*, 118, citing Jan O. Swahn, *The Tale of Cupid and Psyche*, 437–38.

10. Bengt Holbek, *Interpretation of Fairy Tales*, 154–57.

11. Ramanujan, "Toward a Counter-system."

12. Midas Dekkers, *Dearest Pet. On Bestiality*, 155.

13. Judith Kegan Gardiner, *"Fifteen Joys,"* 72; citing *Les Quinze Joies de Mariage* 7.28.

14. Ramanujan, "Toward a Counter-system," 53.

15. Velcheru Narayana Rao, "A Ramayana of Their Own," 119.

16. Sarah Caldwell, "Waves of Beauty," ms., 29.

17. Ibid., 30.

18. O'Flaherty, *Textual Sources*, 97–98.

19. Ovid, *Metamorphoses*, 9.265–301.

20. Ramanujan, "Toward a Counter-system," 53.

21. Rao, "A Ramayana of Their Own," 128.

22. Margaret Mills, "Sex Role Reversals," 192.

23. Ann Grodzins Gold, "Gender and Illusion in a Rajasthani Yogic Tradition," 107, 113, 126.

24. Aeschylus, *Agamemnon* (part I of the *Oresteia*), line 11 (*androboulon*).
25. Aeschylus, *Eumenides* (part III of the *Oresteia*), lines 658–66, 734–40.
26. Wendy Doniger, "Gender and Myth."
27. Rao, "A Ramayana of Their Own," 128.
28. Leavy, *In Search of the Swan Maiden*, 118.
29. Warner, *From the Beast to the Blonde*, 210.
30. Ibid., 227.
31. Jeanine Basinger, *How Hollywood Spoke to Women, 1930–1960*, 20–21.
32. Warner, *From the Beast to the Blonde*, 238.
33. Ibid., 278.
34. Ibid., 217.
35. Doniger, "Sex, Lies, and Tall Tales."
36. Ruth Padel, "Putting the Words into Women's Mouths," 13.
37. Warner, *From the Beast to the Blonde*, 188.
38. Ibid., 209.
39. Ibid.
40. John Stratton Hawley, "Images of Gender in the Poetry of Krishna," 234–35.
41. Paula Richman, *Extraordinary Child*, 218–19.
42. A. K. Ramanujan, David Shulman, and Narayana Rao, eds, *When God Is a Customer*.
43. Edward Said, *Culture and Imperialism*.
44. I owe the ideas at the end of this paragraph to Bruce Lincoln; personal communication, June 1997.
45. Laqueur, *Making Sex*, 67.
46. A. T. Hatto, "The Swan Maiden," 333.
47. Leavy, *In Search of the Swan Maiden*, 22–23, citing Marie Louise von Franz, *Problems of the Feminine*, 1–4.
48. Leo Tolstoi, *Anna Karenin*, part 6, chapter 23, 774.
49. Bal, *Lethal Love*.
50. Harold J. Bloom, *The Book of J*.
51. Adrien J. Bledstein, "Female Companionships," 132–33.
52. S. D. Goitein, "Women as Creators of Biblical Genre," 2.
53. Ibid., 31.
54. Donald Keene, "Feminine Sensibility in the Heian Era," 109, 111.
55. Ibid., 115.
56. Ramanujan, "Toward a Counter-system," 33.
57. Personal communication from Susanne Wadley, March 19, 1997, based on her fieldwork in North India.
58. Padel, "Putting the Words into Women's Mouths," 13.
59. John Gray, *Men Are From Mars, Women Are From Venus*.
60. Keene, "Feminine Sensibility in the Heian Era," 112.
61. *Kathasaritsagara* 17.137–48; C. H. Tawney, trans., *The Ocean of Story*, 2:46.
62. Ramanujan, "Toward a Counter-system," 53.
63. Lila Abu-Lughod, *Veiled Sentiments*.

64. Sabra Jean Webber, *Romancing the Real*.

65. Leavy, *In Search of the Swan Maiden*, 22–23.

66. Toril Moi, *Sexual/Textual Politics*, 100.

67. Edmund Leach, "Animal Categories and Verbal Abuse."

68. Ramanujan, *Folktales from India*, xv. This, too, has its variants: when asked what their "mother language" ("matrbhasha") was, 3 out of 125 Hindi-speaking people recently said, "Devanagari"—not a language at all, but a script, originally the script of Sanskrit, now of many Sanskrit-derived languages, like Hindi. None of them ever referred to a "father language" in Hindi, Urdu, or English. Personal communication from Peter Gottschalk, June, 1997.

69. O'Flaherty, *Women, Androgynes*, 331–32.

70. I owe this excellent formulation to Hugh Urban.

71. Stephanie Jamison, *Sacrificed Wife*, 12.

72. But women too have seed. See O'Flaherty, *Women*, 35–39 and 262–72.

73. Miranda Shaw, *Passionate Enlightenment*, 36–37.

74. Judith Kegan Gardiner, "*Fifteen Joys*," 65.

75. Ibid., 70–71.

76. Ibid., 73, citing *Les Quinze Joies de Mariage* 3.214–24.

77. Ibid., 74.

78. Wendy Doniger, "Playing the Field." Frances Zimmermann agrees that there is a woman's voice in the *Kamasutra*; personal communication, April, 1994.

79. *The Laws of Manu* 9.15.

80. *Kamasutra* 5.1.8.

81. *Kamasutra* 5.1.8, -.17–43; O'Flaherty, *Textual Sources*, 101–4.

82. *Kamasutra* 5.1.52–54; see O'Flaherty, *Textual Sources*, 101–6.

83. *The Laws of Manu* 8.362–3.

84. *Rig Veda* 8.91.4, the song of Apala; O'Flaherty, *The Rig Veda*, 256–57.

85. The *parivrikta*. See Jamison, *Sacrificed Wife*, 99 ff.

86. *The Laws of Manu* 5.154.

87. *The Laws of Manu* 9.77 and .79.

88. Jon Spayde, "The Politically Correct Kama Sutra," 56.

89. Ibid., 57.

90. Gold, "Sexuality, Fertility, and Erotic Imagination," 71.

91. Rosette F. Willig, introduction to *The Changelings*.

92. Sappho, Fragment 31 (from Longinus, *On Sublimity*) trans. David A. Campbell, *Greek Lyric*, 1:79, 81 (the Greek text is on 78, 80).

93. Catallus 51, trans. Francis Warre Cornish, *Catullus, Tibullus, Pervigilium Veneris*, 59, 61 (Latin text on 58, 62).

94. Margaret Williamson, *Sappho's Immortal Daughters*, 156–59.

95. *Letters on Poetry from W. B. Yeats to Dorothy Wellesley*, 71–92.

96. William Butler Yeats, "The Three Bushes," in *Last Poems* (1936–39); *The Collected Poems of W. B. Yeats*, 341.

97. Ibid.

6. Textual Pluralism and Academic Pluralism

1. Warner, *From the Beast to the Blonde*, 279.
2. Ibid., 239.
3. Bruno Bettelheim, *The Uses of Enchantment*.
4. Warner, *From the Beast to the Blonde*, 213.
5. Ibid., 381.
6. Ibid., 213.
7. Ibid., 237.
8. Ibid., 417.
9. Mircea Eliade, *Cosmos and History*, viii–ix.
10. Ginzburg, *Ecstasies*, 28.
11. J. Z. Smith, *Drudgery Divine*, 47.
12. *Kathasaritasagara* 124 (18.5).131–237. The story is translated on 77 ff. of vol. 9 of the Tawney Penzer edition (chapter 124, or 171g).
13. William Witherle Lawrence, *Shakespeare's Problem Comedies*, 42.
14. R. Howard Bloch, *The Scandal of the Fabliaux*, 1–3.
15. Dundes, *Cinderella: A Casebook*, 110–11.
16. The error has been corrected in the 15th Edition of the *Encyclopedia Britannica*.
17. Alan Dundes, "The Psychoanalytic Study of the Grimms' Tales," 60–61.
18. Dundes, *Cinderella: A Casebook*, 110.
19. Warner, *From the Beast to the Blonde*, 362.
20. Dundes, "The Psychoanalytic Study," 60–61.
21. David Henry Hwang, *M. Butterfly*, act 3.
22. Claude Lévi-Strauss, "Split Representation in the Art of Asia and America," 247, 258.
23. Ioan Culianu, review of Ginzburg's *Ecstasies*, *Times Literary Supplement*, December 15, 1989.
24. Ginzburg, *Ecstasies*, 213. Ginzburg actually distinguishes between two different sorts of diffusion, from a common source or not from a common source, but this distinction obscures the basic contrast that I am arguing for here.
25. Ibid., 216–17.
26. Ibid., 280.
27. Ibid., 166.
28. Ibid., 217.
29. See J. Z. Smith, "In Comparison a Magic Dwells," for a critique of the family resemblances theory.
30. See J. Z. Smith, *Drudgery Divine*, on the difference between analogy and homology.
31. Tracy, *The Analogical Imagination*, 102.
32. François Jacob, "Evolution and Tinkering." *Science* 196 (4295): 1161–1166.
33. Ralph Waldo Emerson, *The Heart of Emerson's Journals*, 267.
34. Hartman, "Midrash as Law and Literature," 339.
35. Personal communication from Steve Gabel, November 1994.

36. *Mrs Miniver* (1942), written by James Hilton et al., from the novel by Jan Struther; directed by William Wyler; starring Greer Garson and Walter Pidgeon.

37. Geertz, *After the Fact*, 48.

38. Lévi-Strauss, *Tristes Tropiques*, 160 (Weightman translation, 229).

39. Laqueur, *Making Sex*, 19.

40. Leach, "Anthropological Aspects of Language," 153–66. Speaking of Lévi-Strauss's *The Savage Mind*, he remarks, "Though fascinated by that work I have also felt that some dimension to the argument is missing."

41. Tracy, *The Analogical Imagination*, 118.

42. Lévi-Strauss, *Myth and Meaning*, 8.

43. A. K. Ramanujan, "The Indian Oedipus."

44. Ivan Strenski, *Four Theories of Myth*, 165.

45. Edmund Leach, "Genesis as Myth."

46. I use the phrase "greening" not in its technical slang meaning, of being environmentally aware, but in its broader use indicating a general political correctness. The actual color has already been used to satirize Claude Lévi-Strauss: in 1968, Asger Jorn and Noel Arnaud published, in Paris, an elaborate cross-cultural spoof entitled *La langue verte et la cuite* ("the green tongue and the spoon"), a collection of visual puns on *langue* ("tongue") designating both language and a part of the mouth, as well as on *cuite* ("spoon" and "cooked"): photographs from all over the world of people sticking out their tongues, which the authors had colored green.

47. Lévi-Strauss, *Myth and Meaning*, 25.

48. Mantel review of John Demos, *The Unredeemed Captive*.

49. O'Flaherty, *Women, Androgynes*, introduction.

50. William H. McNeill, *Mythistory and Other Essays*, ix.

51. Dundes, "The Psychoanalytic Study," 60–61.

52. Roland Barthes, *S/Z: An Essay*, 120.

53. D. E. Bynum, *The Daemon in the Wood*, 25.

54. Sigmund Freud, "Where id was, there ego shall be." "The Dissection of the Psychical Personality," 80.

55. Jeremy Treglown, "False to Type: A review of *Cyril Connolly, A Life*, by Jeremy Lewis." In the *Times Literary Supplement*, May 9, 1997, #4910, 7.

56. O'Flaherty, *Siva*, 314–18.

57. Ibid., 318.

58. O'Flaherty, *Other Peoples' Myths*.

59. David Berreby, "Unabsolute Truths: Clifford Geertz," 44–47.

60. Jonathan Walters, personal communication, May 1996.

Bibliography

Sanskrit and Pali Texts

Aitareya Brahamana. Trans. A. B. Keith. Cambridge: Harvard Oriental Series vol. 25, 1929.

Bhagavata Purana, with the commentary of Sridhara. Benares: Pandita Pustakalaya, 1972.

Kamasutra of Vatsyayana, with the commentary of Sri Yasodhara. Bombay: Laksmivenkatesvara, 1856.

Kathasaritsagara (The Ocean of the Rivers of Story). Bombay: Nirnaya Sagara Press, 1930.

——. *The Ocean of Story.* N. M. Penzer, ed. Trans. C. W. Tawney. 10 vols. London: Chas. J. Sawyer, 1924.

The Laws of Manu [Manusmrti]. Harikrishna Jayantakrishna Dave, ed. Bombay: Bharatiya Vidya Series, vol. 29 ff., 1972– .

——. Trans. Wendy Doniger, with Brian K. Smith. Harmondsworth: Penguin, 1991.

Mahabharata. Poona: Bhandarkar Oriental Research Institute, 1933–69.

Milinda Panha. Trenckner, ed. Translated in *Sources of Indian Tradition,* Wm. Theodore de Bary et al., eds. New York: Columbia University Press, 1958.

Ramayana of Valmiki. Baroda: Oriental Institute, 1960–75.

Rig Veda, with the commentary of Sayana. 6 vols. London: Oxford University Press, 1890–92.

Upanishads. In Vasudeva Laxman Shastri Panshikar, ed., *One Hundred and Eight Upanishads* Bombay: Tukaram Javaji, 1913.

Texts in European Languages

Abu-Lughod, Lila. *Veiled Sentiments: Honor and Poetry in a Bedouin Society.* Berkeley: University of California Press, 1988.

Ackerman, Robert. *J. G. Frazer: His Life and Work.* Cambridge: Cambridge University Press, 1987.

Aeschylus. *Oresteia.* Trans. David Grene and Wendy Doniger O'Flaherty. Chicago: University of Chicago Press, 1988.

Aitchison, Joan. *The Language Web: The Power and Problem of Words.* Cambridge: Cambridge University Press, 1997.

Akutagawa, Ryunosuke. "In a Grove." In *Rashomon and Other Stories.* Trans. Takashi Kojima. New York: Liveright Publishers, 1952.

Allen, Woody. "The Kugelmass Episode." In *Side Effects,* 61–78. New York: Warner Books, 1975.

——. "The Scrolls." In *Without Feathers,* 24–28. New York: Warner Books, 1976.

Alter, Robert. *The Art of Biblical Narrative.* New York: Basic Books, 1981.

Appadurai, Arjun et al., eds. *Gender, Genre, and Power in South Asia.* Philadelphia: University of Pennsylvania Press, 1991.

Atlas, James. "The Shadow in the Garden." *The New Yorker,* July 26 and July 3, 1995: 74–85.

Auerbach, Erich. *Mimesis: The Representation of Reality in Western Literature.* Trans. William R. Trask. Princeton: Princeton University Press, 1953.

Bacon, Francis. "The Unity of Religions." In Richard Whately, ed., *Bacon's Essays with Annotations,* 20–44. New York: C. S. Francis, 1857.

Bal, Mieke. *Lethal Love: Feminist Literary Readings of Biblical Love Stories.* Bloomington: Indiana University Press, 1987.

Barthes, Roland. *Mythologies.* Selected and translated from the French by Annette Lavers. London: Jonathan Cape, 1972.

——. *S/Z. An Essay.* Trans. Richard Miller. New York: Farrar, Straus & Giroux, 1974.

Basinger, Jeanine. *How Hollywood Spoke to Women, 1930–1960.* New York: Knopf, 1993.

Baum, L. Frank, Jr. *The Land of Oz: Being an account of the further adventures of the Scarecrow and Tin Woodman . . . A Sequel to The Wizard of Oz.* Chicago: The Reilly and Lee Company, 1904.

Bellow, Saul. *Henderson the Rain King.* New York: Avon, 1976.

Berlin, Sir Isaiah. *The Hedgehog and the Fox: An Essay on Tolstoy's View of History.* London: Weidenfeld and Nicolson, 1953.

Bernheimer, Charles and Claire Kahane, eds. *In Dora's Case.* New York: Columbia University Press, 1990.

Berreby, David. "Unabsolute Truths: Clifford Geertz." *The New York Times Magazine,* April 9, 1995: 44–47.

Bettelheim, Bruno. *The Uses of Enchantment: The Meaning and Importance of Fairy Tales.* New York: Knopf, 1986.

Bialik, Hayim Nahman and Yehoshua Hana Ravnitzky, eds. *The Book of Legends.* Trans. William G. Braude. New York: Schocken Books, 1922.

Bledstein, Adrien. "Binder, Trickster, Heel and Hair-Man: Rereading Genesis 27 as a Trickster Tale Told by a Woman." In A. Brenner, ed., *A Feminist Companion to Genesis*, 282–95. Sheffield, England: Sheffield Academic Press, 1993.

——."Female Companionships: If the Book of Ruth were Written by a Woman . . ." In A. Brenner, ed., *A Feminist Companion to Ruth*, 116–33. Sheffield, England: Sheffield Academic Press, 1993.

Bloch, R. Howard. *The Scandal of the Fabliaux.* Chicago: University of Chicago Press, 1990.

Bloom, Harold J. *The Book of J.* New York: Weidenfeld, 1990.

Bohannan, Laura. "Shakespeare in the Bush." *Natural History* 75 (7): 28–33. See also the French translation ("Shakespeare dans la brousse") and discussion ("Un *Hamlet africain*") by Jean Verrier, *Revue des sciences humaines* 240 (1995): 161–72 and 173–78.

Bonnefoy, Yves, ed. *Mythologies.* Ed. Wendy Doniger. 2 vols. Chicago: University of Chicago Press, 1991.

Booth, Wayne. *The Rhetoric of Fiction.* Chicago: University of Chicago Press, 1961.

Borges, Jorge Luis. "Pierre Menard, Author of the *Quixote*." In *Labyrinths*, 36–44. New York: New Directions, 1962.

Bowden, William R. "The Bed-Trick, 1603–1642: Its Mechanics, Ethics, and Effects." *Shakespeare Studies* 5 (1969): 112–23.

Buber, Martin. *The Legend of the Baal-Shem.* Trans. Maurice Friedman. 1955; reprint, Princeton: Princeton University Press, 1995.

Butler, Judith. *Bodies That Matter: On the Discursive Limits of "Sex".* New York: Routledge, 1993.

Bynum, Caroline Walker, et al., eds. *Gender and Religion: On the Complexity of Symbols.* Boston: Beacon Press, 1986.

Bynum, David E. *The Daemon in the Wood: A Study of Oral Narrative Patterns.* Cambridge: Harvard University Press, 1978.

Calasso, Roberto. *The Marriage of Cadmus and Harmony.* New York: Knopf, 1993.

Caldwell, Sarah. "Waves of Beauty, Rivers of Blood: Constructing the Goddess's Body in Kerala." In Tracy Pintchman, ed., *In Search of Mahadevi: Constructing the Identity of the Great Goddess.* Albany: SUNY Press, 1998.

Campbell, Joseph. *The Hero with a Thousand Faces.* New York: Pantheon, 1949.

Carroll, Lewis. *Alice's Adventures in Wonderland* and *Through the Looking Glass.* In Martin Gardner, *The Annotated Alice.* New York: Bramhall House, 1960.

Catullus. *Catullus, Tibullus, Pervigilium Veneris.* Trans. Francis Warre Cornish, J P. Postgate, and J. W. Mackail. 2nd. ed. revised by G.P. Goold. Cambridge: Harvard University Press, 1988.

Chadwick, H. M. and N. K. Chadwick. *The Growth of Literature.* Cambridge: Cambridge University Press, 1936.

Coe, Michael D. Review of Steven Pinker, *The Language Instinct. The New York Times Book Review*, February 27, 1994: 7–8.

Comaroff, Jean. *Body of Power, Spirit of Resistance: The Culture and History of a South African People*. Chicago: University of Chicago Press, 1985.

Culianu, Ioan. Review of Carlo Ginzburg, *Ecstasies*. *Times Literary Supplement*, December 15, 1989.

Davis, Dena S. "Beyond Rabbi Hiyya's Wife: Women's Voices in Jewish Bioethics." *Second Opinion* 16 (March 1991): 10–30.

Davis, Elizabeth Gould. *The First Sex*. New York: G. P. Putnam's Sons, 1971.

Davis, Nathalie Zemon. *The Return of Martin Guerre*. Cambridge: Harvard University Press, 1983.

Dekkers, Midas. *Dearest Pet: On Bestiality*. Trans. Paul Vincent. London and New York: Verso, 1994.

Delbanco, Andrew. *The Death of Satan*. New York: Farrar, Straus & Giroux, 1995.

Derrida, Jacques. "Violence and Metaphysics: An Essay on the Thought of Emmanuel Levinas." In *Writing and Difference*, 79–153. Chicago: University of Chicago Press, 1978.

Desens, Marliss C. *The Bed-Trick in English Renaissance Drama: Explorations in Gender, Sexuality, and Power*. Newark: University of Delaware Press, 1994.

Detienne, Marcel. *The Creation of Mythology*. Chicago: University of Chicago Press, 1986.

Dillard, Annie. *Encounters with Chinese Writers*. Middletown, Conn.: Wesleyan University Press, 1984.

——. "Lenses." In *Teaching a Stone To Talk: Expeditions and Encounters*, 106–9. London: Pan Books, 1984.

——. *The Living*. New York: HarperCollins, 1992.

——. *Mornings Like This: Found Poems*. New York: HarperCollins, 1995.

Dilthey, Wilhelm. *Pattern and Meaning in History*. New York: Harper Torchbooks, 1961.

Doane, Mary Ann. *Femmes Fatales: Feminism, Film Theory, Psychoanalysis*. New York and London: Routledge, 1991.

Doniger, Wendy. (See also O'Flaherty, Wendy Doniger). *The Bed Trick*. Chicago: University of Chicago Press, forthcoming.

——. "Gender and Myth." In Gil Herdt, ed., *Critical Terms for the Study of Gender*. Chicago: University of Chicago Press, 1998.

——. "The Mythology of Masquerading Animals, or, Bestiality." Arien Mack, ed., *In the Company of Animals. Social Research* 62 (3): 751–72.

——. "Myths and Methods in the Dark." *Journal of Religion* 76 (4): 531–47.

——. "Playing the Field: Adultery as Claim-Jumping." In Ariel Glucklich, ed., *The Sense of Adharma*, 169–88. Oxford: Oxford University Press, 1994.

——. "Sex, Lies, and Tall Tales." *Truth-Telling, Lying and Deceptio* (special issue of *Social Research*) 63 (3): 633–99.

——. "Sita and Helen, Ahalya and Alcmena: A Comparative Study." *History of Religions* 37 (1): 21–49.

——. *Siva: The Erotic Ascetic*. London and Oxford: Oxford University Press, 1973.

——. "Speaking in Tongues: Deceptive Stories about Sexual Deception." *Journal of Religion* 74 (3): 320–37.

——. *Splitting Women in Ancient India and Greece*. Chicago: University of Chicago Press, forthcoming.

——. "Structuralist Universals and Freudian Universals." *History of Religions* 28 (3): 267–81.

——. "A Very Strange Enchanted Boy." Review of Stephen Larsen and Robin Larsen, *A Fire in the Mind: The Life of Joseph Campbell. The New York Times Book Review*, Sunday, February 2, 1992. Letters of protest, with my reply, printed on Sunday, February 23, 1992.

Douglas, Mary. "Children Consumed and Child Cannibals: Robertson Smith's Attack on the Science of Mythology." In Patton and Doniger, eds., *Myth and Method*, 29–51. Charlottesville and London: University Press of Virginia, 1996.

Doyle, Sir Arthur Conan. "Silver Blaze." In William S. Baring-Gould, ed., *The Annotated Sherlock Holmes*. New York: Clarkson N. Potter, 1967, Vol. 2, 261–81.

Durrenmatt, Friedrich. *The Assignment, or, On Observing the Observer of the Observers*. Trans. Joel Agee. New York: Random House, 1988.

Dundes, Alan, ed. *The Blood Libel Legend: A Casebook in Anti-Semitic Folklore*. Madison: University of Wisconsin Press, 1991.

——. *Cinderella: A Casebook*. New York: Wildman Press, 1983.

——. *Little Red Riding Hood: A Casebook*. Madison: University of Wisconsin Press, 1989.

——. "The Psychoanalytic Study of the Grimms' Tales with Special Reference to 'The Maiden Without Hands' (AT 706)." *The Germanic Review* 62 (2): 50–65.

—— and Lowell Edmund, eds. *Oedipus: A Folklore Casebook*. New York and London: Garland Publishing, 1984.

Dyer, Frank Lewis. *Edison: His Life and Inventions*. 2 vols. New York and London: Harper and Brothers, 1929.

Eisenhower, David. *Eisenhower at War: 1943–1945*. New York: Random House, 1986.

Eliade, Mircea. *Cosmos and History: The Myth of the Eternal Return*. New York: Pantheon, 1954.

——. *Myth and Reality*. Trans. Willard R. Trask. New York: Harper, 1963.

——. *The Quest*. New York, 1969.

Eliot, T. S. "*Ulysses*, Order, and Myth." In Mark Schorer et al., eds., *Criticism: The Foundations of Modern Literary Judgment*. New York: Harcourt Brace & World, 1948, 269–71.

Ellison, Ralph Waldo. *Invisible Man*. New York: Modern Library, 1952.

Ellman, Richard. *along the riverrun: Selected Essays*. London: Hamilton, 1988.

Elshtain, Jean Bethke. "Feminist Political Rhetoric and Women's Studies." In John Nelson, Allan Megill, and Donald N. McCloskey, eds., *The Rhetoric of the Human*, 319–40. Madison: University of Wisconsin Press, 1987.

Emerson, Ralph Waldo. *The Heart of Emerson's Journals*. Bliss Perry, ed. Boston: Houghton Mifflin, 1924.

Epstein, Joseph. " 'U. S. A.' Today." *The New Yorker*, August 5, 1996: 68–75.

Erasmus. *Opera Omnia*. Leiden: Cura & impensis Petri Vander, 1703.

Feldmann, Susan, ed. *African Myths and Tales*. New York: Dell, 1963.

Festinger, Leon. *A Theory of Cognitive Dissonance*. Stanford: Stanford University Press, 1957.

Feyerabend, Paul. *Against Method*. New York: Verso/Schocken, 1978.

Fielding, Henry. *Tom Jones*. 1749; reprint, Oxford: Oxford University Press, 1996.

Fineman, Joel. "Fratricide and Cuckoldry: Shakespeare's Doubles." *Psychoanalytic Review* 64:409–53.

Forster, E. M. *Aspects of the Novel*. New York: Harcourt, Brace, 1927.

von Franz, Marie Louise. *Problems of the Feminine in Fairytales*. Irving, Texas: Spring Publications, 1972.

Freud, Sigmund. "The Dissection of the Psychical Personality." In *New Introductory Lectures on Psycho-Analysis, and Other Works*. Trans. James Strachey. London: Hogarth Press, 1960, SE 22 (1932–6): 57–80.

Fuss, Diana. *Essentially Speaking: Feminism, Nature, and Difference*. New York: Routledge, 1989.

Garber, Marjorie. *Vice Versa: Bisexuality and the Eroticism of Everyday Life*. New York: Simon and Schuster, 1995.

Gardiner, Judith Kegan. "*Fifteen Joys*: A Medieval Look at Marriage." *University of Michigan Papers in Women's Studies* 2.4 (1978): 146–65.

Garner, James Finn. *Politically Correct Bedtime Stories: Modern Tales for Our Life & Times*. New York: Macmillan, 1994.

Geertz, Clifford. *After the Fact: Two Countries, Four Decades, One Anthropologist*. Cambridge: Harvard University Press, 1995.

——. "Thick Description: Towards an Interpretive Theory of Culture." In *The Interpretation of Culture*. New York: Basic Books, 1973.

Gellner, Ernest. *The Psychoanalytic Movement, or, The Cunning of Unreason*. London: Paladin Grafton Books, 1985.

——. Review of Rolf Wiggershaus, *The Frankfurt School*, and Klaus-Dieter Krohn, *Intellectuals in Exile*. *Times Literary Supplement*, September 23, 1994: 3–5.

Gilligan, Carol. *In a Different Voice: Psychological Theory and Women's Development*. Cambridge: Harvard University Press, 1982.

Goitein, S. D. "Women as Creators of Biblical Genre." *Prooftexts* 8 (1988): 1–31.

Ginzburg, Carlo. *Ecstasies: Deciphering the Witches' Sabbath*. Trans. Raymond Rosenthal. New York: Pantheon, 1991.

——. "Morelli, Freud and Sherlock Holmes: Clues and Scientific Method." *History Workshop* 9 (1980): 5–36.

Goldberg, Benjamin. *The Mirror and Man*. Charlottesville: University of Virginia Press, 1985.

Gold, Ann Grodzins. "Gender and Illusion in a Rajasthani Yogic Tradition." In Appadurai, Arjun et al., eds., *Gender, Discourse, and Power in South Asia*, 102–35. Philadelphia: University of Pennsylvania Press, 1991.

——. "Sexuality, Fertility, and Erotic Imagination." In Gloria Goodwin Raheja and Ann Grodzins Gold, *Listen to the Heron's Words: Reimagining Gender and Kinship in North India*. Berkeley: University of California Press, 1994.

Goldman, Robert P. "Transsexualism, Gender, and Anxiety in Traditional India." *Journal of the American Oriental Society* 113 (3): 374–401.

Gombrich, Sir Ernst. *The Essential Gombrich: Selected Writings on Art and Culture*. Richard Woodfield, ed. San Francisco: Phaidon Press, 1996.

——. *The Sense of Order*. Ithaca, N.Y.: Cornell University Press, 1979.

——. *Topics of Our Time*. Berkeley: University of California Press, 1991.

Graves, Robert. *Adam's Rib, and other anomalous elements in the Hebrew Creation Myth*. New York: Thomas Yoseloff, 1958.

Gray, John. *Men Are from Mars, Women Are from Venus: a Practical Guide to Improving Communication and Getting What You Want in Your Relationshp*. New York: HarperCollins, 1992.

Hammett, Dashiell. *The Dain Curse*. 1928; reprint, New York: Vintage, 1989.

Hartman, Geoffrey H. "Midrash as Law and Literature." *Journal of Religion* 74 (3): 338–55.

Hatto, A. T. "The Swan Maiden: A Folk-Tale of North Eurasian Origin." *Bulletin of the School of Oriental and African Studies* 24 (1961): 326–52.

Hawley, John Stratton. "Images of Gender in the Poetry of Krishna." In Bynum et al., eds., *Gender and Religion: On the Complexity of Symbols*, 231–56. Boston: Beacon Press, 1986.

Hegel, W. G. F. *Phaenomenologie des Geiste*. 1807; reprint, Hamburg: Felix Meiner, 1952.

Herodotus. *The History*. Trans. David Grene. Chicago: University of Chicago Press, 1987.

Heywood, John. *A Dialogue of Proverbs*. Ed. Rudolph E. Habenicht. Berkeley: University of California Press, 1963.

Holbek, Bengt. *Interpretation of Fairy Tales*. Helsinki: Folklore Fellows Communications No. 239, 1987.

Hollander, John. *Selected Poetry*. New York: Knopf, 1993.

——. *Tesserae, and Other Poems*. New York: Knopf, 1993.

Hope, Sir Anthony. *The Prisoner of Zenda*. New York: Henry Holt, 1896.

Hugo, Victor. *Les Misérables*. Paris: Gallimard, 1983.

Hume, David. *A Treatise of Human Nature*. 1888; reprint, Oxford: Oxford University Press, 1951.

Hutton, Ronald. *The Stations of the Sun*. Oxford and New York: Oxford University Press, 1996.

Hwang, David Henry. *M. Butterfly*. New York: Penguin, 1989.

Iser, Wolfgang. *The Implied Reader: Patterns of Communication in Prose Fiction from Bunyan to Beckett*. Baltimore: Johns Hopkins University Press, 1974.

Jacob, François. "Evolution and Tinkering." *Science* 196 (4295): 1161–1166.

Jagendorf, Zwi. " 'In the Morning, Behold It Was Leah': Genesis and the Reversal of Sexual Knowledge." In David H. Hirsch et al., eds., *Biblical Patterns in Modern Literature*, 51–60. Chico, Calif.: Scholars Press, 1984.

Jameson, Raymond D. *Three Lectures on Chinese Folklore*. Peiping, China: San Yu, 1932.

Jamison, Stephanie. *Sacrificed Wife/Sacrificer's Wife: Women, Ritual, and Hospitality in Ancient India*. New York: Oxford University Press, 1996.

Jennings, Luke. "Nights at the Ballet: The Czar's Last Dance." *The New Yorker*, March 27, 1995: 71–87.

Jorn, Asger, and Noel Arnaud. *La langue verte et la cuite*. Paris: Jean-Jacques Pauvert, 1968.

Kafka, Franz. "Leopards in the Temple." In *Parables and Paradoxes*, 93. Trans. Ernst Kaiser and Eithne Wilkins. Bilingual edition, New York: Schocken Books, 1946.

Keneally, Thomas. *Schindler's List*. New York: Simon and Schuster, 1982.

Keene, Donald. "Feminine Sensibility in the Heian Era." In Nancy G. Hume, ed., *Japanese Aesthetics and Culture: A Reader*, 109–24. Albany, N.Y.: SUNY Press, 1995.

Kierkegaard, Soren. *Either/Or: A Fragment of Life*. Vol. 1. Trans. David F. Swenson and Lillian Marvin Swenson. 1843; reprint, Princeton: Princeton University Press, 1944.

Kittler, Friedrich. "World-Breath: On Wagner's Media Technology." In David J. Levin, ed., *Opera Through Other Eyes*, 215–35. Stanford: Stanford University Press, 1994.

Kristof, Nicholas D. "Big Wolves Aren't So Bad in Japan." *The New York Times*, Wednesday, December 4, 1996.

Kuhn, Thomas. *The Nature of Scientific Revolutions*. 2nd. ed. Chicago: University of Chicago Press, 1970.

Kundera, Milan. *The Unbearable Lightness of Being*. New York: Harper and Row, 1984.

Kuper, Hilda. *The Uniform of Colour: A Study of White-Black Relationships in Swaziland*. Johannesburg, South Africa: Witwatersrand University Press, 1947.

Laqueur, Thomas. *Making Sex: Body and Gender from the Greeks to Freud*. Cambridge: Harvard University Press, 1990.

Lawrence, D. H. *Lady Chatterly's Lover*. New York: Penguin, 1959.

Lawrence, William Witherle. *Shakespeare's Problem Comedies*. New York: Frederick Ungar, 1960.

Leach, Edmund. "Anthropological Aspects of Language: Animal Categories and Verbal Abuse." In William A. Lessa and Evon Z. Vogt, *Reader in Comparative Religion*, 153–66. 4th ed. New York: Harper and Row, 1979.

——. "Genesis as Myth." In Middleton, John, ed. *Myth and Cosmos: Readings in Mythology and Symbolism*, 1–14. Austin: University of Texas Press, 1967.

——. "Jesus, John, and Mary Magdalene." *New Society* 34 (Dec. 1975): 686–88.

Leavy, Barbara Fass. *In Search of the Swan Maiden: A Narrative on Folklore and Gender*. New York: New York University Press, 1994.

Levinas, Emmanuel. *Totality and Infinity: An Essay on Exteriority*. Trans. Alphonso Lingis. The Hague: Martinus Nijhoff, 1979.

Lévi-Strauss, Claude. *Myth and Meaning*. New York: Schocken Books, 1995.

——. *Mythologiques (Introduction to a Science of Mythology)*. I: *The Raw and the Cooked*. Trans. John and Doreen Weightman. New York: Harper and Row, 1969.

——. *The Savage Mind*. Chicago: University of Chicago Press, 1966.

——. "Split Representation in the Art of Asia and America." In *Structural Anthropology*, 245–68. Trans. Claire Jacobson and Brooke Grundfest Schoepf. Harmondsworth: Penguin, 1963.

——. "The Story of Asdiwal." In Edmund Leach, ed. *The Structural Study of Myth and Totemism*, 1–48. Trans. Nicolas Mann. London: Tavistock, 1967.

——. *The Story of Lynx*. Trans. Catherine Tihanyi. Chicago: University of Chicago Press, 1995.

——. *Structural Anthropology*. Trans. Claire Jacobson and Brooke Grundfest Schoepf. Harmondsworth: Penguin, 1963.

——. "The Structural Study of Myth." In *Structural Anthropology*, 206–31. Trans. Claire Jacobson and Brooke Grundfest Schoepf. Harmondsworth: Penguin, 1963.

——. *Tristes Tropiques*. Trans. John and Doreen Weightman. London: Jonathan Cape, 1973.

Lincoln, Bruce. *Discourse and the Construction of Society*. New York: Oxford University Press, 1989.

Loraux, Nicole. "Origins of Mankind in Greek Myths: Born to Die." In Yves Bonnefoy, ed., *Mythologies*, 390–94. Ed. Wendy Doniger. 2 vols. University of Chicago Press, 1991.

Lotman, Yuri. "The Semiosphere." In *Universe of the Mind: A Semiotic Theory of Culture*. Trans. Ann Shukman. Bloomington: Indiana University Press, 1990.

Mantel, Hilary. Review of John Demos, *The Unredeemed Captive: A Family Story from Early America*. *London Review of Books*, October 20, 1994: 20.

McNeill, William H. *Mythistory and Other Essays*. Chicago: University of Chicago Press, 1985.

Mellen, Joan. "The Women in Rashomon." In Donald Richie, ed., *Rashomon*, 179–82. New Brunswick and London: Rutgers University Press, 1986.

Menn, Esther. *Judah and Tamar (Genesis 38) in Ancient Jewish Exegesis: Studies in Literary Form and Hermeneutics*. Ph.D. diss., University of Chicago Divinity School, June 1995.

Michnik, Adam. Interview, *The New Yorker*, December 9, 1996: 52.

Middleton, John, ed. *Myth and Cosmos: Readings in Mythology and Symbolis*. Austin: University of Texas Press, 1967.

Mills, Margaret. "Sex Role Reversals, Sex Changes, and Transvestite Disguise in the Oral Tradition of a Conservative Muslim Community in Afghanistan." In Rosan A. Jordan and Susan J. Kalcik, eds., *Women's Folklore, Women's Culture*, 187–213. Philadelphia: University of Pennsylvania Press, 1985.

Mitchell, Stephen, trans. *The Book of Job*. San Francisco: North Point Press, 1987.

Moi, Toril. *Sexual/Textual Politics: Feminist Literary Theory*. New York: Routledge, 1985.

Morson, Gary Saul. *Narrative and Freedom: The Shadows of Time*. New Haven and London: Yale University Press, 1994.

Mulvey, Laura. "Pandora: Topographies of the Mask and Curiosity." In Beatriz Colomina, ed., *Sexuality and Space*, 53–72. Princeton: Princeton Architectural Press, 1992.

Müller, F. Max. *Lectures on the Science of Language* [delivered in 1861 and 1863]. London: Longmans, Green & Co., 1891.

Narayana Rao, Velcheru. "A Ramayana of Their Own: Women's Oral Tradition in Telugu." In Paula Richman, ed. *Many Ramayanas: The Diversity of Narrative Traditions in South Asia*. Berkeley: Univerity of California Press, 1991.

Nelson, Michael. "One Mythology Among Many: The Spiritual Odyssey of C. S. Lewis." *Virginia Quarterly Review* (Autumn 1996): 619–33.

Obeyesekere, Gananath. *The Work of Culture: Symbolic Transformation in Psychoanalysis and Anthropology*. Chicago: University of Chicago Press, 1990.

O'Flaherty, Wendy Doniger. (See also Doniger, Wendy). *Dreams, Illusion, and Other Realities*. Chicago: University of Chicago Press, 1984.

——. *Hindu Myths: A Sourcebook, Translated from the Sanskrit*. Harmondsworth: Penguin, 1975.

——. "On Translating Sanskrit Myths." In William Radice, ed., *The Translator's Art: Essays in Honor of Betty Radice*, 121–28. Harmondsworth: Penguin, 1987.

——. *The Origins of Evil in Hindu Mythology*. Berkeley: University of California Press, 1976.

——. *Other Peoples' Myths: The Cave of Echoes*. 1988; reprint, Chicago: University of Chicago Press, 1995.

——. *The Rig Veda: An Anthology*. Harmondsworth: Penguin, 1981.

——. *Tales of Sex and Violence: Folklore, Sacrifice, and Danger in the Jaiminiya Brahmana*. Chicago: University of Chicago Press, 1985.

——. *Textual Sources for the Study of Hinduism*. Chicago: University of Chicago Press, 1990.

——. *Women, Androgynes, and Other Mythical Beasts*. Chicago: University of Chicago Press, 1981.

Ovid, *Metamorphoses*. Trans. Frank Justus Miller. Cambridge, Mass.: Loeb Library, 1977.

Padel, Ruth. "Putting the Words into Women's Mouths." *London Review of Books*, January 23, 1997: 12–17.

Parry, Milman. *The Making of Homeric Verse: The Collected Papers of Milman Parry*. Adam Parry, ed. Oxford: Clarendon Press, 1971.

—— and Albert Bates Lord. *Serbocroatian Heroic Songs*. Cambridge: Harvard University Press, 1954.

Patton, Laurie L. *Myth as Argument: The Brhaddevata as Canonical Commentary*. Berlin and New York: Walter de Gruyter, 1996.

—— and Wendy Doniger. *Myth and Method*. Charlottesville and London: University Press of Virginia, 1996.

Peirce, Charles Sanders. "Thirdness." In Charles Hartshorne and Paul Weiss, eds., *The Collected Papers of Charles Sanders Peirce*. 1934; reprint, Cambridge: Belknap Press for Harvard University Press, 1965.

——. "The Reality of Thirdness." In Charles Hartshorne and Paul Weiss, eds., *The Collected Papers of Charles Sanders Peirce*. 1934; reprint, Cambridge: Belknap Press for Harvard University Press, 1965.

Pépin, Jean. "Christian Judgements on the Analogies between Christianity and Pagan Mythology." In Yves Bonnefoy, ed., *Mythologies*, 655–65. Ed. Wendy Doniger. 2 vols. University of Chicago Press, 1991.

Plato, *Laws*; *Phaedo*; *Philebus*; *The Republic*; *The Sophist* [Cornford]; *The Statesman*; *Symposium*; *Timaeus*. All in Loeb Classical Library, Cambridge: Harvard University Press. *Laws*, ed. Robert Gregg Bury (1967); *Phaedo*, ed. Harold North Fowler (1970); *Philebus*, ed. Harold North Fowler (1974); *The Republic*, ed. Paul Shorey (1970); *The Sophist*, ed. Harold North Fowler (1977); *The Statesman*, ed. Harold North Fowler (1975); *Symposium*, ed. W. R. M. Lamb (1983); *Timaeus*, ed. Robert Gregg Bury (1975).

Propp, Vladimir. *The Morphology of the Folktale*. Austin: University of Texas Press, 1968.

Proust, Marcel. *Remembrance of Things Past*. Vol. 2: *Cities of the Plain, The Captive*, and *The Sweet Cheat Gone*. Trans. C. K. Scott Moncrieff. New York: Random House, 1932.

——. *The Past Recaptured*. Trans. Frederick A. Blossom. New York: Random House, 1932.

Rafferty, Terrence. "The Avengers: 'Die Hard with a Vengeance' and 'A Little Princess.' " *The New Yorker*, 29 May 1995: 91–92.

Ramanujan, A. K. *Folktales from India*. New York: Pantheon, 1992.

——. "Hanchi: A Kannada Cinderella." In Alan Dundes, ed., *Cinderella: A Casebook*, 259–75. New York: Wildman Press, 1983.

——. "The Indian Oedipus." In Alan Dundes and Lowell Edmund, eds. *Oedipus: A Folklore Casebook*, 234–61. New York and London: Garland Publishing, 1984.

——. "Three Hundred Ramayanas: Five Examples and Three Thoughts on Translation." In Paula Richman, ed. *Many Ramayanas: The Diversity of Narrative Traditions in South Asia*, 22–49. Berkeley: University of California Press, 1991.

——. "Toward A Counter-system: Women's Tales." In Arjun Appadurai et al, eds., *Gender, Genre, and Power in South Asia*, 33–55. Philadelphia: University of Pennsylvania Press, 1991.

——. "Two Realms of Kannada Folklore." In Stuart Blackburn and A. K. Ramanujan, eds., *Another Harmony: New Essays on the Folklore of India*, 41–75. Berkeley: University of California Press, 1986.

——. "When Mirrors are Windows: Towards an Anthology of Reflections." *History of Religions* 28 (3): 187–216.

——, David Shulman, and Narayana Rao, eds. *When God Is A Customer: Telugu Courtesan Songs by Ksetrayya and Others*. Berkeley: University of California Press, 1994.

Richie, Donald, ed. *Rashomon*. New Brunswick and London: Rutgers University Press, 1986.

Richman, Paula, ed. *Many Ramayanas: The Diversity of Narrative Traditions in South Asia*. Berkeley: Univerity of California Press, 1991.

———. *Extraordinary Child: Poems from a South Indian Devotional Genre*. Honolulu: University of Hawaii Press, 1998.

Ricoeur, Paul. *The Symbolism of Evil*. Trans. Emerson Buchanan. Boston: Beacon Press, 1969.

Rushdie, Salman. *Haroun and the Sea of Stories*. New York: Grant, 1990.

———. *Shame*. London: Jonathan Cape, 1983.

Said, Edward. *Culture and Imperialism*. New York: Knopf, 1993.

Sappho. *Greek Lyric*. Vol. 1 (Sappho, Alcaeus). Trans. David A. Campbell. Cambridge: Harvard University Press, 1982.

Scarry, Elaine. *The Body in Pain: The Making and Unmaking of the World*. New York: Oxford University Press, 1985.

Scott, Joan W. "Gender and the Politics of Higher Education." Inaugural talk for the Center for Gender Studies, University of Chicago, October 18, 1996.

Sedgwick, Eve Kosofsky. *The Epistemology of the Closet*. Berkeley: University of California Press, 1990.

Shakespeare, William. *All's Well That Ends Well, Hamlet, Henry the Fifth, Merchant of Venice, The Winter's Tale*. All citations are from *The Complete Works of Shakespeare*, ed. David Bevington. Glenview, Ill.: Scott, Foresman, 1980.

Shaw, Brent D. Review of Caroline Walker Bynum, *The Resurrection of the Body*. *The New Republic*, April 17, 1995: 43–48.

Shaw, George Bernard. *Saint Joan*. In Warren S. Smith, ed., *Bernard Shaw's Plays*. New York: Norton, 1970.

Shaw, Miranda. *Passionate Enlightenment: Women in Tantric Buddhism*. Princeton: Princeton University Press, 1994.

Shelley, Percy Bysshe. *Shelley's Prometheus Unbound: The Text and the Drafts*. Lawrence John Zillman, ed. New Haven and London: Yale University Press, 1968.

Smith, Cyril Stanley. "Metallurgical Footnotes to the History of Art." In *A Search for Structure: Selected Essays on Science, Art, and History*, 242–305. Cambridge: MIT Press, 1981.

Smith, Jonathan Z. "Adde Parvum Parvo Magnus Acervus Erit." In *Map Is Not Territory: Studies in the History of Religions*, 240–64. 1978; reprint, Chicago and London: University of Chicago Press, 1993.

———. "The Bare Facts of Ritual." In *Imagining Religion: From Babylon to Jonestown*, 53–64. Chicago: University of Chicago Press, 1982.

———. *Drudgery Divine: On the Comparison of Early Christianities and the Religions of Late Antiquity*. Chicago: University of Chicago Press, 1990.

———. "Fences and Neighbors: Some Contours of Early Judaism." In *Imagining Religion: From Babylon to Jonestown*, 1–18. Chicago: University of Chicago Press, 1982.

——. *Imagining Religion: From Babylon to Jonestown*. Chicago: University of Chicago Press, 1982.

——. "In Comparison A Magic Dwells." In *Imagining Religion: From Babylon to Jonestown*, 19–35. Chicago: University of Chicago Press, 1982.

——. "Map Is Not Territory." In *Map Is Not Territory: Studies in the History of Religions*, 289–309. 1978; reprint, Chicago and London: University of Chicago Press, 1993.

——. *Map Is Not Territory: Studies in the History of Religions*. 1978; reprint, Chicago and London: University of Chicago Press, 1993.

——. "Sacred Persistence." In *Imagining Religion: From Babylon to Jonestown*, 36–52. Chicago: University of Chicago Press, 1982.

——. "What a Difference a Difference Makes." In *"To See Ourselves as Others See Us": Christians, Jews, 'Others' in Late Antiquity*. Jacob Neusner and Ernest S. Frerichs, eds. Chico, Calif.: Scholars Press, 1985.

Sorel, George. *Reflections on Violence*. Trans. T. E. Hulme and J. Roth. Glencoe, Ill.: Free Press, 1950.

Spayde, Jon. "The Politically Correct Kama Sutra." *The Utne Reader* (Nov.–Dec. 1996): 56–57.

Spivak, Gayatri. "Can the subaltern speak?" In *Marxism and the Interpretation of Culture*, 271–313. Cary Nelson and Lawrence Grossberg. eds. Urbana and Chicago: University of Illinois Press, 1988.

Stoppard, Tom. *Rosencrantz and Guildenstern Are Dead*. New York: Grove Press, 1967.

Strenski, Ivan. *Four Theories of Myth in Twentieth-Century History: Cassirer, Eliade, Lévi-Strauss and Malinowski*. Iowa City: University of Iowa Press, 1987.

Sullivan, Lawrence. *Icanchu's Drum: An Orientation to Meaning in South American Religions*. New York: Macmillan, 1988.

Swahn, Jan O. *The Tale of Cupid and Psyche*. Lund: Gleerup, 1955.

Tate, James. *Absences: New Poems*. New York: Little, Brown with the Atlantic Monthly Press, 1970.

Taylor, Charles. *Multiculturalism and "The Politics of Recognition"*. Princeton: Princeton University Press, 1992.

Teilhard de Chardin, Pierre. *Christianity and Evolution*. London: Collins, 1971.

Terrace, H. S. *Nim*. New York: Knopf, 1979.

Thurber, James. "University Days." In *The Thurber Carnival*, 222–23. New York and London: Harper, 1931.

Tolstoi, L. N. *Anna Karenin*. Trans. Rosemary Edmonds. Harmondsworth: Penguin, 1954.

Trollope, Anthony. *Kept in the Dark*. 1882; reprint, New York: Dover Publications, 1978.

Tracy, David. *The Analogical Imagination: Christian Theology and the Culture of Pluralism*. New York: Crossroads, 1981.

——. *Dialogue with the Other: The Inter-Religious Dialogue*. Louvain: Eerdmans, Peeters Press, 1990.

——. *On Naming the Present: Reflections on God, Hermeneutics, and Church.* Maryknoll, N.Y.: Orbis Books, 1994.

——. *Pluralism and Ambiguity: Hermeneutics, Religion, Hope.* Chicago: University of Chicago Press, 1987.

Twain, Mark. *Pudd'nhead Wilson and Other Tales.* R. D. Gooder, ed. Oxford and New York: Oxford University Press, 1992.

Tyler, Royall. "The Origin of Evil." In Marius B. Peladeau, ed., *The Verse of Royall Tyler*, 13–15. Charlottesville: University of Virginia Press, 1968.

Unsigned, "The Explosion Point of Ideology in China." In Knabb, Ken, ed. and trans., *Situationist International Anthology.* English edition of *Internationale Situationiste* (Paris, 1967), no. 11. Berkeley: Bureau of Public Secrets, 1981, 185–94.

Updike, John. *The Centaur.* New York: Ballantine, 1991.

Warner, Marina. *From the Beast to the Blonde: On Fairy Tales and Their Tellers.* London: Chattos and Windus, 1995.

Waugh, Evelyn. *A Handful of Dust.* 1934; reprint, Harmondsworth: Penguin Books, 1951.

Webber, Sabra Jean. *Romancing the Real: Folklore and Ethnographic Representation in North Africa.* Philadephia: University of Pennsylvania Press, 1991.

White, David. *Myths of the Dog-Man.* Chicago: University of Chicago Press, 1991.

Whitman, Walt. "A Noiseless Patient Spider." In *The Complete Poems of Walt Whitman.* Harmondsworth, England: Penguin Education, 1975.

Wiley, Bell Irvin. *Johnny Reb: The Common Soldier of the Confederacy.* Baton Rouge: Louisiana State University Press, 1978.

Williamson, Margaret. *Sappho's Immortal Daughters.* Cambridge: Harvard University Press, 1995.

Willig, Rosette F., ed. and trans. *The Changelings: A Classical Japanese Court Tale.* Stanford: Stanford University Press, 1983.

Wilson, Horace H. *Essays and Lectures, Chiefly on the Religion of the Hindus.* London, 1846 (originally published in *Asiatic Researches* 1828 and 1832).

Yeats, William Butler. *The Collected Poems of W. B. Yeats.* London: Macmillan, 1965.

——. *Letters on Poetry from W.B. Yeats to Dorothy Wellesley.* London: Oxford University Press, 1940.

Zeitlin, Froma. "Signifying Difference: The Case of Hesiod's Pandora." In *Playing the Other: Gender and Society in Classical Greek Literature*, 53–86. Chicago: University of Chicago Press, 1996.

Ziegler, Karen. "Creation Myths: Bridge to Human Wholeness." In *FryingPan* (Jan. 1980): 12–18.

Zohar, *The Book of Enlightenment.* Trans. and introduction by Daniel Chanan Matt. New York: Paulist Press, 1983.

Index